READING
DANCE

READING
DANCE

Judith
Mackrell

MICHAEL JOSEPH
LONDON

MICHAEL JOSEPH LTD

Published by the Penguin Group
27 Wrights Lane, London w8 5TZ
Viking Penguin Inc., 375 Hudson Street, New York, New York 10014, USA
Penguin Books Australia Ltd, Ringwood, Victoria, Australia
Penguin Books Canada Ltd, 10 Alcorn Avenue, Toronto, Ontario, Canada M4V 3B2
Penguin Books (NZ) Ltd, 182–190 Wairau Road, Auckland 10, New Zealand

Penguin Books Ltd, Registered Offices: Harmondsworth, Middlesex, England

First published 1997
10 9 8 7 6 5 4 3 2 1

Set in 9.5/13 Adobe Palatino by
Rowland Phototypesetting Ltd Bury St Edmunds, Suffolk
Printed in England by Clays Ltd, St Ives plc

A CIP catalogue record for this book is available from the British Library

ISBN 0 7181 3851 1

The moral right of the author has been asserted

This book is for everyone who's ever kept me company at a dance performance – especially Simon.

Contents

List of Illustrations

1 Marie Taglioni in *La Sylphide*. Lithograph by J. H. Lynch from a drawing by A. E. Chalon (The Board of Trustees of the Victoria & Albert Museum)

2 Martha Graham in *Strike* (Soichi Sunami/Hulton Getty)

3 Subathra Subramaniam dancing Bharatha Natyam (Subathra Subramaniam)

4 The Kirov Ballet in *Swan Lake* (Leslie E. Spatt)

5 Bronislava Nijinska's *Les Noces* (Photographer unknown. The Royal Opera House Archives)

6 Margot Fonteyn in *The Sleeping Beauty* (Hulton Getty)

7 Martha Graham in *Cave of the Heart* (Dance Collection. The New York Public Library for the Performing Arts. Lenox, Astor and Tilden Foundations)

8 Mark Morris in *Dido and Aeneas* (Tom Brazil)

9 Vaslav Nijinsky in *L'Après-midi d'un faune* (Bert/The Board of Trustees of the Victoria & Albert Museum)

10 Sylvie Guillem and Adam Cooper in *Hermann Schmerman* (Clive Barda/The Performing Arts Library)

11 Antoinette Sibley and Anthony Dowell in *The Dream* (Zoë Dominic)

12 Darcey Bussell and Eddie Shellman in *Agon* (Leslie E. Spatt)

13 Carolyn Brown in *Walkaround Time* (James Klosty)

14 Oskar Schlemmer's *Triadic Ballet* (Photo Archive C. Raman

Schlemmer, Oggebbio, Italy/© 1996 The Oskar Schlemmer Theatre Estate, 79410 Badenweiler, Germany)

15 Les Ballets Trockadero de Monte Carlo in *Swan Lake* (© Lois Greenfield, 1995)

16 Merce Cunningham and his dancers in *Quartet* (© JoAnn Baker, 1986)

Acknowledgements

I am very grateful to Barbara Newman, who has allowed me to quote extensively from her invaluable book *Striking a Balance* (see Sources on p. 255).

Many thanks also to Debra Craine and Christopher Butler for reading the manuscript.

Introduction

At any dance performance there will always be one person, and probably many more, enthusing how beautiful or interesting the movement is, how skilled or extraordinary the dancers, but muttering that they've no idea what it all means. Viewers who might be noisily confident when judging a play or a film often turn uncharacteristically coy when confronted with choreography. They suspect that there's a secret body language into which they haven't been initiated, a code they don't quite get.

In fact, the only basic skill that's needed for reading dance is a curiosity about the event – a willingness to let the movement play on our senses, to let its rhythms charge up our pulses and to let its pictures range around our imaginations.

But a suspicion of dance will often interfere with the simplest of our responses, and our desire for meaning adds to our wariness. Is some esoteric information being communicated by that complicated flurry of steps? Are those six dancers suddenly doing the same movements because they've formed a private gang? When three women dance with one man, are they all vying for his attention or are they two couples, lesbian and straight? If that man is lying down, is he meant to be exhausted or simply on a different geometrical plane from the rest?

Of course, it's natural to interpret human activity. But what are the right kinds of meanings to look for in dance? If there is a language of dance, how do we understand what it's saying?

Over the last few decades we've learnt to be wary of asking such questions. Dance, like any other cultural activity, is shaped by aesthetic, social, biological and psychological forces whose effects are under constant debate. The language of art has become a war zone for competing academics.

But there are practical issues within the huge question of how dance communicates that *are* up for discussion. Does dance speak in ways that are different from the other arts? What can dance actually tell us? How should we look at different styles of dance? What exactly is the dance object under discussion? These are questions which we take with us to the theatre and they are all part of the business of reading dance.

WHERE DANCE BEGINS AND ENDS

Part of the problem for dancephobes is that dance *looks* quite similar to the way people act in the real world, even while it's extravagantly deviant from normal behaviour, and the point of these fit human bodies doing whimsically impractical things seems irritatingly obscure. Yet for dance addicts the fact that movement keeps sliding between reality and artifice is a source of its power. It means that dance can tell serious truths about men and women, even though it may be using intensely mannered choreography to do so. It also means that the dancers' solid, sweaty flesh can be transformed into pure images of beauty.

In some ways the language of dance is richer than that of the other arts. Like music, it constructs rhythms and phrases, but it also gives these elements visible form. It creates colour, line and shape like painting or sculpture, but it moves them around through space and time. It has cinema's freedom to flip between the real and the symbolic, but its performers are living, breathing people. It can achieve the emotional intensity of an opera or play, yet it isn't confined to a single geographical language.

On the other hand, compared with the verbal arts, dance may seem frustratingly dumb.

Take a love affair. A novel, a play or a film is capable of analysing its lovers' actions in logical detail: it can negotiate the emotional maze that lies beneath the plot's surface; it can place the characters in distinct social and political spheres. A dance can't do these things with anything like the same precision. But as the most physical of all art forms, it can do one thing better – it can let us experience the affair as it is lived in the flesh.

THE STORIES DANCE CAN TELL

In any dance work audiences may get an instant grasp of a relationship just in the way that two characters move together. Their lifts and balances may be as delicate as a caress or as harsh as a blow, while the touch of a hand may seem to scorch the other's skin. The lines of the dancers' movements may be harmonious or disruptive. There may be tension or trust in the way that the space between them is charged. The rhythms of their movements may hum with desire, or be snagged by the jagged edges of danger.

In his ballet *Mayerling* (1978) Kenneth MacMillan charts a neurotic sexual wasteland through the series of *pas de deux* in which his emotionally disintegrating hero dances with the various women in his life. The rough cruelty with which Rudolf handles his wife speaks of a morbid self-disgust; his coarse manipulation of his discarded mistress is a brutal mix of lust and powerplay, and the see-sawing rhythms and distorted lines of the duets with his dark angel Mary Vetsera show greed and tenderness fighting with sensuous exhaustion.

In Mark Morris's *Dido and Aeneas* (1989) the mourning chorus of dancers in Act II seems to tread the pulse of Dido's grief at her lover's betrayal. They cross the stage in trembling steps with their bodies flattened into archaic two-dimensional positions – torsos twisted, heads averted, palms flat. The extreme stylization of their movements suggests both resignation and dignity, while at the same time the unnatural torque of their bodies and the blind turning of their heads portray extremes of torment and despair.

But eloquent as these images are, they are not literal statements of fact or emotion and most dance leaves itself wide open to interpretation. Choreographers themselves rarely start out with a single narrative idea which they then 'translate' into movement – a step is dictated just as much by the flow of the movement and the music as by any dramatic motive. Many are interested, surprised or charmed by the various interpretations their audiences draw from their choreography.

Because of this fluidity dance can't be trusted with very detailed facts – as the choreographer George Balanchine famously said, there are no mothers-in-law in ballet. Any work with a complicated scenario has to rely on extended programme notes or include text or film to develop its plot. But choreographers don't set out to be writers. The point of dance language is that it gives physical form to fantasy, feeling and sense, not to logical ideas. (Which doesn't mean that dance is not susceptible to logic.) It gives us images of the individual ways that people inhabit their skin and the world around them – whether they be Aurora balancing serenely on her points in *The Sleeping Beauty* (1890), princess of all she so graciously surveys, or the ruthless, reckless 'Eurocrash' dancer who dashes her body through an assault course of rolls and falls with the brutalized energy of the late twentieth century.

Dance condenses moments of human conduct and behaviour – but some of the greatest dance works have no narrative at all. These often seem close to visual art and music. We discuss the patterns made by dancers in terms of architecture, balance and line; we talk about individual bodies having sculptural form and of dance phrases building rhythm, harmony and flow. And because we prize the purely formal qualities of these works, we call them abstract.

Yet this term contradicts a basic truth about dance, which is that it is always human. Choreography is created out of individual bodies and personalities, not out of neutral paint, metal or ink. Bodies are the way we communicate. We read people's histories in their faces and we read their intentions through their gestures. We make up stories about them, so of course we make up stories about dancers. Balanchine, despite being the twentieth century's greatest popularizer of 'abstract ballet', said, 'Put a man and a girl on the stage and there is already a story. A man and two girls, there's already a plot.'

In the body language of dance, even the purest movement will express something. A dancer's flying leap may induce a physical lift in us as we watch (audiences frequently enact their own private, tiny dances during a performance), while a dying fall may carry the weight of resignation or despair. A hypnotically repetitive sequence of steps will bring a suspension of time and place;

a passage of quick, rhythmically uneven dance will make our hearts beat faster.

Some choreographers, though, may try to bleach out the physical drama of dance. In the post-modern choreography of the 60s and 70s simple runs, walks and gestures were performed in a strictly functional manner, and often ordered into geometric patterns that mimicked the cleanness of abstract painting or sculpture. Audiences weren't meant to interpret the movement or to become distracted by the individual personalities of the performers (even though they must actually have found themselves fascinated by one dancer's poise, amused by another's features or struck by a third's resemblance to their cousin, and so on).

LOOKING AT DIFFERENT STYLES

The premise of post-modern dance was that it required a style of viewing very different from ballet or early modern dance – and every other dance genre also proposes its own ideal way of seeing. If audiences are not meant to look for flying jumps and romantic agonies in 60s minimalism, they're also not intended to expect raw emotion or realistic drama in the ballet repertoire of the nineteenth century.

When we view the language of classical ballet we're meant to be ravished by its qualities of proportion, nobility and grace. The proud line and effortless airy flights of the dancers' bodies deny the mundane world. Their confident symmetrical patterns rarely distort themselves to express raw sex or brutal pain. And within the studied perfection of the classical language they are judged as failures if their feet are not stretched to a quivering point, if their arms are not graciously moulded, if their legs are weak and their heads swim during *pirouettes*.

Modern dance, by contrast, makes a virtue, even a religion, out of individual deviations. All the many different languages it has developed during the twentieth century express personal, rather than idealized, notions of human conduct and they embrace a range of private dance aesthetics. Martha Graham's tense angles and driven falls, Merce Cunningham's quizzical gestures and asymmetric rhythms imply very contrasting ideas of what the body can and should be doing. These also differ radically from the low-key pedestrian dancing of the post-modern 60s and 70s, which, with its casual dress and its denial of sex and spectacle, would have appalled – and then bored rigid – any nineteenth-century balletomane.

WHO DOES THE LOOKING?

This introduces another obvious variable into the way we read dance – for if each style proposes its own ideal viewer, then each viewer proposes his or her own ideal dance. We all bring our own prejudices, passions and blind spots to the theatre. When I watch Marius Petipa's *Sleeping Beauty* I bring all the baggage of a white English middle-class woman brought up in the late twentieth century and I view the stage completely differently from, say, a St Petersburg nobleman in the Maryinsky Theatre a hundred years ago, a second-generation British Asian living in London today or a fan of post-modern dance who cannot watch ballet without flinching at its gilded artifice.

THE OBJECT WE LOOK AT

What is certain is that the work I see will never be the same as the one viewed by my neighbour. Even if we both come to the theatre with similar values and expectations, we'll inevitably notice different details in the performance. We will scan the stage differently, make different connections between events, and the more that's happening on stage, the more likely our versions will diverge.

What heightens the uniqueness of our response is the ephemeral nature of the product. Despite sophisticated advances in video and notation, there's no completely satisfying way of reproducing a live dance performance. The complexity of what happens in a theatre on a particular night is lost for ever because there's no common object (like a book or a film or a painting) against which we can test our memories and opinions.

Some dance works, of course, have a longer shelf life than others. Nineteenth-century classical ballets are more familiar to the general public than many contemporary dance works because they've been around for longer and are performed much more frequently. Yet these works are certainly not set in stone, and Petipa and his collaborator Lev Ivanov would have trouble recognizing some aspects of their ballet *Swan Lake* (1895) in the versions we see today. One reason is that the nineteenth century had no comprehensive system of dance notation to record its ballets, and when works were passed on to new dancers individual steps, and even whole dances, were altered. Another reason is that the choreography is now danced differently.

Dancers' bodies change and we can only imagine how the technique of the stocky ballerinas of Petipa's time differed from that of today's streamlined athletes. And while we now regard the choreographer's steps as sacrosanct (and protected by copyright), in Petipa's day dancers used to change them freely to suit their individual techniques. In fact, when Petipa climaxed the Act III *pas de deux* of *Swan Lake* (1895) with a string of thirty-two *fouettés* (whipping turns), it wasn't just because these steps seemed dramatically and compositionally apt. It was because his ballerina Pierina Legnani was one of the few dancers of the day who could get her legs around this difficult technical trick and audiences insisted on seeing her perform it at every opportunity. Other less sturdy and co-ordinated dancers had to substitute their own favourite stunts when they performed this role – though, of course, many of today's dancers can knock off *fouettés* with double or triple turns in the middle without apparently turning a hair.

In the same ballet Petipa also gave a lot of dancing to a minor character, the Prince's friend Benno, since Pavel Gerdt, who was the Prince in the first performances, was getting too stiff and short-winded to partner his ballerina and dance all the steps himself. With today's Olympic-standard male dancers, the Prince dances every step he can get hold of, and Benno may not even get a mention in the cast list, his role is so reduced.

The set, the costumes, the style of acting, the interpretation also change with different productions of the classics. One reason why these ballets survive is that they are made new – for better or for worse – each generation. Even within the same generation different dancers will produce different readings of the same roles. For any piece of choreography is always coloured by the dancers' personalities, by their bodies, their responses to the music and by the strengths and limits of their techniques. And that is perhaps what sets dance most vividly and mysteriously apart from the other arts – it is only alive in the bodies of those who perform it. The poet W. B. Yeats saw this truth as a kind of metaphysical conundrum when he pondered, 'How do you tell the dancer from the dance?' in 'Sailing to Byzantium'. But for choreographer Merce Cunningham it's a practical fact of life: 'You can't describe a dance without talking about the dancer. You can't describe a dance that hasn't been seen, and the way of seeing it has everything to do with the dancers . . . that's the trap.'

What both men are saying is that dance is the art of the moment. It exists in the gaze of those who are watching and the bodies of those who perform it. What we dance addicts hope for at every performance is the combination of the dancers' perfect execution and our own perfect attention to what's happening on stage. What we remember afterwards may only be a set of images, emotions and ideas which have been sparked by that combination. *Reading Dance* is about how we get hold of those pictures, feelings and memories, how we interpret them and finally how we judge them.

Part One: READING STYLE IN DANCE

From one week to another a dance venue might programme a charming reconstruction of an eighteenth-century ballet, a dance-theatre piece where performers clamber around a massive steel-and-Perspex set, or a triple bill of Ashton ballets. The works spanned by today's repertoire have been spawned by different centuries and by different continents. And many of them demand that we read the body in very different ways.

The characteristic shapes, rhythms and gestures of one dance style will carry ideas of beauty and offer images of human behaviour that are very different from those of another. We should no more expect filigree footwork from an 80s company shod in Doc Martens than we should be surprised by the sexual politics of nineteenth-century Russian ballet. Sexual difference – female grace and lightness contrasted with male strength and support – is inscribed in the very muscles of classical dancers, as are aristocratic notions of beauty. When we read the body of the classical dancer, we're not only identifying the steps and positions that make up its style. We're taking on board a whole set of aesthetic principles and moral values.

To identify these and to fill in the background of other dance styles, Part One of this book is a preliminary historical tour, pointing out landmarks in the social context, the philosophies and the body languages of different dance forms. This tour unapologetically takes in many of my favourite works and is guided by my own interests and interpretations. It also concentrates on choreography that can be seen in the current Western repertoire, making no claims for historical, social or geographical completeness. There are encyclopaedias and reference books already covering the ground admirably, and I want my own more limited range of facts to act as a frame for the most important subject in dance: the human body and all the different ways which it has found to decorate and express itself.

The history of Western theatre dance has been dominated by classical ballet – which has been performed on stages for over three centuries. During this time it has told very different stories, held different notions of beauty and portrayed very different kinds of people. Even some of the steps that form its basic vocabulary have come in and out of fashion. But it still remains the most academic and rigorously codified of all Western dance forms. Its movements stem from a basic grammar which is handed on from generation to generation and which forms the basis of all classical teaching and much of ballet's choreography.

THE CLASSICAL BODY

The human body is a stubborn, tightly knit and earth-bound mechanism that doesn't naturally adapt itself to the wide, turned-out positions of ballet or to its soaring lines. So every day, in ballet schools and companies all over the world, dancers put themselves through a ninety-minute class that will laboriously coax their bodies into ballet's stylized shapes, while at the same time preparing them for feats of balance, co-ordination and strength. (It's always said that if dancers miss one class, they will notice the effect in their own dancing; if they miss two, their teacher will notice; and if they miss three their public will notice.)

The daily routine of class is meant to instil in dancers a near-religious dedication. Anna Pavlova said of her training in St Petersburg that it was like 'a convent whence frivolity is banned and where merciless discipline reigns'. Some great dancers, though, may choose to override convention. According to ballet director Julian Braunsweg, the English ballerina Alicia Markova in middle age

never attended class and walked through every rehearsal, usually in a fur coat and high heeled shoes. 'I did class for thirty years. If my body isn't good enough now, it never will be,' she said. Before a performance she flexed her long, delicate feet, clenched and unclenched her hands and then moved on to the stage as if blown by a gentle breeze.

For the dedicated, though, class begins at the barre, where the dancers perform a graduated series of exercises that warm up the feet and muscles (crucially round the groin and in the thighs and calves), so that the legs can rotate easily in the hip sockets and lift free from the ground in the classic turned-out shapes of ballet.

Away from the barre, the dancers perform *adagio* (a series of slow balances) where their legs lift and fold through, *arabesques* (a balance on one leg where the other leg is stretched to the front or back), *attitudes* (where the lifted leg is bent) and *développés* (where a lifted bent leg unfolds slowly and majestically up to graze the dancer's nose or ear). Then come *pirouettes* (turns in a variety of positions), *petit allegro* (the brilliant, speedy steps that make up the embroidery of ballet), *petite batterie* (the tiny beaten jumps that get the dancers airborne), and finally *grand allegro* (the big jumps like *grand jeté* and *grand jeté en tournant*).

The steps are universally known by their French names since it was in France that ballet was formulated as a language. A teacher can thus rap out a string of snappily accented instructions (*glissade, pas de bourrée, coupé, jeté*) and have a room full of students launching into a unison flurry of steps where they slide, run, shift weight and jump from one foot to the other. Though individual teachers may stress different nuances, may even add their own variations on a step, the basic vocabulary of ballet doesn't alter. You could put a dancer from anywhere in the world in a class and he or she'd be able to join in.

Not only do most of ballet's steps look the same the world over, so too do its basic principles of demeanour and design. The following are six of the most important.

ONE: GRACE

In ballet much of the movement is powered from the centre of the dancer's body – the muscles of the solar plexus, buttocks and lower back – but the effort remains invisible. The dancing must look as if it's generated by a secret motor that runs smoothly within the body's inner core. A difficult movement should certainly never be accompanied by visible strain, like the hefting of shoulders, the flexing of biceps or the bracing of thighs. Nor should dancers ever visibly wince from any pain they're (frequently) suffering from strained muscles or battered feet. (Some dancers dangerously pride themselves on the machismo of their suffering. Legend has it that when Pavlova once finished a particularly quick bright solo she left a trail of bloody footprints behind her as she exited – the stigmata of the profession.)

TWO: TURN-OUT

Pure classical dancers never adopt a natural, casual stance, and the most extreme stylization of their bodies is caused by 'turn-out'. This term describes the rotation of the arms and legs in their sockets so that dancers present a wide, open view of their bodies to the audience. In the legs, the rotation is so extreme that the knees are swivelled out to face to the side, and when the dancers stand in a basic 'first position' their heels will touch and their toes also point sideways, creating a near-straight line with the feet.

All the other positions of the feet (upon which every ballet step is built) are variations on this stance. In 'second position' the feet are placed hip-width apart to provide a secure base, in 'fifth' they are tightly crossed, toe to heel, enclosing a taut coil of energy that's poised to spring the dancer into action.

To echo the feet the arms are braced in long, light curves that are either held out in front of the body ('first'), or spread to the side ('second') or upwards to frame the face ('fifth').

This turned-out, symmetrical body stance isn't simply designed to set dancers apart from ordinary mortals. It also gives the body a confident demeanour and makes it appear both larger and more legible on stage. A turned-out leg can rise much higher and much further away from the body than a turned-in leg, dramatically increasing the scale of the movement, while the mechanics of turn-out also make it easier for dancers to move fast in all directions without averting their face and body from the audience.

THREE: THE VERTICAL AXIS

If the dancers' limbs radiate outwards, their heads and torsos form vertical lines – aspiring towards the heavens and disdaining the earth. Rarely do you see pure classical dancers crouch over double, or fall to the floor, unless they are miming death. The length of their body line is exaggerated by their tautly stretched legs and feet, and by the women actually dancing on point.

FOUR: THE DENIAL OF GRAVITY

Classical dancers spend as much time as possible either in the air or appearing to float just above the ground. They seem to be less hampered by gravity than other mortals. The women's point shoes allow them to skim the floor in little running steps or to freeze in balances. Both sexes arc through the air in high leaps that land in softly cushioned *pliés* (bent legs) rather than clunking heavily back to the floor. Both have to whip through multiple turns without looking dizzy, and men have to lift women as if they were no more than a drift of blossom. A raised leg in *attitude*, *arabesque* or *développé* must appear to float upwards without strain and even the supporting leg must never appear to buckle under the dancer's weight. In fact, ballet dancers don't typically stand or balance on a bent leg (as classical Indian dancers do). Their limbs are stretched for maximum resistance to the earth.

The extreme stylization of the body helps to create this apparent weightlessness. In many *attitude* positions, for instance, the dancer's lifted leg is bent, with its knee raised higher than its pointed foot, and this slightly tilted horizontal plane cocks an extra snook at gravity, making the whole leg appear to float. The arms raised in a curve over the head also create the illusion that the dancer is being lifted out of his or her body. The straight supporting leg doesn't actually seem to be bearing any weight at all.

The illusion of weightlessness is also intensified by the fact that classical movements rarely take the shortest route. A jump, an arch of the back, a circling of the leg will all pass through the highest possible point, the widest arc – as if the dancer has all the time and energy in the world and there are no forces pulling or constraining the movement.

Often the most heart-stopping moments in ballet are those where the body seems to be moving in two contradictory directions at once. In a high jump called a *cabriole* (usually performed by men) the dancer almost sits in the air with his legs thrust in front of him performing a fast scissoring movement. The movement has a sharp forward attack – yet at the same time the dancer may also arch his back luxuriantly backwards as if airily, even negligently, denying the effort of his legs.

FIVE: ORNAMENTATION

Ballet is the most lavish and unpractical kind of dancing. Steps are embellished at every point with little angles of the shoulder or head, decorative arm movements, beats and flourishes of the ankles and feet. As the dancers twist and turn their bodies, they show them off to us from every possible angle. Sitting in our seats we rarely see a flattened two-dimensional picture – but a mobile, three-dimensional sculpture.

SIX: DECORUM

Ballet not only contrives to display the body in the most pleasing and harmonious arrangements, it also rarely chooses to express raw emotion. Love, cruelty and madness are conveyed through the most decorous of dance metaphors. Ballet is, in fact, the natural dance expression of a culture that prefers to idealize rather than expose the body.

EARLY COURT BALLETS

Ballet's aristocratic values are actually woven deep into its ancestry, because it developed out of the dance, song and music spectacles that were staged in the great Renaissance courts of Europe. Monarchs and nobility during the sixteenth and seventeenth centuries all appeared in these lavish court entertainments, whose choreographed dances allowed them to parade their personal elegance on a mass scale. In preparation for these appearances, they devoted hours to mastering the little running steps, turns, jumps and elegant hand gestures which their dancing masters had lifted out of peasant folk dances and then polished into smooth, dextrous choreography. They also had to memorize the complex patterns which the steps traced across the floor, enabling large groups of dancers to move together in an intricate human geometry.

These court ballets were highly elaborate and often featured astounding scenic devices. One of the earliest recorded was the 1581 extravaganza *Ballet comique de la Reine Louise*, which was performed in front of Henry III at the Palais de Bourbon in Paris and which lasted from ten at night until four the next morning. The plot was taken from Homer's story about the enchantress Circe, and was also a political allegory condemning the civil wars and religious conflicts that were tearing France apart. The ballet's choreography thus delicately offered images of elegant harmony to oppose the scenes of battle and sorcery. At one point Queen Louise and her ladies, dressed as naiads, were carried in on a three-tiered fountain to dance with twelve pages; and in the grand sequence that closed the ballet, lines of naiads and dryads danced through forty different geometric dance patterns.

At this point in ballet's history, the dancing body was little more than a graceful but limited instrument for displaying personal grace and social skills. But by the eighteenth century ballet had moved from the court to the theatre and most dancers had become professional. With far more extensive training, their technique developed exponentially. Different dancers mastered new steps and added them to the vocabulary, establishing many of the staple jumps and turns of today's classical language.

In the early eighteenth century this burgeoning range of steps was mostly contrived to show off the dancers' technique and to create decorative interludes for operas. But towards the end of the century dancers and choreographers were beginning to explore ballet's dramatic potential by inventing more expressive gestures and trying to suggest character through varying the movement's pace and attack. Jean-Georges Noverre, a French choreographer passionately determined to elevate dance into a dramatic art, argued for ballets where the movement 'should speak with fire and energy'. Envisioning this, he suggested how one might choreograph a scene where a 'troupe of fauns' was pursuing a 'band of nymphs' (a popularly erotic theme for ballet) and the movement could give 'an air of ferocity to some of the fauns, to others less passion, to these a more tender air and lastly to the others a voluptuous character'.

By 1828 the Italian dancer, choreographer and teacher Carlo Blasis was able to publish his *Code of Terpsichore*, which analysed the mechanical basis of ballet technique and laid down principles for its efficient instruction. It's from this point that we date modern ballet, partly because it had reached such technical sophistication, and partly because we can readily see versions of many of the works choreographed after this date (unlike pre-1830 ballets, which are only now being slowly reconstructed).

ROMANTIC BALLET

In the first half of the nineteenth century ballet started cutting loose from its mortal coils. Ballerinas all around Europe began imitating sylphs and ghosts and attempting to deny the solidity of their flesh with dancing that aspired to weightlessness and delicacy of line rather than dazzling technical show. In ballets that no longer aimed to display the magnificence of court, promote political loyalties or decorate opera stages, dancers dreamed of the supernatural and the spiritual. Bodies attempted to become light as air.

As London's *Morning Post* commented in 1843:

Formerly dancers' evolutions were as precise as those of soldiers . . . Now [they] have discovered that the line of beauty in dancing is like that of Hogarth in painting – and that the more it is waving, undulatory, and inclined, the more it is graceful and captivating. They have gone one step further and laid down this axiom, that dancing excels exactly in proportion as it resembles flying.

Romantic ballet was in vogue.

This new style was born out of a radical technical innovation – women's new-found ability to dance on the tips of their toes. Wearing shoes toughened by a little cotton stiffening and a line of darning, dancers like Marie Taglioni could, by dint of hard muscular effort, perch so high on their toes that they seemed to be hovering above the ground. Ballerinas came to be viewed not simply as skilled and pretty acrobats, but as creatures of freedom and mystery, fragile inhabitants of another world. To Romantic poets and intellectuals, who yearned fashionably after the Ideal, these dancers seemed miraculously to garb the Spirit in physical form.

The popularity of Romantic ballet was fuelled by a public avid for sensation and fantasy. After the middle-class monarch Louis-Philippe had been installed on the French throne, ballet at the Paris Opéra became a private enterprise. No longer in thrall to the tastes of courtiers and kings, all of its new productions had to appeal to the general public – and what the public wanted was high gothic melodrama.

From the early nineteenth century most of European culture had been in the grip of Romanticism. An unsettling climate of political instability, scientific change and creeping industrialism produced a fashion for escapist art. People wanted stories that would fictionalize their terrors of the unknown as well as channel their desires. They wanted to ignore the privations of mass urban living and retreat into tales of perfect love, magical escapade and exotic adventure.

Ballet plunged into this vogue for the supernatural and the marvellous with a frenzy. The new fairy heroines skimmed the stage on the tips of their toes in white gauze frocks. The new heroes were men weary of social convention, who pursued these females with a kind of madness. While the heroines' eerie beauty tormented their pursuers' senses, their ghostly delicacy put them for ever out of the heroes' reach.

New technology in the theatre made it possible to present these visions of seductive mystery with a potent realism. In the Paris Opéra gas lamps with large reflectors that softened and diffused light were installed, creating pools of moonlight and enticing shadows. They lent magic to the stage machinery of trap doors and wires, with which dancers miraculously appeared and disappeared, and gave extra verisimilitude to the smoke machines, explosives, waterfalls, etc., that conjured the ballets' haunting settings.

This lighting also exaggerated the poetry of the dancing, and one of the by-products of Romantic ballet was a gush of colourful, hectic prose from the pens of critics and fans who sought to re-create the marvels on stage. 'To describe Marie Taglioni one would have to tip a hummingbird quill into the colours of the rainbow and inscribe it on the gauze wings of a butterfly,' raved one French writer, Jules Janin, along with many others who rarely referred to these dancers as real women but as birds, feathers or moonbeams.

A similarly overwrought idealism also afflicted painters and illustrators, who showed ballerinas perched weightlessly on flowers or twigs, tipped forward in some impossibly off-balance position as if supported by a passing summer breeze. Careless of the rules of anatomy, these dancers were drawn with skins translucent in a pearly light, with feet absurdly tiny. There was no suggestion of muscle and sinew in their bodies; their limbs were so delicately rounded they couldn't possibly have borne the dancers' weight (see illus. 1).

The reality was bloodily and exhaustingly different. When Marie Taglioni was preparing for her stage début in 1822, her father Filippo (a dancer and choreographer) forced her to practise for six hours a day until she was almost unconscious with exhaustion. Her biggest challenge was learning how to achieve the new feat of toe-dancing with grace and apparent ease. Since ballet shoes didn't have the solidly blocked ends that allow today's dancers to balance on their toes with relatively little effort, Taglioni and her rivals were actually having to hold themselves up on their toes by brute muscular power (though Taglioni was famous for being able to conceal the strain with unusually graceful arms, a gently pliant torso and a sweet, airy jump).

The lightness and fluency of Taglioni and her peers was aided by the fact that turn-out had increased since the eighteenth century. (Some dancers used to stand for long periods in a box which forced their feet and legs to rotate outwards; others used to lie on the floor and have their maids or lovers stand on their hips. According to American dance writer Deborah Jowitt, 'Carlotta Grisi said sourly that those times Jules Perrot stood on her hips while she lay face down on the floor with legs spread were the erotic high points of their liaison.') But however it was achieved, greater turn-out allowed the dancers to raise their legs higher as well as facilitating faster steps, higher jumps and more rapid changes of direction. Lighter, more loosely fitting dresses also allowed the dancers much more freedom in the torso and thighs – so that they could sway, jump and turn with greater ease.

The Romantic line is much softer than the 'classical' line which developed towards the end of the nineteenth century. Instead of holding a rather four-square position, with limbs fully stretched and energy radiating out through the body, Romantic dancers seemed almost to drift. Their torsos didn't rise to a stiff vertical but angled gently forward; their arms didn't lie in a long curve but were delicately bent at the wrist and elbow as if scarcely supporting their own weight. Their legs, although lifted a little higher than those of their eighteenth-century sisters, didn't soar. And the dancers rarely held a position. They flowed from one pose to another, as if the movement was eddying through them.

As well as dancing on their toes, ballerinas were highly valued for their *ballon*, their ability to jump softly and lightly through neat springing steps. They were admired too for their staying power in *adagio* sequences, where they had to maintain their control through a series of charmingly variegated balances. But despite their pleasing modesty and grace, they were also admired for sex.

Though the prototype for the Romantic ballerina was the elusive ghost or sylph, this didn't mean these dancers lacked erotic appeal; it simply made their sexuality more tantalizing. One of the first works to herald Romanticism proper was the Ballet of the Nuns in Act II of the opera *Robert le Diable* (1831) whose heady mix of death, sex, beauty and blasphemy aroused its audience to unusual scenes of frenzy. The moment when a chorus of dead nuns rose from their graves was described by Hans Christian Andersen in terms of shocked and delighted hyperbole: 'By the hundred they rise from the graveyard and drift into the cloister. They seem not to touch the earth. Like vaporous images, they glide past one another. Suddenly their shrouds fall to the ground. They stand in all their voluptuous nakedness, and there begins a bacchanal.'

These women, flesh and not flesh, alive and dead, inviting yet remote, could hardly appeal more to men raised in an era of repressive social propriety and sexual double standards. They represented licensed fantasy; they were danger and desire incarnate.

In fact, there was a more earthy side of Romanticism which admitted the pleasure of the flesh without the need for spiritual or supernatural seasonings. Instead it found its fantasy in the gypsy, the peasant and the exotic. Taglioni's great rival was Fanny Elssler, prettier and more voluptuous than the thin, chaste-looking Marie, whose famous *cachucha* (a Spanish dance with Eastern influences) involved a lot of stamping, heel-tapping and seductively supple twists of the body.

The French writer Théophile Gautier raved about her: 'What fire! What voluptuousness! What ardour!', while another critic, Charles de Boinge, was slightly shocked in his enthusiasm: 'Those contortions, those movements of the hips, those arms which seem to seek and embrace the absent lover, the mouth crying out for a kiss, that thrilling, quivering, twisting body . . .'

Other stars were Fanny Cerrito, renowned for her soaring

jumps, brilliant point work and unusual speed, and Carlotta Grisi whose speciality was impersonating Eastern maidens from temples and harems.

These glamorous, mysterious and unconfined women were often set against lesser heroines from ordinary middle- to upper-class society. With their conventional beauty and domestic ways, the latter were always being ousted by their more exotic, dead, or elusive sisters – they represented all that the male audience (and possibly the female audience) was trying to escape.

There was no mystique attached to the male heroes of the ballet, who were mostly valued for their ability to partner their ballerinas and keep the plot going. Even though, during the eighteenth century, male dancers ranked as equal stars to female, and even though the mid years of the nineteenth century did not lack male talent, men simply couldn't compete with the cult of the Romantic ballerina. Gautier wrote savagely that, 'Nothing is more abominable than a man who displays his red neck, his great muscular arms, his legs with calves like church beadles, his ... heavily masculine frame shaken with leaps and *pirouettes*. For us a male dancer is something monstrous and indecent.'

So poorly esteemed were men that some choreographers had women dancing the heroes of their ballets, performing *en travesti* – and adding a salacious twist to their admirers' fantasies. The imbalance between male and female roles has often been cited as a reason for Romanticism's rapid decline. The stories and the choreography were too one-sided, the imagery too weighted towards the exquisite, the feminine, the febrile. Certainly by the late 1850s Romantic ballet had wasted itself into an over-formulaic spectacle – and the public's interest had transferred to opera.

Given the genre's relatively short-lived popularity and the lack of any reliable notation to record individual works, it's not surprising that few Romantic ballets survive. However, *Giselle* and *La Sylphide* are classics of the repertoire still.

Neither ballet is performed as it was originally choreographed and, of course, no performances today can replicate the novelty of those first stagings. Television gives us a far more sophisticated diet of spectacle and sex than ballet can ever supply, and we're accustomed to far more bravura displays of dance than those early delicate exercises in point work. But both ballets show the range and power of the Romantic imagination, dramatizing with intense poignancy their heroes' desire to lose their everyday selves in the arms of some otherworldly beauty. And both show how vividly dance can give shape to our strangest impulses and dreams.

La Sylphide

This work was choreographed by Taglioni's father in 1832 to show off Marie's exemplary point work and *ballon*. Its scenario is archetypally Romantic – and chilling. It tells the story of a young Scots crofter, James, who is engaged to the pretty girl next door, Effie. On the eve of their marriage he's visited by a Sylphide who gives him a fatal taste for the sublime. He abandons Effie and pursues the Sylphide into her woodland home where they sport in bliss with her sister sylphs. James is desperate to possess her and is tricked by the evil witch Madge into throwing a magic scarf over the Sylphide's wings. Instead of making her human, it makes her wings drop off and she dies. Ideal beauty cannot live in the mortal world. James's anguish is given a terrible ironic twist at the ballet's close as a wedding march passes by celebrating Effie's union with his more steady-headed neighbour Gurn.

The version we mostly see today was choreographed, after Taglioni's, by the Danish choreographer August Bournonville in 1836 with a score by H. Lovenskjold. (Bournonville actually partnered Marie Taglioni during the years he danced in Paris.) One of the main differences between the two stagings is in the male dancing. Bournonville was never so completely in thrall to the ballerina cult as his colleagues, and during his long career with the Royal Danish Ballet steadily fostered the art of male dancing. The flying open-chested leaps and deft springy footwork given to James and his friends rank in grace and elegance with the sylphs' skimming point work and floating arms.

But the ballet's opening makes it clear who is the star attraction. The curtain rises to show James sleeping in a chair with the Sylphide watching by his side. Her pose is archetypally Romantic – her delicately inclined cheek rests against an exquisitely crooked finger, her elbow nestles on the back of her other hand. A daintily pointed foot peeps out from under her drifting skirts. She seems poised for flight even though her body leans desirously towards James. When she dances, she travels along a charmingly mysterious flight path, fluttering forward and back in little running steps or tiny, gusty jumps, her feet tightly crossed together, her arms floating upwards through the air.

The tug between dreams and harsh fact is so powerfully imagined in this story that it survives updating. A 1994 version by the British company Adventures in Motion Pictures relocates the ballet to a high-rise estate in Glasgow, where James is an out-of-work welder with a drug habit. He is seduced by a Sylphide (looking like a grubby New Age traveller) and runs away with her to a nearby bit of wasteland. Like his prototype, he longs to make this strange creature his own and his solution is to cut off her wings with garden shears. The sylph twitches bloodily, agonizingly to death – giving a grisly new literalness to the old Romantic trauma of idealism massacred by reality.

Giselle

This work was originally choreographed by Jules Perrot and Jean Coralli in 1841 to a score by Adolphe Adam, though the stagings we see today are mostly based on Petipa's reworkings during the second half of the nineteenth century. Here the source of the hero's bewitchment is a beautiful and naïve peasant girl. Count Albrecht, bored and a little alienated, sees Giselle as an escape from life at court and pretends to be a peasant to engage her affections. She falls in love. When she discovers his real identity she loses her mind, and in some versions kills herself with Albrecht's sword, in others dies of a broken heart. Shattered by remorse, Albrecht visits her grave where the ghost of Giselle dances lovingly with him. But the lovers are swept up by a band of Wilis – ghosts of other jilted maidens, who punish deceitful men by forcing them to dance to death. Giselle manages to keep Albrecht alive until dawn when she and the Wilis vanish, leaving Albrecht to ponder his folly and loss. In Act I Giselle's dancing has a folk element of buoyant jumps and springing hops that portray her pretty exuberance. But written into the rhythms of these movements is also a suggestion of her ethereal destiny. In her signature *ballotté* (a jump with a high rocking movement from one foot to another) Giselle seems to hang in space for an extra couple of heartbeats at the apex of each jump, as if already anticipating the airy spirit she'll become.

When she picks up the hem of her skirt and hops daintily on one toe across the stage, her lifted foot tracing a pretty circle as she does so, she is partly performing one of the nineteenth-century ballerina's most popular stunts. But she's also anticipating the way her running steps and hops will graze the floor with ghostly lightness during the second act (as well as denying, at some painful cost to the real-life ballerina, the harsh fact of a hundred-odd pounds of body weight bouncing up and down on a few square inches of toe).

In Act II Giselle's ghost appears almost to rise from the earth as with her hands crossed on her heart she begins to whirl like a dervish, one leg floating up behind her into *arabesque*, her arms drifting forward. As her speed intensifies, she seems to be unravelling the last of her mortal coils, transforming herself into pure spirit.

When Albrecht first sees her he tries to touch her, but she drifts past even as she stretches her long arms towards his embrace. Each dancer seems to be bound by different laws of time and space. Even when he finally holds her in *arabesque* her body leans forward while her arms waft from side to side as if she's about to leave him. When he lifts her through the air on a long, low arc she seems to be only temporarily caught between his hands, not solid, resilient flesh but unstable spirit.

The British ballerina Moira Shearer explains that in this second act

all you have to convey is absolute lightness like gossamer blown away, with just the slightest suggestion of the human element of the character when she realizes Albrecht is there … if you show too much towards him, you're cancelling out your own death in a way. Margot used to run all the way down the line of the Wilis and go *whomp*, throw her arms out to protect him . . . it was too much as if she were really living . . . for this act . . . it's got to be much smaller, almost with your head down a little bit . . . knowing this is all you can do as your spirit self.

When the Swedish choreographer Mats Ek rewrote *Giselle* in 1982 he made Giselle a far more earthy, gawky peasant than the pure exquisite heroine of the original. He emphasized the brutal physicality of her village community – locked into a cycle of birth, copulation and death – as a contrast with the effete court. And his image of visionary transcendence in Act II – the White Act – was not of ghosts and graves but of a lunatic asylum where poor mad Giselle and her other betrayed sisters were all locked away.

NINETEENTH-CENTURY CLASSICAL BALLET

If the ideal woman in Romantic ballet was a dead martyr or a sylph, in the classical ballet of late nineteenth-century Russia she was a princess. If the setting for *Giselle* or *La Sylphide* was a woodland glade, in classical ballet it was often a court. If the desired qualities in Romantic ballet were ethereal grace and exotic dash, in classical ballet they were technical glitter and aristocratic finesse. If Romantic ballet had been fed by the fantasies of a bourgeois audience, classical ballet was fed by the gilded images of court power. Paid for by the Tsar, created primarily to entertain him and his entourage, the Imperial Ballet of Russia was a reflection of the court's splendour, one among many screens behind which the Tsar's illusion of eternal power could be protected from the reality of an increasingly restless middle class.

As the imaginative energy drained out of Romanticism in mid-nineteenth-century Western Europe, the creative focus of ballet shifted north and east. In Denmark August Bournonville began developing a body of work that mixed Romanticism, local folk tale and naturalism in a formula unique to the Royal Danish Ballet. In Russia, though, ballet evolved along the course already set by France and Italy, drawing on the melting pot of talents that had been lured to Russia from Western Europe ever since the late eighteenth century.

MARIUS PETIPA

It was a Frenchman, in fact, the dancer and choreographer Marius Petipa, who was most responsible for taking Russian classicism to its apogee of sophistication during the five decades that he was ballet master for the Imperial Ballet in St Petersburg.

His work, naturally, developed out of the themes and preoccupations of the early nineteenth century. As a dancer he'd performed in many of the early Romantic ballets, including *Giselle*, and their images of death, madness and the supernatural remained potent for him. His own works frequently pivoted around the contrast between corrupt reality and its visionary alternative. In *La Bayadère* (1877), for instance, the heroine, Nikiya, after being killed off by her jealous rival Gamzatti, returns to haunt the hero in an opium dream – a vision of reproachful beauty surrounded by dozens of identically lovely dead maidens. In *Swan Lake* (which Petipa choreographed in collaboration with the Russian dancing master Lev Ivanov in 1895) the Swan Princess Odette also occupies a white magical world which acts as a chastely beautiful rebuke to the materialism and moral treachery of the court. Even the golden girl Aurora in *Sleeping Beauty* becomes, temporarily, a vision so that she can lure the prince to her bedside and have him kiss her out of her enchanted sleep.

Petipa's ballets were, however, far less simple in scale and conception than the earlier Romantic ballets. Typically three or four acts long, they often resembled nineteenth-century opera in their labyrinthine complexities – and absurdities – of plot. Rajah's palaces, temples, harems, shipwrecks, fights, chases, dream sequences were common fare, playing to audience demand for grand spectacle and dramatic excess, opulent costumes and gorgeous settings.

The public also expected to be dazzled by the dancers, particularly the principals, who embodied all that was glamorous and powerful. The hierarchy of the Imperial Ballet was as strictly graduated as that of court. The grandest stars, who were allowed to deck themselves out in their own jewellery during a performance, dominated the stage, flanked by soloists, demi-soloists, coryphées and finally the humble *corps de ballet*. (Gazing out at the audience, the dancers would see their own ranking system reflected in the auditorium, with the Tsar and his family occupying the grandest seats, surrounded by nobility, court officials and, in the poorest seats, the ordinary public. The court was reflected in other ways too. Much of the choreography was constructed around parades, grand entrances and ceremonials which were mirrors of court rituals and allowed the dancers, like the nobility, to show off their elegant costumes and manners.)

Within this hierarchy Petipa constructed elaborate stage pictures. He wove the dancers of the *corps* through intricately patterned dances, carving the stage into circles, squares, lines, diagonals and rosettes. These figures would then freeze to frame the dances of individual soloists and principals – the stars of the ballet moving in a galaxy of lesser dancers.

Symmetry and order were the gods of Petipa's classicism. Each ballet was structured to maintain a balance between sections of mime and pure dance, between classical movement and folk or national dances and between group dances and *pas de deux*.

The structure of each *pas de deux* was also rigidly codified. It began with an *adagio* where the man supported his ballerina through her most beautiful poses. This was followed by a male variation – featuring his most effective jumps and turns (these became more athletic as men regained some of their old ascendancy), then a female variation which showcased her point work and solo balances, and finally a firework coda where man and woman reached a climactic pitch of virtuosity together.

This formulaic approach was basic to the decorous way in which ballet had traditionally approached sex. It was rare for men to do more than support their ballerinas with their hands. Bodies did not press or entwine, they rested gently and chastely against each other. Codifying the structure of every *pas de deux* meant that every meeting, every love affair and every betrothal followed the same carefully bounded stages. It limited the dangerous effects of individual passion and unlicensed desire.

Order was also written into every detail of the dancers' moves. The language Petipa used was taught every day in the classroom, and he upheld its rules. It was a language that shaped the human body into harmonious shapes and rarely allowed the stark impress of emotion to disturb its graceful lines.

It was, though, a constantly evolving style. Eighteenth-century Russian ballet was grounded in the rather four-square, correct style of French dancing, but over the decades, new colours were added. The Russians themselves added a more flamboyant arching and twisting of the body, characteristic of their own national dances. The Swedish teacher Christian Johansson introduced faster and more detailed footwork when he started teaching in the 1860s, and also expanded and refined the men's technique. Guest appearances by Italian ballerinas in the 1880s and 90s further advanced female technique with their unusually powerful point work, dashingly athletic jumps and turns.

Their virtuosity was made possible by developments in the technology of ballet shoes which were now fortified by a stiffened box for the toes – giving far greater protection and support to the foot. The ballerina was no longer a fey sprite, floating from one balance to the next, but was empowered to perform a new range of bravura feats and had a whole new language to speak. She could playfully hop, jump and skip on her toes; she could angrily jab her point into the ground; she could ethereally skim the floor in even longer strings of *bourrées* (light running steps danced on the toes) than her Romantic sisters; she could trace a teasing circle with the point of her toes; she could control more effectively the rise from flat foot to full point. She could also turn multiple *pirouettes* and *fouettés* on point and she could hold her balances for much longer with her legs lifted increasingly high. (Heights, though, were still modest, compared to our own dancers' skyscraper extensions. The Russian ballerina Alexandra Danilova records that even in 1912 it was considered 'rather daring, a little bit vulgar' to lift the leg too high. '"You are not in the circus," our teacher would scold if our legs went much above the waist.')

Because of the ballerina's new abilities the whole nature of male–female partnering changed, with the man no longer just gently embracing the woman or dancing alongside her, but aiding and abetting her through bravura displays. By supporting her at the waist or holding her hands he could help her zip through fast or slow turns, let her swoon into backbend or freeze in a triumphant *arabesque*. (The ballerina's shortened tutu showed off these new tricks and dramatized her strengthened legwork.) And as the dancers' confidence and strength increased, more of these positions began to be held in the air – in a fast-developing vocabulary of lifts that gave the illusion they were triumphantly conquering space.

Classical ballet in all its aspects thus became grander – the dancers were aristocrats of the stage, arrogantly in charge of their physical destiny. The drifting torso of Romantic ballet was now lifted tall, the arms were held in more forcefully etched positions, the legs radiated greater power and the steps were more gorgeously embellished.

Just as Petipa coaxed his stars to reveal more and more of their brilliance, so he developed his *corps de ballet* into a virtuoso collective instrument. In *Sleeping Beauty* he turned it into a kaleidoscope of abstract patterns which sometimes crystallized into dramatic images – as in the Vision Scene, where dozens of women became a human maze, forming corridors and barriers around which the Prince pursued his elusive image of Aurora. In his staging of *Giselle* the chorus of Wilis were briefly an army of vengeful ghosts criss-crossing the stage, their stretched arms and legs in *arabesque* slicing through space with the deadly force of bayonets. Lev Ivanov, Petipa's collaborator, was a master at suggesting natural forces and powerful emotions through his own more organic patterning of the *corps*. In his Act IV of *Swan Lake* (Petipa choreographed Acts I and III) the chorus of Swans whirled round the stage on the wings of their agitation and distress; in the Dance of the Snowflakes in the first act of *The Nutcracker* (1892) the dancers blew up an exquisite snowstorm as they danced in eddying circles.

But Petipa's own use of the *corps de ballet* in Act III of *Bayadère* probably remains the most sustained and extraordinary instance of the power of group magic in nineteenth-century ballet. As dozens of identically dressed dancers glide on to the stage, one after another, performing the same sequence of steps and balances, we are stilled into the same trance state that has overtaken the ballet's opium-smoking hero Solor. Dancers appear to be reflecting each other in an infinity of mirrors, creating the illusion of endless space while the slow, steady repetition of movements suspends all sense of time.

Though Petipa's primary aim as choreographer was to dazzle the audience with his own ingenuity and with his dancers' brilliance, the movement vocabulary he and Ivanov developed was capable of registering vivid states of emotions and subtleties of character. Even if the palette of classical ballet wasn't wide, its colours could still be intense. Nikiya in *Bayadère* is an Indian temple dancer who moves with an ersatz Oriental sinewyness – her back arching lavishly and her arms freed from academic correctness into supple, serpentine curves. In *Swan Lake* the contrast between the heroine Odette and evil seductress Odile is shown by soft dancing set against hard, by modesty set against flash.

Swan Lake

Odette is in fact a princess who's been turned into a swan by a wicked enchanter and can only be released by an oath of true love. Prince Siegfried encounters Odette by a lake, falls in love and swears eternal faith. But back at his court, Odile appears, disguised as Odette. She bamboozles the Prince into swearing his love for her, and Odette's chances of escape are ruined. The Prince races back to the lake and he and Odette leap into its waters together, to the grand, cathartic climax of Tchaikovsky's score.

The doomed but exquisite Odette in her pure white tutu clearly descends from the heroines of Romantic ballet. Her semi-bird nature is dramatized by powerful undulations that make her arms ripple like great wings, by the way she ducks her averted face into her shoulder when she first meets the Prince and by the shy abruptness that characterizes her initial movements. Though her classical dancing also marks her out as an archetypal Ballerina Princess, certain nuances continue to emphasize her unique character. When she balances on point, her free foot beating

rapidly against her other ankle, the feathery speed of the movement emphasizes her wild nature, and the ecstasy of her growing
love for the Prince. When she stretches out her leg in high
développé, it has the unfolding slowness of a sigh. When her whole
body arches back against his and her outstretched leg sinks slowly
down to the floor, the rhythm is of someone relaxing into a
moment of perfect but unaccustomed trust.

The Danish ballerina Toni Lander has spoken of how Odette
is probably falling for the Prince 'without the knowledge of what
falling in love is' and how the great moments of their *pas de deux*
in Act II contain 'moments of pure joy . . . and then this fear of
what's going to happen, and sorrow for the future'. When Odette
beats her foot, Lander says, 'For me it was almost like shivering.
The Portuguese say, "When I'm happy I'm crying," and that's
what is meant by this *battu*.'

In Act III Odile attempts to impersonate Odette but can only
distort her movements. She never sinks against anyone but is all
confidence, resistance and attack. The rippling effect in her arms
is performed faster and harder, so that she's more like a bird of
prey than a graceful swan. While Odette's face is nearly always
turned away or downcast, Odile's is triumphantly scouring the
crowd for applause. While Odette, like earlier Romantic sylphs,
seems to pass through poses, seems almost to tremble for the
need of support, Odile looks as if she could balance in *arabesque*
for ever, her limbs stretched, her back lifted with the force of her
implacable will. And while the flourishes that decorate Odette's
dancing are exquisite, Odile's signature move is one of the most
notorious tricks in the repertoire, the thirty-two whipping *fouetté*
turns that clinch her seduction of the Prince and work the watching crowd into a lather of anticipation.

One hundred years after Petipa and Ivanov's production, British
choreographer Matthew Bourne staged a new version of *Swan
Lake* that gave the ballet a radical gender twist. Odette became a
male Swan and Odile a louche sexual freebooter (called the
Stranger), the two characters representing not so much the object
of the Prince's love, as the freedom and power which his own
cramped upbringing at court so drearily lacked. The Prince

became a much more complex character than the original Siegfried as the ballet showed him losing his reason in pursuit of these two alter egos. But Bourne's version also created a compelling new image of the Swan and his male *corps de ballet* as powerful and dangerous creatures – their beauty a wild and frightening force of nature.

As in most stagings of the 1895 *Swan Lake*, Bourne's two leading roles (Odette/Swan and Odile/Stranger) were performed by the same dancer, with extreme differences in style having to register contrasting characters. In Petipa's *Sleeping Beauty* Aurora too has to pass through three very different manifestations, all registered by the same dancer within a single role.

Sleeping Beauty

Sleeping Beauty (also set to music by Tchaikovsky) is in every way a more compact and contained ballet than *Swan Lake*, featuring less of the wild terrain of gothic melodrama. Its locations are nearly all the beautifully decorated interiors of a palace and its ideals are ultimately those of civilization and sweet reason rather than otherworldly love. Its threats too come from the neatly externalized force of Evil – the Wicked Fairy Carabosse – rather than the demons of sexuality and fantasy that lurk within the characters' minds.

The whole structure of the ballet is also based around the court. Not only is most of it set within the court of King Florestan, but each of the main protagonists is attended by their own mini-courts, and the way in which these are organized is crucial to the telling of the ballet's tale. In the Prologue Florestan's court is ordered strictly according to rank. Everyone except the King yields to his or her superior, and every gesture and every processional entrance seems codified according to palace etiquette. We're alerted to the fact that this rather stuffy palace has little connection with the outside world. Certainly, in forgetting to invite the bad fairy Carabosse to the christening of Baby Aurora, it has shown itself fatally forgetful of Evil.

Carabosse's opposite number – the benign Lilac Fairy – rules over a dancing court. She's surrounded by minor fairies, and by solo fairies and their cavaliers, who all frame her in densely patterned dances. Each of the solo fairies is the keeper of a special virtue which she bestows on Aurora and which is illustrated in the individual style of her dancing.

The Fairy of Purity moves with a studied modesty. Her gracefully lifted arms curve from side to side and her feet move with pretty hesitant rhythms. Her other signature move is the classical mime gesture for purity where one hand brushes the other arm in a slow sweep from forearm to fingertips. The Fairy of Vitality has a quick *piqué* attack, her arms making little flickering gestures. The Fairy of Generosity scatters invisible largesse (in fact, her original – French – name Miettes Qui Tombent means falling breadcrumbs and refers to an ancient Russian tradition where scattering breadcrumbs on a girl baby's cradle ensures her happy motherhood). Fairy Eloquence's fingers trill and quiver in front of her mouth like a songbird and Temperament travels the stage with rapid changes of direction, her arms and hands pointing decisively around her. The Lilac Fairy at their centre is all confidence and grandeur, her body opened wide, her arms stretched and her legs swinging out into space.

When Carabosse intrudes on the christening, usually accompanied by much smoke, she is surrounded by her own courtiers who leap and fawn around her in a grotesque parody of palace etiquette. In many productions she turns on the Fairies and caricatures them savagely, imitating the pretty little gestures that denote their virtues.

By the time Aurora is a young woman Florestan's court has become less inert, filled with the Princess's friends and the pastoral charm of the Garland Dance (which often features some children in its winding patterns). But Carabosse's curse still prevails; Aurora pricks her finger and the whole palace falls into a deep sleep. In Act II the ballet moves, briefly, out of doors, to Prince Florimund's court, one hundred years later. Manners have become less formal; the Prince's court is having a shooting match and they dance and play blind man's bluff. But, like Siegfried in *Swan Lake*, Florimund has his mind on other things. The old Romantic ideals of love and adventure are still poisoning the minds of ballet heroes. When the Lilac Fairy shows him a vision of Aurora he races off to wake her with a kiss.

Act III celebrates the betrothal of Aurora and her Prince, the vanquishing of Evil and the heralding of a new order where ceremony is yoked to courage and love. Young and old, courtiers and ordinary folk, real and fairy-tale characters unite in a final dance presided over by the Lilac Fairy. Aurora herself has been transformed from a charming adolescent to a mature woman. (In the classic double-language of fairy tale, the spindle on which she pricked her finger has prepared her for sexual awakening.)

When we first see her in Act I Aurora's dancing is very animated, fast and pretty, with almost capricious changes of rhythm and direction – as British ballerina Darcey Bussell puts it, 'She's very girly and sparky and hey come on.' But at the centre of that youthful joyousness there is also a serious test, where she suddenly has to assume the dignified authority of a grown-up princess.

The Rose Adagio (which also happens to be one of the most notorious technical challenges in the ballerinas' repertoire) is the moment in the story when Aurora is introduced to the four Princes who've come to court her. She has to dance with all of them, twice, displaying a gracious adult manner appropriate to the situation and certainly not betraying any terror at the steps she has to perform – which actually *are* terrifying.

Balancing on point in *attitude* Aurora has to take the hand of the first Prince, then let it go and balance on her own while the next Prince comes forward to take her hand, and so on. The second time this passage occurs, Aurora is promenaded through a single turn before again having to hold her balance as the Princes switch over.

Most dancers can do these balances quite happily in a studio with a barre close by for support. But the fact that Aurora has to bring off a total of eight in a situation where she's completely exposed in the centre of the stage, when her toes are screaming for a rest, and there is the possibility of a nervous Prince tugging her off balance, makes the Rose Adagio an unnerving prospect. Today we might look askance at the politics of a situation where a woman is so publicly handed from man to man. But in the context of the ballet it's a powerful metaphor for Aurora's fledgeling royal authority as she transcends the terrors of the moment.

In Act II Aurora dances as a vision of herself. The *attitude* and *arabesque* poses that dominated her movement in Act I return in a slower, more ethereal form. Her dancing is rhythmically calmer, the transition between steps more fluid. Royal Ballet Aurora Viviana Durante says the challenge is to 'dance as if you're not there' or, as her colleague Lesley Collier describes it, 'as if you're fading in and out of the steps'.

By Act III Florimund and Aurora are betrothed and they dance together in a set-piece *pas de deux*. This is a technical showstopper (certainly as we see it today) including slippery fish dives where the ballerina revolves in a *pirouette* and ends in a flying balance, perched at the Prince's waist with her whole body curving parallel to the floor. But it also features Aurora's signature balances in their grandest possible style as her limbs stretch extra inches, her back arches and she moves with lovely stateliness through music which, as Collier says, makes Aurora appear 'grand and erotic and lovely'.

TWENTIETH-CENTURY BALLET

Only a decade after Petipa had brought classical ballet to an elegant apotheosis in *Sleeping Beauty* the twentieth century overtook its aristocratic certainties with waves of political and artistic upheaval. The pressure to 'make it new' and to find an individual voice was as passionate a force in dance as it was in music, painting or literature. Choreographers started to think in terms of inventing their own language rather than diligently reprocessing what they'd learnt in class and on stage. They looked for beauty and truth in new lines and rhythms. They allied themselves to avant-garde movements in music, theatre and art. They rewrote the hallowed structure of the old two- to four-act classical ballets. They scorned the old fairy-tale identities of ballet heroes and heroines. Some of them even made ballets that didn't have plot or characters at all.

The dancing body suddenly assumed a whole set of different possibilities and images. No longer aiming for the traditional ideals of nobility and grace, it was free to imitate a much wider range of characters, to let raw emotion puncture its perfect façade and to draw different shapes in the air. Legs and arms no longer had to obey the sacred principle of turn-out; they could be turned inwards or bent at extreme angles to the body. The torso no longer had to be kept scrupulously erect and steps no longer had to generate virtuoso effects.

Such changes of course happened in a context very different from the tenaciously privileged and nostalgic Tsar's court. And for those choreographers who tried to make them within the sphere of classical ballet – rather than daring the new frontiers of modern dance – it was often difficult to find dancers willing to share their new vision. Ballet training is conservative by nature, which means that choreographers such as Vaslav Nijinsky who were struggling to articulate a new vision of ballet frequently had trouble getting dancers to act as their raw material. Live bodies are far less malleable than paint or print – if dancers have been turning out their legs and rounding their arms for twenty years, it's hard for them suddenly to screw their toes inwards and hold their arms at right angles.

Thus, Bronislava Nijinska records that rehearsals for her brother's extraordinary and ferociously difficult *Rite of Spring* (1913) often provoked outright rebellion. Not only were the movements upsettingly unfamiliar, but Nijinsky insisted they be executed with a precision that seemed eccentrically authoritarian to dancers used to some personal freedom of style. His exhausted and demoralized cast sometimes refused to rehearse at all, while the irate Nijinsky interpreted their genuine inability to do certain steps as sabotage.

The revolutionary choreographer is dependent not only on willing dancers but also on a sympathetic management. He or she may create any number of subversive steps in the studio but be powerless to show them on the stage. When Mikhail Fokine was still trying to remake classicism within the staid Maryinsky Company (the Imperial Ballet of St Petersburg), he was thwarted by notions of propriety that now seem absurd. His 1907 ballet *Eunice* was set in Ancient Greece and featured Fokine's early experiments with antique Greek movement. With his crusading zeal for realism, Fokine wanted the dancers to perform barefoot. The horrified management drew in its skirts and insisted they wore tights with toe-nails painted on. Some of the ballerinas too were appalled by Fokine's refusal to let them wear their prize personal jewellery on stage as they'd been accustomed to.

Not surprisingly, Fokine could only think about truly radical changes once he'd left the tradition-encrusted Imperial Ballet and taken his chances with the publicity-seeking and erratically inspired genius of Serge Diaghilev. In 1909 this most famous of ballet impresarios plucked the hottest and most restive talent from the Imperial Ballet and took it to Western Europe. With an immaculate grasp of artistic fashion, he not only encouraged the emerging choreographic talents of Fokine and Nijinsky but allied them with the newest names in painting and music. Les Ballets Russes became famous for its chic, exotic, sometimes scandalous *Gesamtkunstwerks* where new choreography was performed to new music and accompanied by sometimes brazenly shocking designs. Composers like Stravinsky, Milhaud, Debussy, Ravel and Satie were all in the Diaghilev stable and his list of collaborating painters reads like a *Who's Who* of modernism – Picasso, Rouault, de Chirico, Braque, Matisse. (Though such names didn't come cheap. When another would-be impresario met Diaghilev in 1917 he noticed that the latter's 'highly polished shoes had enormous holes in the soles. You could see his socks which were just beginning to wear through. "Never become a ballet impresario, young man," said Diaghilev. "It never pays." ')

While the old Imperial Ballet had performed largely for the Russian court and the claques of balletomanes – all notoriously conservative in their tastes – Diaghilev's Ballets Russes catered to a fashion-conscious audience of artists, intellectuals, socialites and bohemians. It is certain that as a purely commercial operator Diaghilev was not always as free, as disinterested or uniquely bold in his artistic judgements as he liked to suggest. Radical experiments in ballet flourished in Russia during the early years of the Revolution and Diaghilev's rival outfit in Europe, Les Ballets

Suédois, directed by the less famous Rolf de Maré, produced works that were perhaps more dangerously avant-garde.

But arguments about revolutionary supremacy aside, it is certain that the break-up of the old ballet institutions and monopolies allowed new ideas to flourish. Almost every modernist movement of the early twentieth century had its effect on ballet. The movement in Nijinsky's *Rite of Spring* can be seen as a daring exercise in primitivism; Nijinska's *Les Noces* (1923) was influenced by constructivist design and theatre practice; Balanchine's *Prodigal Son* (1929) was an expressionist morality tale. The 1917 ballet *Parade* displayed strong cubist and futurist influences in its juxtaposition of real-life elements and theatrical spectacle. Jean Cocteau's chaotic libretto revolved around a group of circus artists trying to lure the public into one of their performances. Picasso's designs, with their famous circus drop-curtain, included a tilting skyscraper growing out of the back of one dancer and a pantomime horse costume for another. Leonid Massine's choreography incorporated everyday mime and mechanistic gesture into the dancing, and Satie's music featured the sound of sirens, pistol shots and typewriters. (It was seeing *Parade* that prompted the poet Apollinaire to coin the term 'surrealism'.)

So what did these new ballet languages look like? Although by the beginning of the twentieth century Petipa's ballets had come to seem stale, this next generation of choreographers still respected the fundamental discipline of classicism. They all took daily ballet classes and most danced willingly in the old repertoire. But they needed to expand their inherited language, and to do that they took it apart and added to it to suit their individual vision.

MIKHAIL FOKINE

Fokine's new vision of ballet was based on a revolutionary commitment to realism. His condensed one-act works were unified round a single theme and were shorn of the rampant spectacle that marked the worst excesses of the nineteenth century. He believed passionately that music and design should reflect the ballet's setting (no more Indian temple dancers wearing tutus and diamonds) and that the style of movement should accurately reflect character and plot. When his subject was Greek the movement was influenced by the silhouetted figures on Ancient Greek vases; when it was Russian it was influenced by indigenous folk dancing. The old codified mime of nineteenth-century ballets was replaced by freer and more natural gestures, and even virtuoso dance passages were motivated by dramatic expression. In the big *pas de deux* in *The Firebird* (1910) the dancers still performed demanding lifts and balances – but the movements were all about struggle. While the hero was trying to hold the beautiful powerful bird, she was quivering to escape, her head was agitated and her arms staccato with resistance even as she held a conventional *arabesque*. In *Le Spectre de la rose* (1911) Nijinsky, as the perfumed fantasy hero, performed some of his most spectacular jumps but they were also breathtaking images of lightness and strangeness, and their masculine power was softened by tendrily curving arms and gestures where he seemed according to his sister 'to be fanning the air, creating the aroma of a rose'. (Nijinska, later reviving the rivalry that existed between Nijinsky and Fokine, actually claimed these were the dancer's own improvements on the latter's originally rather 'banal' choreography.)

Fokine's pursuit of realism also led him to integrate his leading dancers far more closely with the rest of the ensemble. They weren't allowed to wow their public with needlessly virtuoso solos, but only dominated the stage when the drama required. Crowd scenes and national dances were authentically performed. The dancers didn't move in the geometric blocks of Petipa's day but in asymmetrical groups that were constantly changing formation.

The point of Fokine's ballets was that they looked very different from each other, although they had in common a simplified and loosened form of classicism. It's a matter of debate how much this style was indebted to the American dance revolutionary Isadora Duncan (see Chapter Two: Reading Modern Dance) who appeared in St Petersburg several times between 1904 and 1909 and certainly impressed Fokine. Her fluid, apparently spontaneous movements, her bare feet, uncorseted body and New World seriousness, her scorn for the meaningless 'gymnastics' of nineteenth-century ballet must all have seemed a bracingly radical alternative to the fusty traditions and intellectual vapidness at the Maryinsky. Yet if Fokine took courage from Duncan, his own choreography had been moving, of its own accord, in a similar direction.

Whatever the origin of his ideas, Fokine's early dances were all attempts to make his dancers' bodies more expressive. Although his own dancers still often turned out their legs, spun *pirouettes*, held *arabesques* and jumped, these movements had a new pliancy and versatility. They could be ethereal and delicate in *Les Sylphides*, snaky and supple in *Schéhérazade* (1910) or boisterously grotesque like the monsters in *The Firebird*, and the lines of the steps of were made bolder, more vivid by stripping away purely decorative detail, like multiple beats on the jumps or highly embellished travelling steps. They were also mixed with a rich repertoire of non-academic dance and gesture. In many of his ballets Fokine dared to let his dancers simply run or walk – where that was the most appropriate action. In his Greek and exotic ballets he allowed his dancers to yield to gravity, so that they might lie or crouch on the floor and have their feet planted firmly on the ground rather than skimming it or trying to escape its pull.

Les Sylphides

Originally called *Chopiniana*, this ballet was retitled for its 1909 première in Paris. It is Fokine's homage to Romanticism, and while it doesn't, like most of his ballets, tell a story, its movement, music and design all distil the essence of early ballets like *La Sylphide* and *Giselle*.

Set in a woodland glade (originally by a ruined chapel), its cast features one man, the Poet, three ballerinas and a female *corps de ballet*. The women all wear the long white tulle skirt of the Romantic period and their little gossamer wings seem to waft them through Chopin's music. The choreography has no formal *ports de bras* (arm positions) or grandly expansive poses but reverts to the delicate, undulating lines of Romanticism. Arms and legs appear almost boneless; the body tilts wistfully forward; the head is modestly averted on sweetly sloping shoulders and the dancers perform hopping jumps and skimming *bourrées* that create a mood of magical serenity and ease. In her autobiography *Choura* Alexandra Danilova recalls it as a 'difficult' ballet to dance because 'it's sexless. You must be a creature of the air, not a woman – a weightless body with beautiful arms. I used to imagine Chopin lying on his back on the top of a hill, staring up at the blue sky. A white cloud drifts into view and passes, then another comes.'

In each section a different cloud, a different Romantic image moves across the stage. In the Valse, for instance, the ballerina opens out her arms as if she's parting the misty air. In the Mazurka the ballerina is a livelier sylph, darting and skimming in unpredictable lines, while in the *pas de deux* she is a bird or a butterfly as she flutters round her partner, hovering in his arms.

The *corps de ballet* frame the main dancers, holding hands and linking arms in asymmetrical patterns that recall Duncan's nature-inspired dances rather than the demonic Wilis in *Giselle*. Fokine's ballet is about intimacy and trust rather than diabolic deception, about simple beauty rather than show. Everybody touches everybody else and glances at each other from time to time, maintaining the sympathy of the group. American choreographer Mark Morris, star of the post-modern vanguard of the 80s and 90s, finds the ballet's sweetness utterly beguiling. 'I love the manners of it The way that people are always checking out what everyone else is doing, "Is it all right with you if I do this? Of course, go ahead." '

Petrushka

Made in 1911 this ballet condenses mime, classical ballet and folk dancing into a fable about power. It is set in a street fair in the 1830s where a puppeteer is showing off his three puppets, a pert Ballerina, a stupid, vain and cruel Moor and Petrushka, a sad, gauche clown. The ballet moves between the bustling colourful street scenes to the world of the puppets where Petrushka, forlornly in love with the Ballerina, is being tormented by the Moor. In increasing anguish the puppet understands that however deep his love he can never escape the trap of his grotesque body. The puppeteer encourages his puppets to act out their love triangle to its grim conclusion in order to amuse his public. The two rivals fight and Petrushka is killed. The public, half believing him to be real, gape with horror and the puppeteer tries to prove that he was only a wooden doll. But above his tent appears the spirit of Petrushka shaking his fists in a mixture of triumph and pain as he's finally liberated from the cage of his puppethood.

Fokine said that he wanted the dances in the street fair not to appear 'staged' but as if they 'arose spontaneously from an overabundance of emotions and gaiety'. Possibly influenced by Stanislavsky's methods at the Moscow Art Theatre, Fokine devised individual movements for each fairground performer and member of the crowd, making every gesture an expression of their character, while his designer Alexandre Benois created over a hundred different meticulously researched costumes and Stravinsky incorporated old folk melodies into his score.

The Russian dance writer André Levinson, who saw the ballet in Paris, described the period detail of its setting and costumes:

> The square swirls in holiday intoxication: beauteous nursemaids in *sarafins* and *kokshniks* stream by spreading their arms and waving their hands; coachmen in colourful *poddyovkas* with lace on their hats click their heels . . . while elegant ladies accompanied by stately officers in three-cornered hats . . . fastidiously observe the crude amusements of the common flock through their lorgnettes.

But even more novel than the detailed realism of the crowd was the psychological truth of the choreography given to each of the three puppets.

The Ballerina is almost a parody of a nineteenth-century Russian star as she prances flirtatiously on her points like a mechanical doll. (Alexandra Danilova says of her, 'Let's be honest, she's a gold-digger, she goes where the money is.') The Moor's dancing is bold and crude, the brazenly extreme turn-out of his legs is a sexual invitation as he stamps his feet and flaunts his gaudy strength. The role of Petrushka, certainly as danced by Nijinsky in the first performances, was the most drastically new – completely inverting all the premises of classical ballet with its lolling head, disjointed limbs, knock knees and stiff hands and its virtual exclusion of traditional steps. Ungainliness may have been used for comic or grotesque effect in ballet before, but never as a carefully conceived, expressive language for a main character.

For Nijinska her brother's performance was a supreme example of his eerie ability to transform himself:

When Petrushka dances, his body remains the body of a doll; only the tragic eyes reflect his emotions, burning with passion or dimming with pain. The heavy head carved out of a wooden block hangs forward, rolling from side to side, propped on the shoulder. The hands and feet are also made of wood and Vaslav holds his fingers stiffly together inside black mittens like wooden paddles.

An impassioned central performance can still reveal the intense drama of Fokine's ballet, though some of his other works have lost their power to shock. *Schéhérazade*, for instance, whose orgiastic writhings once looked titillating and exotic now usually appears as stilted and chaste as an early silent movie; *Spectre de la rose* can seem like a dainty, art-nouveau curio. Yet there's a core to the ballets that remains stubbornly powerful – some resonance in the original scenario that's made enduring by its conjunction with the score or by its position in ballet legend.

In 1993 France-based choreographer Angelin Preljocaj created his own version of *Spectre*, dovetailing its gentle Victorian fantasy with a much rawer contemporary sexual encounter. One half of the stage was screened behind gauze, a dim romantic area of dreams in which two dainty women danced coquettishly with two gorgeously masculine lovers. Outside a tough muscular woman danced with a beautifully androgynous man, her face doped in a sleeper's trance even as her aroused body grappled with his. Past and present, dream and reality, assault and consent mingled in this double-take on erotic fantasy, bringing an old ballet into sharp focus.

In 1994 British choreographer Richard Alston premièred a stripped-down version of *Petrushka* set to the piano version of Stravinsky's score with all of the carnival drama cut out. The ballet became an archetypal encounter between the Outsider and the Crowd, the Petrushka figure dancing alone in an untouchable space, his body straining and jerking at painful angles, his gaze scouring strange horizons as four amiable, uncomprehending couples flirted and danced around him.

VASLAV NIJINSKY

Of all the early-twentieth-century classical choreographers, Vaslav Nijinsky pushed most urgently and uncomfortably against the grain of tradition. Originally a dancer with the Maryinsky Theatre and then with Les Ballets Russes, he was encouraged by Diaghilev to become a choreographer. The seriousness with which he committed himself to inventing a new language is demonstrated by the fact that for his first ballet he demanded more than 120 rehearsals, to create little more than ten minutes of dance. The result was, however, the most extraordinary ballet of its time.

L'Après-midi d'un faune

Set to Debussy's tone poem in 1912, this ballet was designed by Léon Bakst as an impressionistic image of a pagan idyll. The stage looked like a huge mottled canvas in greys, russets and greens with the nymphs' dresses and Nijinsky's darkly blotched tights blending with the backdrop.

This flattened stage image was part of the curiously calm temper of the work. Nijinsky's first break with tradition was to avoid setting his movement to the rhythms of Debussy's music, simply using its lush colours and atmosphere as a sound world for the dance to play in. His second was to flatten the dancers' bodies into two-dimensional shapes that denied the special three-dimensional brilliance and graceful curves associated with classicism. The ballet was like a moving bas-relief in which figures were seen in profile, their torsos twisted, their palms flattened, their bare feet flat against the floor and their limbs angled stiffly in imitation of figures in Ancient Greek vases or wall carvings. (Marie Rambert, who danced briefly with Ballets Russes before forming her own company in London, recalls in her autobiography *Quicksilver*, "The walking was all done on one line parallel to the footlights, the whole foot on the ground. It was an incredibly difficult position to achieve, let alone use in walking or changing direction.')

The ballet's story is simple. A faun idly watches a group of nymphs bathing and becomes enamoured of one. He tries to capture her and she runs away, leaving behind her scarf on which the aroused faun lies to indulge in a triumphant but solitary orgasm. Unlike Fokine, who aimed for psychological detail in his story-telling, Nijinsky reduced his own drama to a basic physical outline. He used no decorative or virtuoso ballet steps, and his dancers displayed very little heightened emotion. Often they held their poses for several long seconds, or performed very primitive steps. When the faun attempts to seduce the nymph she crouches on one bent knee, and though her head inclines towards him in some hint of acquiescence, her body angles back in fear. The faun's own sexual release comes simply but blatantly in a single thrust of his pelvis as he lies on the floor.

This austerely stylized conception reduced ballet to geometry, to a play of lines and rhythms. (Critic Lynn Garafola suggests Nijinsky might have been influenced by Moscow theatre director Vsevolod Meyerhold with his use of static, stylized postures, depersonalized character and totalizing design.) Not surprisingly, the sculptor Auguste Rodin found the ballet profoundly interesting:

Nijinsky has never been so remarkable as in his latest role. No more jumps, nothing but half-conscious animal gestures and poses. He lies down, leans on his elbows, walks with bent knees, draws himself up, advancing and retreating, sometimes slowly, sometimes with jerky angular movements. His eyes flicker, he stretches his arms, he opens his hands out flat, the fingers together, and as he turns away his head he continues to express his desire with a deliberate awkwardness that seems natural. Form and meaning are indissolubly wedded in his body, which is totally expressive of the mind within. [see illus. 9]

Though the movement was so stylized as almost to deny the dancers' gender, the eroticism of Nijinsky's scenario was extreme for its times. There was no love interest to soften its meaning, no swashbuckling adventure, as in *Schéhérazade*, to distract from its intentions. Most of the public approved, though the critic of the French paper *Le Figaro* reported, 'We are shown a lecherous faun whose movements are filthy and bestial in their eroticism and whose gestures are as crude as they are indecent.'

In 1953 American choreographer Jerome Robbins produced his own interpretation of Debussy's score in *Afternoon of a Faun*, which portrays the encounter between two dancers at the ballet barre with the proscenium as an imaginary mirror.

The Rite of Spring

The criticisms of *Faune* would in retrospect have seemed mild to Nijinsky compared to the furore created by his 1913 ballet *The Rite of Spring* (original French title: *Le Sacre du printemps*). This epic collaboration with Stravinsky plumbed a fierce, unsettling primitivism in its sound and music, while at the same time creating utterly new languages for the twentieth century. The scandal generated by its first performance has become a byword for all battles waged by courageous avant-garde artists against crass philistines and we read almost enviously of the brouhaha at its première where supporters and attackers fought openly. Amidst the general laughter, shouting, whistling and jostling, one fashionable woman slapped her neighbour, someone else called Ravel, who was in the audience, a 'dirty Jew' and various noisy wits retitled the ballet *Le Massacre du printemps*, while others called out for doctors and dentists.

The scenario of the ballet was as archetypal as *Faune*'s (a pagan tribe celebrates a fertility ritual at the climax of which a sacrificial virgin dances herself to death), but this time the inspiration was Russian folk tradition. Stravinsky built parts of his score out of traditional Russian melodies, though he treated them in such a way as to make them unrecognizable, changing time signature between bars, for instance, so unpredictably that neither Nijinsky nor his dancers could actually count the music. (Marie Rambert, trained in the rhythmic movement exercises of Dalcroze, had to be brought in to help them figure the score out and became known by the nickname Rythmichka.)

Stravinsky also made the orchestra sound like a different breed of instruments. As Nijinsky's biographer Richard Buckle has described, strings and woodwind were used in extreme registers, with special effects demanded from the rest of the players – shrieks from the brass, flutter-tongued flutes, wild pulsing from the tuba and instruments playing against each other in different rhythms. The churning juggernaut power of the music, with its coruscating colours and clashing rhythms, established that this piece was no nostalgic vision of some past Eden. It showed the barbarity of human life, the cruelty of the tribe, the subservience of the individual to the forces of nature.

The ballet's characters were appropriately generic, tribal members known only as Elders or Virgins, and the language which Nijinsky created for them seemed like an assault on classical rules. The legs were so turned in that the feet were pigeon-toed, and when the dancers jumped they seemed hardly to leave the ground before they were driven back into the floor. Their energy was compressed inwards instead of radiating outwards; their bodies trembled and their gestures were heavy and harsh. As the French writer Jacques Rivière, one of the ballet's most ardent supporters and most detailed witnesses, argued, 'The body is no longer a means of escape for the soul. On the contrary it collects and gathers itself around it, it suppresses its outward thrust . . . chained to the body, spirit becomes mere matter.'

Nijinsky organized his dancers into tight groups who danced to different rhythms, some running in circles, others jumping *en masse*. They seemed fuelled by a blind collective urgency which was far from the calm certainties of late-nineteenth-century ballet. (The choreography actually anticipated much of what was to happen in modern dance in the 30s when choreographers were giving shape to forces of depersonalization which they saw at work in twentieth-century society and also creating images of the Freudian unconscious.)

Yet if this was ballet with its emotions flayed, its body wrung out, it was still constructed with the discipline of classicism. Though Nijinsky's dancers looked nothing like the fleet, perfectly manicured fairies of *Sleeping Beauty*, their bodies still showed the training of generations and evoked the principles of nineteenth-century ballet by the force with which they inverted them – their

flexed feet and angled limbs clearly posed in relation to the classical language. Jacques Rivière wrote,

If we can but stop associating grace with symmetry and *arabesques* we
shall find it everywhere in . . . *Sacre* . . . even in the dance of the Chosen
Maiden, in the short and abortive tremors that agitate her . . . in her
frightful waits, in her prisoner-like and unnatural gait and in that arm
raised to heaven in . . . a gesture of appeal, threat and protection.

And this was only twenty-three years after another chosen virgin,
the privileged little Aurora, balanced confidently on one toe, graciously extending her hand to each of her four suitors – the whole
world at her fingertips.

   Nijinsky's *Rite* only received thirteen performances, though
Stravinsky's score went on to acquire the status of a sacred text
for choreographers. Many different dances have been made to it,
ranging from the one-woman endurance test of Molissa Fenley's
solo version, made in 1988, to Michael Clark's *Mmm* (1992) which
juxtaposed the original music with punk rock and featured
astonishingly ferocious movement that gave Stravinsky the
urgency and eroticism of a contemporary rock score.

BRONISLAVA NIJINSKA

As Nijinsky's sister and as a dancer in some of his ballets, Nijinska
had been the willing, if long-suffering, raw material on which he
had hammered out his new dance language. Her own works,
not surprisingly, echoed some of Nijinsky's ideas, but they also
travelled beyond them.

Les Noces

Like *Rite* this 1923 ballet portrays a universal human ritual, a
simple peasant wedding, in which a nervous bride and groom, a
crowd of parents and guests all play their prescribed parts in the
business of pairing the sexes and sending a young woman from
her family home to the house of strangers in order to bear
children.

As in Nijinsky's ballet, there is no sentimental gloss to this ritual. Though Stravinsky said his score was intensely religious, Nijinska took an essentially feminist view of her subject, seeing clearly the pain and terror often involved in such marriages. The decor on which she insisted was drab and strictly functional: simple benches and platforms and dull, earth-brown costumes. The women wore point shoes, but not as a concession to classical, airy beauty. Rather, Nijinska wanted to 'elongate the dancers' silhouettes and make them resemble the saints in Byzantine mosaics'. The points were also never used for display. One dance was made for the friends of the bride as they plaited her two long braids of hair – binding her up ready for her new world. As their feet criss-crossed in quick *bourrées*, they didn't appear to be skimming the floor but to be stabbing fiercely downwards. Nijinska said this was to capture the action of plaiting, but, as many have noted, their action also prefigures the pain and violence of the bride's impending sexual initiation.

As in *Rite* too, the language is generic, it makes no concessions to individual characterization or virtuosity. Men and women often dance the same steps, which are as weighted, angular and powerful as those of Nijinsky, and the dancers usually move in groups. The design of the ballet is architectural – focusing less on the lines and shapes of single bodies than on the pyramids, mounds, triangles and squares created by dancers moving together in units (see illus. 5). This constructivist design is one aspect of the ballet's revolutionary nature; the other is its narrative method. Nijinska, even more than her brother, had found a way of using pure dance to express emotion without resorting to mime. The drama of the work is all in the line and force of the steps, and in the shapes in which the dancers are composed. The sheer mass of the guests and the authoritative presence of the parents seated high on their platform make a powerful contrast to the lone tender state of the bride – suggesting the frightening weight of family and community. As the ballet progresses, we see male dancers grouped apart from female and elders watching from a distance the orgiastic celebrations of the younger guests in an archetypal division of genders and generations.

Stravinsky's score, which mixes a sanctified stillness with an irresistible, rhythmic force, has proved almost as attractive to choreographers as *Rite*, though no versions have matched the oblique tenderness and terror of Nijinska's work, nor her ability to bind the music's ferocity in such tight formal structures. Angelin Preljocaj's 1989 version is a more contemporary and explicitly political deconstruction of the marriage rite, featuring five couples and five tailor's dummies. As the real women tremble on the verge of wedlock in a mix of desire and dread, their men struggle unsuccessfully to make them compliant and complacent, then gladly retreat to the embraces of the obligingly passive and virginal dummies.

Nijinska's female take on classicism is significant not only because it is choreographically so fine, but also because it is so rare. There have been very few women choreographers in ballet, which, unlike modern dance, has been creatively and administratively dominated by men. Certainly Diaghilev never quite knew how to place Nijinska. He found her stubborn artistic integrity difficult to accept from a woman and was not always quick to appreciate and understand her work. In fact, he was, with unconsciously self-damning irony, often heard to remark, 'What a choreographer Bronia would have been if only she were a man.'

GEORGE BALANCHINE

George Balanchine too was trained at the Maryinsky school and also spent the early years of his career in the Diaghilev stable, after abandoning a revolution-torn Russia in 1924. One of his first ballets, *Prodigal Son* (1929), showed that he could turn out highly coloured, dramatic ballets like the best of Diaghilev's choreographers. It retold the biblical parable in often violent expressionist language, with the errant hero discovering temptation at the feet of the archetypally erotic Siren. With her towering head-dress (designed by Rouault) and long red cloak, with her drastically arched back and scissoring limbs, she presented a formidable icon of sexuality, while her drunken acolytes were like the bizarre

grotesques of a George Grosz painting, bald-headed and moving
with an obscene, crouching gait.

There are aspects of this ballet's choreography that anticipate
not only 30s modern dance, but more directly the ballet–modern
crossover in Kenneth MacMillan's and Glen Tetley's movement
– where the classical language is distorted and exaggerated for
erotic or emotional effect. But Balanchine was not much interested
in pursuing the expressionist line. Famously he went on to create
ballets which were a triumphant affirmation that dance didn't
have to follow a story-line at all – it could simply be about
itself.

After Diaghilev's death in 1929 and the break-up of Les Ballets
Russes Balanchine ended up in America. In 1933 he founded the
School of American Ballet, which over the years evolved into one
of the world's great ballet companies, the New York City Ballet.
It was a company that was devoted almost exclusively to the
development and presentation of Balanchine's own style – itself
a fusion of nineteenth-century Russian classicism and twentieth-
century America.

Balanchine himself said of his work, 'You discover that what
you are doing is really Petipa', and the principles of classical ballet
are at the basis of nearly everything he made. Some of his ballets
deliberately evoke the past – *Theme and Variations* (1947), for
instance, is like an abstract of *Sleeping Beauty* where a dazzlingly
tutued Ballerina is partnered by a Prince and attended by a mini-
court (four female demi-soloists, eight *corps de ballet* dancers and
their partners). But the hierarchies of this establishment are not
dictated by inherited rank – they don't evoke the Tsar or Louis
XIV – they are based on talent. All the dancers in a Balanchine
ballet hold their position on stage only by virtue of their ability
to dance.

The steps they perform in this work also conjure echoes of
Petipa – a gracefully winding chain of women recalls the fairies
in the Vision Scene; a little running step ending with the Ballerina's foot pointed daintily in front is a classic Aurora pose. But
as the American critic Arlene Croce has commented, the Ballerina's solo variations are 'Aurora rewritten in lightning' and the
whole of the ballet has a speed and an attack that are wholly

modern. The dancers may strike classical positions, but they move from one to another with hardly a beat between. Their steps are multiplied, their rhythms are syncopated and their phrases condensed – so that we see a line of women swinging their legs up so high and fast it's almost a cancan.

What Balanchine found in America was a tempo of life exhilaratingly different from Old Europe. He was enchanted by American jazz music and dance, and, like Stravinsky, he was constantly drawn to its syncopated rhythms, its wit and casual, demotic attitude. Some of his most characteristic steps are jazz-inspired – sleazy hip thrusts, taunting pin-up girl poses, kicking legs and minxy gestures of the hands. He adored New York's towering, streamlined buildings, finding in them an American spirit that was 'cold, luminous, hard as light'. He was charmed by America's brashness and by its huge democratic entertainment industry. (He choreographed numbers for eighteen musicals and five movies as well as a circus routine for fifty elephants.) And he found the athleticism of its dancers irresistible. These were not docile Russians trained to emulate the manners of princesses and kings, they were part of baseball and jive culture, and Balanchine learnt to exploit their peculiar lanky grace. As Edwin Denby wrote of *Agon* when it was premièred in 1957, the ballet's 'basic gesture . . . has a frank, fast thrust like the action of Olympic athletes and it also has a loosefingered goofy reach like the grace of our local teenagers'.

Unlike the curvy women favoured by nineteenth-century balletomanes or the delicate sylphs of Romanticism, Balanchine's favoured performers were 'big girls with long legs'. His dancer was typically long-limbed, very slender, with a small, neat head. Both women and men were groomed for speed, flexibility and daring rather than for old-fashioned delicacy and decorum. And Balanchine worked profound changes into classical technique to bring about a new line and power. Legs were encouraged to fly up to ear level or jut at extreme angles, and if that meant forcing the hip up from its traditionally correct alignment, that was fine. Jumps and steps moved so fast that dancers had no time to bring their heels down to the floor as they landed (traditionally dancers use the whole foot to cushion a landing and to press up for take-off – Balanchine's dancers only used the ball of the foot, saving precious mini-seconds). As they raced across the floor there was often no time for the arms to curve into a graceful frame, they were used more efficiently, almost like those of a runner. Point work for the women was also a way of moving faster and looking taller – there was nothing ethereal about a *bourrée*. As New York City Ballet ballerina Tanaquil LeClercq has put it, dancing Balanchine was all a matter of 'Zip round. Fast. Nothing slow, no *adaaahgio* . . . Kick, wham, fast, hard, big.'

In this new streamlined technique Balanchine allowed for no stagy manners, no bleeding hearts, no personal mannerisms. The ballet was all in the steps and the score, and the dancers were simply expected to dance and listen as accurately as possible. Some dancers, like Gelsey Kirkland, found this tantamount to artistic fascism – she wanted to interpret her roles and find meanings beyond the surface of the steps. But though Balanchine produced many star dancers and wrote intimately tailored roles for them, he wasn't interested in cultivating stars. The casts for his ballets were not advertised in advance; the works took precedence.

Agon

This ballet, choreographed in 1957, may be the most perfect synthesis of old and new in Balanchine's *œuvre* – both in its music and its dance. Stravinsky's score was based on the kind of sixteenth- and seventeenth-century court dances from which classical ballet first developed. But while we can still hear the old measures and melodies of those dances, they are fractured, made dissonant. Equally, though we can see any number of familiar ballet steps in Balanchine's choreography, they are so 'deformed', and so compacted that they strike us even four decades on as surprising and new.

The ballet is a suite of dances for twelve performers wearing black-and-white practice clothes and there is no scenery. The stage waits to be filled with the shapes and the energy of the movement. Most of the dancers appear in teams, dancing with each other or coolly competing, and sometimes they dance in couples – most particularly when the stage clears for a brief climactic *pas de deux*.

Edwin Denby's first review of the ballet sounds almost dizzy from the energy generated by its highly pressured style and speed. He describes men's steps that explode like 'pistol shots', adding

Each phrase, as if with a burst, finds its new shape in a few steps, stops, and at once a different phrase explodes unexpectedly at a tangent ... The explosive thrust of a big classic step has been deepened, speeded up, forced out further, but the mollifying motions ... have been pared down ... the conciliatory transitions have been dropped.

In the ballet's big *pas de deux* the dancers' athleticism turns dangerous and erotic as all the classical manoeuvres of balance and support are exaggerated or inverted. The man lifts the woman's leg up behind her and presses her head back to meet it in a gesture that is both brutal and intimate. She balances in a classical *arabesque*, while he lies on his back at her feet, holding on to her standing leg and rotating her, her leg sweeping arrogantly above his head.

In the *Agon pas de deux* Balanchine seems to be rewriting the male and female roles in ballet – the woman is far more powerful, more sassy here than her nineteenth-century sisters, even though she remains within the man's manipulative embrace. But as critic Deborah Jowitt has suggested, whether you were a principal or a member of the *corps*, a woman or a man in Balanchine's ballets, you were all equal within the music. For Balanchine the music was the ground and the inspiration for every work – the dancer's job was to give shape to its different parts. (More about his use of music will be discussed in Part Two.) Anyone who watches a Balanchine ballet will know that it is like seeing the structure, arguments, rhythms and phrasing of the score take physical form in the dance.

Concerto Barocco

In this 1941 ballet, for instance, two women soloists take the part of the two solo violins in the first movement of Bach's double violin concerto, merging and separating like the two lines of melody. In a later passage the darker, deeper melody of the second violin plays under the first and one of the women is correspondingly replaced by a man, who supports and embraces his ballerina.

Specific dance images also correspond directly with the music, as Edwin Denby has described in one of the most famous passages of dance criticism ever written:

At the climax [of the *adagio* movement] against a background of chorus that suggests the look of trees in the wind before a storm breaks, the ballerina, with limbs powerfully outspread, is lifted by her male partner, lifted repeatedly in narrowing arcs, higher and higher. Then at the culminating phrase from her greatest height he very slowly lowers her. You watch her body slowly descend, her foot and leg pointing stiffly downward, till her toe reaches the floor and she rests her full weight at last on this single sharp point and pauses. It is the effect at that moment of a deliberate and powerful plunge into a wound, and the emotion of it answers strangely to the musical stress.

FREDERICK ASHTON

It's always argued that if Balanchine created a distinctively American style of ballet – long, lean, fast, hard and cool – it was Frederick Ashton who developed the essence of the 'English' style – detailed, lyrical and neat. But one choreographer doesn't make a national style, and both Ashton and Balanchine were responding to the native temperament of their dancers when they made their work. Balanchine said it was the vast plains of America and the huge Russian steppes that made Russians and the Americans move on so large a scale, and it may be true that the island English naturally move small. Equally Americans tend to take bold steps into space, claiming it as their own territory, while the English typically dance as if they have a pocket of air surrounding them and they're anxious not to intrude on anyone else's terrain.

But there are historical as well as geographical reasons for the smallness of the English style. In the first half of the twentieth century, when English ballet was in its infancy, it had very small stages to perform on. Ballet Rambert, founded by Marie Rambert in 1926, used to appear at the Mercury Theatre, whose stage was eighteen foot square. Sadler's Wells, the first home of the Royal Ballet (founded by Ninette de Valois in 1933 and originally called the Vic-Wells Ballet), was larger but still couldn't comfortably hold a full-cast *Swan Lake* or *Sleeping Beauty*.

English training also encouraged a small-scale deftness of movement. When de Valois set up her own school – ultimately to become the Royal Ballet School – she insisted that her pupils studied British folk dance, believing that a country's native dances should colour its ballet style. So English dancers learnt the rhythmic intricacies, the quick steps and calm carriage of the old country dances. They not only became adept at moving fast in a small space but also developed powerful feet. Ballerina Antoinette Sibley recalls that her contemporaries in the late 50s and 60s 'were very strong on point work. The Russians at that time had a wonderful jump and wonderful backs, but their footwork was very weak . . . [Ashton's choreography, with its] jumping on point and quick footwork, is all talking with the feet.'

But Ashton, who was born in Peru, and whose favourite dancers were Russian (Pavlova) and American (Duncan) was frequently driven mad by the reticence which was the negative side of English neatness. (He choreographed first for Ballet Rambert and later for the Royal Ballet.)

It was so hard to get them out of themselves. I had such a struggle with Fonteyn she went home to her mother once and said, 'That man's mad,' because I used to push her around so much to try and make her more malleable. Even de Valois had it, you could give her a dance that was meant to go all over the stage and she would do it in the palm of her hand.

Though Ashton's movements were never as rangy or spacious as Balanchine's, within their own small scale they were intensely mobile, sensuous and free. The roots of his style were possibly even closer to Petipa than Balanchine's were – Ashton would sit at performances of *Sleeping Beauty* saying he was taking a lesson in choreography. But if nineteenth-century classicism is plainly visible in his ballets, it is intensified and made more brilliant by torrents of beaten jumps, complex rhythms and tiny steps flowering out of each other. It is also loosened up, made sexy, spontaneous and lavish. Though Ashton's dancers may move through academically correct positions, their arms also ripple in opulent curves, their torsos swoop and their heads rapturously angle and turn.

If Balanchine put classicism under pressure, stretching its lines, forcing its curves into drastic angles and revving up its power, Ashton made it swoon and fizz. Old films show that during his brief dancing career he was a joyously exuberant mover with springing jump and a hyperactive torso. (The latter was partly acquired from his studies with Nijinska, who in every class exercise had her dancers twisting their torsos in counterpoint to their legs and feet.) Many dancers who worked with Ashton spoke of how he'd ask them to demonstrate a sequence they'd learnt in class, and how he'd then pull it apart, changing its rhythms, embellishing its steps and adding poetic oddities of detail – like the nodding motion of the ballerina in *Symphonic Variations* which makes her look like some big exotic bird dipping her head in the stream of the music; or the quivering interlacing arm movements of the water sprite in *Ondine* (1958), which look as if she's splashing through water.

Isadora Duncan's early example may also have encouraged Ashton to create a style where every movement had a slightly improvised air, as if it was being created by the pressure of emotion or by the simple pleasure of dancing. In a *pas de deux* from the 1956 ballet *Birthday Offering* the ballerina steps into a regally classical balance – a pose that could be straight out of the Rose Adagio – but then on a voluptuous impulse she sighs her poise away into wanton backbend. When she and her partner *bourrée* together across the stage, their torsos lean back in some kind of ecstasy. Just before he died Ashton complained that dancers weren't always willing to lose themselves in his choreography: 'Dancers today are afraid of letting themselves go, they're afraid of looking camp.'

Symphonic Variations

Ashton could be both rigorous and spare, as this 1946 ballet shows. This was the first work he made after the Sadler's Wells Ballet had moved on to the large stage of London's Royal Opera House and it was as much about space as about dancing. Six dancers in plain Greek tunics were set against a limpid green-washed backdrop – like remote Olympian beings in an idealized spring. They either threaded their way through César Franck's score in long, clear skeins of movement or simply paused, letting the music eddy around them.

Long curving lines were drawn across the stage by the men bearing the women in low lifts. Dancers in twos and threes entwined their limbs into intimate sculptures. Fast beaten jumps were performed in concentrated bursts even while the dancers maintained their divine calm. In repose they often stood with their torsos curved to the side, one arm stretched over the head, the other slicing across the body to make two parallel lines. This was a shape as classically pure as anything in nineteenth-century ballet, but unlike any position ever seen in the traditional vocabulary.

The ballet had no story, but its concentration and clarity demanded an air of transcendence from the dancers. They had to dance as if the movement was their special element, the place where they were most consummately at ease. As Antoinette Sibley has described it, 'It's what heaven must be like. It's fulfilment, peace, happiness, beauty. It's not abstract. It's not steps. It's intoxication of everything that's beautiful on another, not human, plane.'

Despite the beauty of *Symphonic Variations* and other plotless works, however, Ashton is best known for his narrative ballets and for his ability to reinvent steps so that they become the language of character.

He was a self-confessed romantic and some of his most inventive movements were images of love. Yet while his contemporaries in the 60s and 70s often resorted to split-crotch lifts and Herculean jumps to choreograph desire, Ashton squeezed intense

drama out of the smallest details. In his 1976 retelling of Tur-
genev's *A Month in the Country* one step is used to express extreme
desire, but it is painted completely differently for the two women
who dance it, both of whom are in love with the same man (the
young tutor Beliaev). When Vera, the young girl, throws herself
into his embrace, her back foot beats rapidly against her supporting ankle to suggest her naïve fluttering ecstasy. When Natalia
Petrovna, her guardian, is later held by Beliaev in a long lift, her
foot also quivers ecstatically in the air. But the rhythm here is a
deep, sobbing spasm, and as her back swoons against his chest
her body speaks eloquently of the doomed, adult intensity of her
love.

In the *pas de deux* which Ashton created for Oberon and Titania
in *The Dream* (1964) the fairies' warring pride is sharpened by the
hard, spiky lines of their limbs and by a taut, stand-offish energy
in their partnering. The space between them bristles with mutual
rejection. But once their argument is settled, Titania's body then
seems to melt and yield and the fierce linearity of her *arabesque*
dissolves in sensuous curves – her arms rippling, her back arching,
her head inclining freely towards Oberon who bends gently over
her.

Love even touches the many comic roles Ashton has written.
Bottom in *Dream* and Alain in *La Fille mal gardée* (1960) both make
us laugh with their clumsy attempts at classical dancing – they
get their feet in a muddle, miss their timing, grab their partners
in ludicrous positions and Bottom even trots round the stage on
a pair of hobbledehoy points. But these jokes aren't just the standard fare of ballet parody. The characters are earnestly attempting
lovely or clever steps; they understand the poetry that's so
impossible for them and so casually performed by others. And
there is such musical wit in their misses and such almost-
virtuosity in their failures that they acquire a real poignancy.

Ashton's impulse towards story-telling is shared by other major
British choreographers – perhaps because the literary and dra-
matic tradition is so dominant in British culture. Both Antony
Tudor and Kenneth MacMillan pushed the language of ballet

even harder than Ashton, testing the boundaries of what it could express.

ANTONY TUDOR

Tudor, who began choreographing with Ballet Rambert before he moved to the American Ballet Theatre in New York, aimed for a Proustian subtlety in his work. He wanted his characters to experience more complex passions than those of the heroes and heroines of nineteenth-century ballet. He wanted to put them into situations that demanded a more sophisticated moral response than the black-and-white scenarios of *Sleeping Beauty* or *Swan Lake*, and he wanted to put them in environments which seemed close to the audience. Ashton used to speak with some envy of the 'depth charge' of Tudor's works.

Like Ashton, Tudor stayed with the basic language of classicism, but he stripped away its decorative virtuosity so that the lines and rhythms of the steps spoke directly. He choreographed movements of the head, arms and hands with absolute precision so that every gesture had a psychological motivation. When Antoinette Sibley first worked with him in *Jardin aux lilas* she was astonished to discover that 'every single finger is important' in the choreography, 'every detail'. Toni Lander recalls that he could demonstrate what he wanted from a character just in 'a shoulder lifting or going forward'.

Jardin aux lilas

This ballet was made in 1936 and reflected Tudor's interest in contemporary theatre, particularly a play by Eugene O'Neill called *Strange Interlude*, which was narrated through stream-of-consciousness dialogue. The ballet's story centres on a woman, Caroline, who is engaged to a man she doesn't love and meets her real lover for one passionate last encounter at a garden party. Her friends try to prevent this meeting, as does her possessive fiancé who also happens to be bidding farewell to his own mistress. In a series of brief encounters Tudor shows desire struggling with convention, freedom with necessity and love with constraint. The engaged couple dance together with deadly politeness – their partnering little more than a clasping of hands, their bodies perfectly upright. When Caroline is alone with her lover, she clings to him. They walk together in fierce plunging steps, furtively turning their heads to check they're not being watched. When they dance together her body arches in passionate curves. The fiancé's mistress is angry at being ousted, and at one point she repeatedly jumps into the fiancé's arms – literally throwing herself at the man she still loves. The chorus of friends meanwhile move, between the couples, dancing in a nodding and waving trio which has the exact rhythms of malicious gossip.

Towards the ballet's close Caroline and her lover meet the fiancé and his mistress. The fiancé snatches hold of Caroline, but as he moves to kiss her she falls back in a dead faint and everything on stage freezes. In a kind of out-of-body solo Caroline wanders between the others, casting desperate looks at them before returning to her swoon. From then the ballet slides towards its inevitable grim conclusion. Caroline kisses her lover farewell, her fiancé reclaims her by putting a cloak over her shoulders and then, as she reaches out one last time for her lover, the fiancé presses her arm firmly and coldly back down to her side.

At times the ballet's drama is conveyed through a near-invisible language of constraint and denial. Maude Lloyd, who danced Caroline in the first production, has described it as follows, 'You have to convey that you are feeling emotion without showing it . . . it was the tiniest gesture this drawing back you had to do . . . You can feel people's muscles tensing on stage even if you can't see them. Sometimes you have to show your emotions with your back to the person you're emoting about.' Her contemporary, the American dancer and choreographer Agnes de Mille, has remarked how 'Embraces and filigrees of arm movements, faint rubbings-out, like little sighings or half heard exclamations . . . are never mere decorations but evocations and echoes . . . each step is wreathed with doubts, regrets, aspirations, until the dancers seem literally to be moving through the human mind.'

The ballet was set in Edwardian England and its most revolutionary move was to portray such ordinary events within the frame of classical dance. The latter was normally considered to be the language of fantasy, while the new modern dance was regarded as the appropriate vehicle for realism. As Hugh Laing, who danced the original Lover has said, 'People weren't tearing their hair and falling on their knees and all that nonsense. They were just behaving like rather refined people of the upper or lower middle class and not in any way fairy princes or princesses ... they are all classical steps ... there is not any modern movement. It's all your *glissades*, your *arabesques*, your *attitudes*.'

KENNETH MACMILLAN

MacMillan, who began choreographing for the Royal Ballet in the mid-50s, strained hardest of all against the traditional ballet formula. He was, in fact, very good at making witty and beautiful plotless ballets, and stylistically he learnt a lot from Ashton. As ballerina Lynn Seymour says, they were 'both into doing these intricate, footsy solos ... all sort of knitting downstairs and not able to drop a stitch'. But it was in his narrative works that he pushed ballet to speak in new ways. In *Different Drummer* (1984) he used jerky, expressionistically distorted movement to underline the alienation of his hero. In *Anastasia* (first choreographed as one act in 1967 and extended to three in 1971) he used grainy old film sequences to show the heroine sifting through memories of her childhood and the Russian revolution; in *Isadora* (1981) he had an actress speaking Duncan's words while a dancer danced her movements. His subject matter was bold, even shocking, grappling with rape, incest, madness and murder, while his favourite characters were driven to death by the excesses of their desires and obsessions.

Romeo and Juliet

Even his most popular ballet, *Romeo and Juliet*, pushed the conventions of the Romantic ballet beyond what was considered, in 1965, to be comfortable. The balcony *pas de deux* in Act I contains some of the most purely lyrical dancing in the repertoire, but its lifts and holds are ecstatically sexual. It starts with Juliet taking Romeo's hand and putting it on her heart so that he can feel how hard it is beating. This is followed by a sequence of steps that are, as the original Romeo, Christopher Gable, says, 'all slightly off balance and turning and reeling. You know that minute when you know that you are hugely . . . attracted to someone . . . and they're feeling the same way . . . it's like stars bursting in your head.'

At moments in the ballet MacMillan dares to let his dancers be absolutely still. When Romeo and Juliet first see each other they do nothing but look, and when Juliet is trying to think how to deal with the appalling prospect of her forced marriage to Paris she simply sits on the edge of her bed and stares into blackness. Lynn Seymour, the original Juliet, describes how she actually had to convince MacMillan that this device would best portray Juliet's panic: 'If you're in a predicament like that, it's very hard to think. She's in a terrible tension at the time. Something's got to happen. It's like squeezing yourself together until suddenly you snap your fingers, you find the only thing to do.'

MacMillan also allows his dancers to look grotesque. In the final scene Romeo simply lugs the dead Juliet despairingly around the stage. At first he tries to make her dance with him because he can't believe she's dead, then he pulls her around like a 'big piece of dead meat' (MacMillan's image). Gable recalls, 'I used to drag Lynn around the stage and she'd just let her legs fall apart, all open and exposed and vulnerable and ugly.'

Manon

Manon, which MacMillan made in 1974, also follows (and then subverts) the familiar conventions of a three-act story ballet. It is set in the eighteenth century, it uses specially arranged music by Massenet and it retells Abbé Prévost's tragic story of Manon Lescaut and her poet lover Des Grieux through some of the most limpidly classical movement MacMillan ever created. The first solo where Des Grieux expresses his sudden passion for Manon is both elegant and moving. He declares himself in a series of controlled *arabesques*, their formality belied by the yearning stretch of his extended arm and the beseeching turn of his head. In the lovers' first bedroom *pas de deux* the lyricism is swept to dangerous extremes by the dancers' passion – during one astonishing lift Des Grieux runs with Manon, then releases her in a slither of movement, so that she slides along the floor while he is falling down on top of her.

But love and sex in this ballet are inseparable from greed and power. Manon can't resist the flattery and money thrust at her from every man she meets, and to show this MacMillan creates a series of outrageously, cynically inverted male/female dances. Conventionally when a man shows off his ballerina it's a metaphor for his love. In *Manon*, though, it's a metaphor for carnal display and acquisition.

In the *pas de trois* in Act I where Manon is being sold off by her brother to the vicious Monsieur G.M. every manoeuvre is a *double entendre*. When Lescaut supports his sister he also manages to press her close to G.M.; when he holds out her leg, G.M. takes it, kisses and caresses her foot; whenever he lifts her, it's in a position best designed to show off Manon's charms and to bring her close to G.M.'s waiting embrace.

In Act II, when Manon has been thoroughly corrupted, G.M. looks on in satisfied ownership as a group of men pass her between them, manipulating her limbs so that her body is flaunted in a shockingly sexual manner. As we watch Manon being reduced to little more than a stripper in a booth, we too are reduced to being voyeurs.

In Europe other choreographers have also attempted to update the genre of narrative ballet. French choreographer and founder of Ballets des Champs Elysées Roland Petit made a speciality of elegantly condensed symbolic dramas, such as *Le Jeune Homme et la mort* (1946), with its libretto by Jean Cocteau, and *Carmen* (1949). Maurice Béjart – also French, though based for twenty-seven years at Brussels' Monnaie Opera House – has mixed theatrical spectacle and high-energy choreography to narrate a huge range of stories – from a version of Wagner's *The Ring* (1989), to a life of Nijinsky (*Nijinsky, Clown de Dieu*, 1971) and a homage to Charlie Chaplin (*Mr C*, 1992) (see Chapter Sixteen: Judging the Work).

*

The history of classical ballet was until the mid-twentieth century exclusively white and exclusively Western. But over the last few decades companies as widely spread as China, Japan, South Africa, Australia and Cuba have been dancing *Swan Lake* and *Giselle*, and have been training dancers to rival any talent from Europe. Many companies have also evolved their own national/racial brand of classical dance, so that contemporary Chinese ballets, for instance, draw heavily on the unique tumbling and conjuring skills of their national acrobats.

In America ballet remained, for many years, an unrepresentatively white art despite the available riches of black dance talent. But in 1971 Arthur Mitchell created a home (and pressure group) for it in Dance Theatre of Harlem – a company of mostly black dancers.

DANCE THEATRE OF HARLEM

Dance Theatre of Harlem was founded in the belief that ballet training is universal and that black bodies dance as beautifully as white, so much of its repertoire – including several Balanchine and Diaghilev ballets – has always been unrelated to colour. But any company has its own style of moving, whether it is based in Moscow, Paris or Harlem, and Mitchell never wanted to deny the physical and cultural roots of his own dancers. DTH's classicism has thus developed a physical, expressive flamboyance that's been dubbed 'Afro-Russian' and some of its repertoire investigates the possibilities of black classicism.

Some of its modern ballets draw on the syncopated rhythms and snappy hip-and-shoulder moves of black jazz dances as well as the volatile energy of urban street and club dance. Some like Geoffrey Holder's *Banda* (1982), a Haitian funeral scene, draw on the vast scope of black culture and mythology. And two of the best known are the company's stagings of the classic works *Giselle* and *Firebird*, which relocate the works to non-white, non-European contexts.

John Taras's *Firebird* (1982) retains only the score and scenario of Fokine's original production and Geoffrey Holder's designs place it firmly in a tropical forest where the Firebird herself is a glorious scarlet bird with plumed head-dress and a fantail ruff. Her dancing is leggy, preening and flouncing, with a hint of the show girl, while the monsters mass with a ferocious voodoo menace.

Frederic Franklin's staging of *Giselle* (1982) retains the old choreography, but relocates the ballet to a Louisiana plantation where Giselle is the daughter of a slave family and Albrecht the son of a free black landowning family. The class gap is less extreme than in the original (hence mildly weakening the plot), but the new setting does give a vivid dramatic twist to the ballet – forcing audiences to see fresh things in it. In Act II the swamps where Giselle's grave is set add a chilling new layer of mystery and superstition to the Germanic original.

WILLIAM FORSYTHE

The American choreographer William Forsythe, who took over the Frankfurt Ballet in 1984, once said that the vocabulary of classical ballet does not date, only the way that it is used: 'I can just as well use it to write the stories of today.' But after immersing himself in the theoretical writings of post-structuralist thinkers like Derrida and Foucault, Forsythe actually arrived at a new choreographic position where he deconstructed the language of ballet – creating what he has called an 'aesthetic of perfect disorder' in which all parts of the body became manic with energy.

In the works he made during the 80s this aesthetic involved wrenching classical positions apart at the joints, shoving them off balance and turning them upside-down. Dancers didn't simply point a foot, they jabbed it wildly into the floor; *pirouettes* didn't spin predictably in one direction but turned ferociously back on themselves. Big movements didn't ride on a string of little steps but slammed one after the other through the body. The dance was angled, slanted, twisted and rarely still, and the stage as a whole could flip from a single dancer's broody twitching to a frenetic pitch of activity where many dancers competed simultaneously for the audience's attention.

The point of this language wasn't to evoke some extreme psychological state. Forsythe's dances were rarely about recognizable characters or plot but about rewriting the rules of classicism. They were also about dismantling the inbuilt codes of the ballet performance – particularly the traditional complicity that has existed between dancers and audience. From the beginning Forsythe never put his dancers on stage to charm the audience. For one thing, his preferred low-level lighting always made them hard to distinguish from each other (he liked to play with the idea of things seen and not seen on stage). For another, the dancers appeared too absorbed in their own activities to spare a smile or a glance into the auditorium. When they'd finished moving they might look briefly at the others, they might hang around the sides of the stage with their hands on their hips or fidgeting with their shoes, or they might just turn their backs and stroll off.

No one was trying to seduce the public, no one was attempting to move it. It was as if the audience were spying on a class or a rehearsal, not a performance, and as if its contact with the dancers was simply the electric, abrasive energy that blazed off the stage.

In many works even this 'contact' between dancers and audience was subverted by elements of surreal theatre, which disrupted the surface of the dance. In the first part of Forsythe's 1988 piece *Impressing the Tsar* part of the stage was covered by a chessboard littered with tiny gold towers and cones, and the dancers, dressed variously in period costume and modern gear, performed a ritual dance of powerplay and death.

In *Interrogation of Robert Scott* (1986) a TV screen showed a man apparently under interrogation, while several voices – live and recorded – spoke in layers, asking questions, piecing together fragments of knowledge. The dancers held pieces of paper as they moved, which possibly had instructions written on them. No one seemed to know exactly where the dance was leading.

In his most recent works Forsythe has unravelled the classical vocabulary even more minutely by deconstructing dance into tiny squibs and surges of movement, as in his 1995 piece for the Royal Ballet, *Firstext*.

Firstext

For this ballet, the stage of London's Royal Opera House was stripped right back to its bare walls, revealing a backstage jumble of cables and flats – with no place for illusion, mystery or glamour to flourish. The first dancer (Sylvie Guillem in the original cast) appeared alone. A long arm rippled in a sequence of tiny jointed moves, as she crouched gracefully down and a leg shot forward past her ear, like some strange quivering antenna. As five other dancers joined her, their limbs also slid and curved through complex unpredictable patterns, impelled by thousands of questioning impulses. When they partnered each other, it was like two mobile jigsaw puzzles connecting, their limbs interlocking with a playful jockeying of position. Out of nowhere, moments of casual grace froze into focus (like a classical *attitude* simultaneously performed by three dancers) and then dissolved back into the buzz of group activity.

This new phase of Forsythe's choreography is a close cousin of the 'release' style (see Chapter Three: Reading Post-modern Dance) favoured by several of today's modern choreographers, in that the movement seems to flow through the dancers' bodies, pursuing its own currents of activity rather than being forced into specific lines and shapes. At the same time the positions of classical ballet remain the deepest conduits of energy in the dancers' limbs, so that even as the movement eddies around it seems to flow most naturally and easily through turned-out legs, stretched feet and lifted torsos. To anticipate Chapter Three, it is like classical ballet meeting Trisha Brown.

The most questing and daring early pioneers of modern dance were women. And what they did to the dancing body wasn't just create new languages for it to speak, but make it a site of liberation and self-expression. Thus San Francisco-born Isadora Duncan danced barefoot in the late nineteenth century while others were still shod in stiff ballet slippers; she threw away her corsets while others were still sewn into tight, spangled tutus; she even bared her breasts and performed when visibly pregnant. She provoked in her audiences a storm of wonder, lust, reverence – and sometimes hilarity – as her body arched and swayed in celebration of Freedom, Nature and Art.

Martha Graham, who began choreographing in New York in the late 20s, scorned feminine lyricism or seductive show in choreography that was as terse as her dancers' scraped-back hair and plain jersey frocks. Affronted by her choreography's angular lines, abrupt phrasing and high seriousness, many early viewers took the cartoonist's line that 'If Martha Graham gave birth, it would be to a cube.'

What gave pressure to these women's intense and rebellious individuality was not just the fact that they were women claiming a language for themselves in an art form dominated by male choreographers. It was the fact that they worked outside the system. They didn't put their bodies through the traditional commands of ballet class but trained them in the steps and exercises they'd invented for themselves. They weren't limited by making works to suit the repertoire of a large company but created for themselves and a select band of dancer-acolytes. They had no conservative male management to appease. They ran their own show at every level.

This made them even more revolutionary than Nijinsky, who

always regarded himself as an artist rooted in classical tradition and used to speak dismissively of the *ad hoc* nature of Duncan's recitals. 'Her performance is spontaneous,' he argued to his sister, 'and is not based on any school of dancing so cannot be taught ... it is not art.' In return, although Duncan admired Nijinsky as a dancer – suggesting once that they should mate and produce baby dance geniuses – she was generally contemptuous of ballet. She thought it was little more than a form of 'sterile gymnastics' that distorted the natural beauty of the human body. 'Look – under the skirts,' she cried, 'a deformed skeleton is dancing before you.' At times she refused to call herself a dancer because she felt the term had too many associations with cheap entertainment.

Duncan and Nijinsky's mutual suspicion defines the gap that separated modern dance from ballet during the first half of this century. Devotees of the former thought ballet was both deadened by tradition and made frivolous by fantasy and display. It was too geared to showing off ballerinas' legs and telling fairy tales to be able to express the hearts and minds of modern men and women. How could it claim to be art? The latter saw modern dance as a group of motley performers doing perversely ugly things with their bodies and trying, absurdly, to portray the state of the world with their arms and legs – all without serious training at a ballet school.

ISADORA DUNCAN

Actually Duncan and the women who followed her did have some training – but it tended to be pieced together from a range of sources. Duncan attended ballet classes as well as studying an arty form of gymnastics. She was also wildly enthused by the late-nineteenth-century vogue for Ancient Greek art and closely studied figures on statues, wall paintings and vases. She never claimed her dances to be authentic re-creations, though: 'If I am Greek, it is the Hellenism of Keats.' And she liked to suggest that her dances were largely inspirational – gushing out from her own passions and from her rapt communings with nature.

Trees, hills, wind and waves gave her the idea of a dance swept by large, fluid and simple motions. In the recitals she gave across America and Europe between 1897 and 1927 she would place herself on a bare stage, draped with grey voile curtains and softened by pink lights. Either alone or flanked by a group of young girls (the Isadorables), she would perform simple dance steps like a waltz or polka and ordinary movements like running, skipping and walking that were elaborated by held poses or by passages of mime (strewing flowers, playing with a ball). These moves were made extraordinary by the ecstatic quality of her bearing, the eloquence of her gestures, the unusual pliancy of her body and by her sheer physical charisma. To audiences used to seeing dancers perform routine stunts Duncan's beauty lay in the fact that she used her body as a single expressive instrument. Frederick Ashton once said, 'She had a wonderful way of running, in which she, what I call, left herself behind and you felt the breeze running through her hair and everywhere else.'

Fokine was also impressed by her – not only because her use of Ancient Greek poses paralleled his own interest in Greek, Egyptian and folk movement but also because he delighted in her courage to be plain and direct in her dancing. 'Duncan,' he enthused, 'reminded us of the beauty of simple movements.' Her bare feet, her bending torso and her natural gestures all found their way into his work – not necessarily as direct imitation, but as part of a new choreographic *Zeitgeist*. When Fokine wrote years later about the fact that arms are 'not pictures on the wall but horizons', he might have been speaking of the gestures with which she conjured up an impression of light, space and wind.

Duncan didn't invent a systematized dance language, but reclaimed the power of moving naturally. While ballet tries to conceal the fact that the solar plexus is the source of its power, Duncan's choreography revealed it as the motor of her movement. Her gut powered her bending torso and her runs and turns; it initiated the downward thrust of her bare feet and the ardent reach of her strong rounded arms. It gave the whole body a central focus.

Duncan was also, from all accounts, musical. As one of her most passionate admirers, Marie Rambert, said, 'When Isadora danced you felt as though she was carried by the music without any effort on her part.' Though her steps looked simple, they resonated with the passion with which she set them to music – and also with the music she dared to use. In the late nineteenth century it was established practice to use only composers who wrote professionally for dance. Duncan, however, raided the repertoire for great scores. To the revered climaxes of Brahms and the well-loved melodies of Chopin she made dances that spoke of Nature and of revolution.

Her gods were Havelock Ellis, Nietzsche and the pagan Greeks. Dance for Duncan was the route to personal and national liberation. 'I see America dancing beautifully, strong with one foot poised on the highest point of the Rockies, her two hands stretched out from the Atlantic to the Pacific, her fine head tossed to the sky, her forehead shining with a crown of a million stars.'

With her body swathed in a simple Greek tunic, her strong bare limbs declaiming an emotional rhetoric or showering rose petals, Duncan became a symbol for free, exalted and sensuous womanhood. When she was young, students in Germany pulled her flower-covered carriage through the streets in worship. But some viewers didn't buy it. George Balanchine spoke of her in 1921 as a 'drunken fat woman who for hours was rolling round like a pig'. And when she died in 1927 people described her as a flabby, prematurely aged woman with badly dyed hair. But for an important few she paved the way for a new female art.

RUTH ST DENIS

One of Duncan's admirers, Ruth St Denis, said of her dancing, 'In one arm's movement was all the grace of the world; in one backward flinging of her head was all the nobility.' St Denis also was inspired to change the world through dance and used to describe herself (in terms that rivalled Duncan's for almost comic high seriousness) as a 'rhythmic and impersonal instrument of spiritual revelation'. Coming out of a career in music hall at the turn of the century, her style mixed popular dance steps and gymnastics with a muddle of exotic influences like gyrating hips, snaking arm movements and a curving torso. With this – actually rather titillating – style, she, her partner Ted Shawn and her company of dancers dramatized scenes of Indian gods achieving spiritual awakening or evoked the beauty of the inner life in abstract choreography.

Despite her elevated aspirations St Denis was a woman of the theatre – brilliant at using scarves, skirts, jewels and lighting to flatter her own half-naked, gorgeously flexible body; adroit at giving her audiences a sensually charged entertainment even while surrounding the whole event with a spiritual aura. Like Duncan she is remembered as a woman who staged her own unique vision of dance. But unlike Duncan she trained other performers to equal and eventually outstrip her – including Martha Graham, who went on to become the most powerful and influential of the founding mothers of modern dance.

MARTHA GRAHAM

It's a curious quirk of history that Graham, raised in a strict Presbyterian household in California, should have taken up a career in dance at all, let alone performed with St Denis's exotic troupe. Yet she learnt many things during her seven years with that company – how to stage a stylish show using simple lighting and drapes, how to make her dancers look good. She also learnt what to avoid. She didn't want to create dances that fluttered round some half-baked mystic notions; she wanted to express the soul of modern America. She didn't want to make dances that flattered and coaxed. She wanted her choreography to express stern truths about the real world. Her father, a doctor with psychiatric interests, once told her that 'movement never lies'. It became Graham's creed.

The language that Graham invented was, like Duncan's, forged out of her own body. It was shaped by her own strong legs, wide pelvis and long, lean torso; it took its dramatic tone from her own darkly eloquent eyes and pale, haunting face (see illus. 2).

American dancer and choreographer Agnes de Mille, who knew and worked with Graham, describes her even as a young woman as having a 'skull-like head . . . Its deep-set eyes . . . gaunt cheeks and long, well-defined jaw looked to me even then like a death's head – until one considered the eyes. And one returned to them again and again. Her eyes flashed light.'

Like Duncan's movement, Graham's dance was rooted in the gut. It was based on the principle of contraction and release, in which the torso curved inwards, sucked against the spine, then expanded forwards, on the ebb and flow of the breath. These movements could be slow and resonant as a sigh, abrupt and agonized as a sob, or quick and percussive as gasps. They allowed the dancers to throw their torsos around with unnerving violence and speed, spiralling into headlong falls, arching forward or back as if they were shot, dropping to their knees with their whole body weight hinging backwards.

What exaggerated the drama of these movements was that they visibly battled with gravity. Ballet dancers in all their guises as fairies and princesses were in perpetual flight from the floor, jumping from it, skimming it on their toes. Graham's dancers, literally women of this earth, were constantly returning to it.

In states of terror, exhaustion or passion they would, in dozens of artful ways, fall to the floor where they might crawl, roll or simply lie. When they jumped they didn't give the impression of flying but of only momentarily defying gravity, their pounding, wrenching leaps weighted by the earth's pull. Their strong limbs didn't float but articulated the struggle and effort of dance. Above all their bare feet were in constant contact with the floor. Un-sheathed by ballet slippers, they became sensitive percussive instruments – the slap of the feet against the floor and the drumming of the heels giving new rhythms and dynamics to the dancing.

A Graham class didn't begin with the barre, as in ballet, but with the dancers seated on the floor, body and limbs stretching away from gravity, then sinking back into it. When they rose to dance they held their bodies in a new way – their legs and feet not turned out like ballet dancers' or artificially turned in as in Nijinsky's *Rite of Spring*, but in the natural parallel stance of ordinary people. What stylized their limbs was the tension running through them and the jagged lines in which they were held. While the limbs of classical dancers created a play of curves, Graham's dancers flexed their feet and hinged their joints into sharp angles, their bodies braced for action. As they danced, their movements weren't stitched into fluid phrases but left as terse statements, the edges of each move blunt and raw.

And each move meant something. Even Graham's exercises for class were powered by emotional expression and had names like 'Pleading', 'The Laugh' or 'The Cry'. Her corrections in the studio were comments like, 'When you contract from the floor you are in the image of a *pietà* and the earth is the mother that cradles you.' Form was content, the emotion shaped the dance. When a dancer spiralled her torso she was dramatizing her character's confusion in the contradictory tug of her body; when she fell to the floor she was in despair or erotic delight.

Lamentation

In this remarkable solo, made in 1930, Graham's body became a pure expressionist statement. Shrouded in a dark tube of tricot, tied at the waist with string, and with only her face, hands and feet showing, she sat with her feet braced against the floor while her body keened from side to side in terrible motions of grief. Her body's lines were made more drastic by the tension and pull of the material enclosing it. De Mille recalls that, 'every movement look[ed] as if it was carved in stone, the costume became not so much yardage as a sculpture by . . . Henry Moore'. Stripped down to the urgent lines and shapes of emotion, the choreography was the dance equivalent of Kandinsky or Munch. If Graham had been a painter, she might have produced *The Scream*.

Graham, of course, was influenced in other ways by her times. Her dancing took on board the syncopated rhythms and angularities of jazz dance; her austere plain lines reflected a growing functionalism in the design and architecture that surrounded her. Some of her angular hieratic poses were, like Nijinsky's, a stripped-down version of earlier Greek dance fashions and of the orientalisms of St Denis. She was impressed by the rhythms of both North American Indian dances and South American dance rituals. And she may in part have been influenced by the primitivist-inspired expressionism of the German choreographer Mary Wigman.

Graham was also deeply engaged in the politics and philosophies of the twentieth century. Her early dances were made during the Depression years and they reflected the tension between individual life and social forces. For her, the struggle to make a new dance language was bound up with a duty to express the modern condition. In 1929 she wrote, 'Life today is nervous, sharp and zigzag; the old expressions could not give it form,' and in 1936 she demanded that audiences must 'allow themselves to be reached by economy, simplicity and necessity of line rather than by intricacy of detail or story values ... if you want to be both entertained and lulled into a false sense of security, then modern dance is not for you.'

Steps in the Street

In this 1938 work the chorus of eleven dancers is like an army of the poor and dispossessed, crossing the stage in lines, diagonals, single or double file. During the opening moments the dancers are walking backwards, faces twisted down to one shoulder, and their open mouths seem to scream a protest into the palms of their lifted hands. Later they march with clenched fists raised in protest, or jump on the spot, feet beating against the floor. The soloist, dressed in uniform black like the others, is at times a part of this march. At others she stands at its head, or else forces her way back between their ranks – her solitariness distilling the anger and pain of the crowd.

During the 40s Graham fell under the spell of Jungian psychology and her dances became increasingly inward and symbolic. She made dances around a range of heroines from history and myth, all of whom represented some powerful female archetype – Medea as the jealous revenger, Clytemnestra as the betrayer and murderess and St Joan as the martyr.

In nearly all of these works Graham was both the raw material and the star. She dragged the emotions of her characters out of her own body and heart, and she performed them with a coruscating intensity. 'Dance,' she once said, 'is a fever chart of the heart' – meaning her own. As with Duncan, most of Graham's disastrous love affairs found their way into her work – her own experiences of jealousy and delight, and her terror of old age given motive and flesh.

Around her, though, the company changed. Graham's first dancers were all women who'd devoted their lives to her. They were tough and committed movers, dedicated to truth and hard physical graft. (Several of them suffered a variety of internal ailments as a result of the punishing physical regime of Graham's schedule, and they earned the nickname 'the Graham Crackers' because of their apparently fanatical acceptance of fatigue and pain.)

This single-sex group gave Graham's early language a universal quality; it was dance for Everywoman. And there were, of course, no distracting sexual relationships or romantic duets. But as Graham's dances moved inward, became more sexual and psychological than political, she gradually introduced men into her company. For a while they tended to be puppet males representing macho strength with their huge leaps and almost comically tough poses. Paul Taylor, who danced with Graham from 1955 to 1961, claimed unflatteringly that they 'were usually stiff foils or something large and naked for women to climb upon'.

But even during Taylor's time Graham's language was being softened and diversified. She accommodated a more balletic fluency in her phrasing; she softened the tense ferocity of her movements into more full-bodied steps; the gestures expanded and grew easier. And she began slowly to exploit the dance range of which her men were capable. Robert Cohan, who also danced with her from the late 40s through to the early 60s, said that she had a 'marvellous way of working with men'; she wanted to 'pull the movement out of them'.

(Taylor was more critical, and always tried to resist the rather mystic idea of maleness that Graham liked to instil into her male dancers. Once he and his colleague (a very young Glen Tetley) stayed behind after class as Graham, dressed in a beautiful kimono and still fearsomely charismatic at sixtysomething, tried to explain some essential secret of their movement. She said that they should hold their heads as if 'something were elevating your ears and . . . releas[ing] the animal brain . . . so that the movement is totally strong and male . . . I want you to be animal and male.' Tetley has admitted he was 'dazzled by this and thought, "The Goddess. The mother of God! Yes."' For Taylor, though, it was just another example of Graham's vague and self-important mysticism. 'What a pile of shit . . . Why can't she just say keep your back straight and your chin up?')

During the course of Graham's long career, the look of her stages became less plain as her movement became more varied. In her early works she rarely used sets, and there was little colour in her costumes. The spare, dissonant effects in her dance were reflected in her choice of tersely contemporary music. She favoured percussive sounds that, like her dance, laid bare their own gestures. But, as she became more interested in specific characters and plots, both the dancing and the staging became more detailed and Graham proved herself as much of a revolutionary in theatre production as in dance.

Most of her sets were designed by Isamu Noguchi and they came to define the style of her productions almost as uniquely as her movement, stripped down to the same level of expressive form. They were never backdrops or scenery and they rarely gave more than a suggestion of realistic setting, but they occupied the stage on their own terms as sculptures. At a compositional level they created a play of lines which echoed the forms of the choreography. At a physical level they provided platforms and surfaces around which the dancers could move. And at a symbolic level they seemed to plug into the many layers of Graham's narrative, giving visual form to the characters' passions and mapping the inward geography of their minds and hearts.

Cave of the Heart

Made in 1946 this was a horrifying study of jealousy which Graham made when she herself was tormented by her relationship with her husband-to-be Eric Hawkins. (It also illustrated her fascination with the darkest reaches of human nature. She'd say to her dancers, 'Show me how low a person will go. Let me see the depths to which she is capable of sinking; the heights will take care of themselves.') It was based on the story of Medea's revenge after Jason betrays her with the Princess of Corinth, but typically it distilled the plot into archetypes of character and emotion.

Noguchi created for Medea a huge, delicate, metallic cage which radiated quivering spikes and suggested at various times the aura of her magic powers, the trap of her passions and also the sun to which she finally returns. Early on, Medea lies in wait behind this cage, staring balefully through its spikes as Jason dances with the Princess. When she emerges she dances a terrible movement where a leg and an arm curve in and out in angry figures of eight, as if she's winding herself up for revenge. She falls backwards to the floor in a slow, agonized spiral. Minutes later, she performs a retching movement with her torso and pulls a bright red ribbon from her breast which she then stuffs into her mouth. According to de Mille, 'Noguchi said that she is dancing with the snake [of jealousy] in her mouth, then she spits it out . . . like blood.' After this comes a concentrated solo of animal fury and pain when she runs in a *bourrée* on her knees and then crouches, trembling over the floor, her knees vibrating, 'like a hungry insect in a spasm of evisceration and digestion – an effect which made the blood run cold'.

Finally Medea returns to her cage and puts it on, the spikes wavering round her like insect wings as she hovers over the dead bodies of Jason and the Princess. Then she climbs up one of the several stone solids that mark out the stage and stands in a red light, having returned to the sun where she burns in the fires of her own hatred (see illus. 7).

Graham's narrative style was completely unlike the logically plotted ballets of the nineteenth century. It was closer to Japanese Noh theatre and Ancient Greek drama in the way it moved between inner and outer reality, between violent physical action and spiritual turmoil – while its characteristic use of narrative flashback and montage was almost cinematic. In *Deaths and Entrances* (1943), based on the lives of the Brontës, the characters were presented simultaneously as adults and children who contemplated each other across the years. Digging one level deeper, they represented not only the Brontës but also the archetypal family, so the role of Heathcliff also represented a generic lover called the 'Dark Beloved' as well as a Father Figure. In 1984 Graham described this work as 'speaking to anyone who has a family', as being 'a modern psychological portrait of . . . women unable to free themselves of themselves, to follow their heart's desire'.

Her characters were never solid individuals but the 'Selves' of modernist art and psychology – assembled out of different conflicts, voices and impulses. Sometimes different dancers even represented different aspects of the same person. These complex, questioning, driven characters inhabited a world that was part myth, part fantasy, part history, part contemporary reality. Only fifty years on from *Sleeping Beauty*, they were centuries removed from its courtly brilliance and moral certainties. In investigating her own language of dance, Graham was also investigating the place of women in the modern world.

MERCE CUNNINGHAM

His build resembles that of the juvenile *saltimbanque* of the early Picasso canvases. As a dancer his instep and his knees are extraordinarily elastic and quick; his steps, runs, knee bends and leaps are brilliant in lightness and speed. His torso can turn on its vertical axis with great sensitivity, his shoulders are held lightly free and his head poises intelligently. The arms are light and long; they float but do not often have an active look.
– Edwin Denby, *Herald Tribune*, 1944

Merce Cunningham was the next great innovator in modern dance and, like Martha Graham, he made choreography out of the way he looked and danced. Compared to the terse, unitary statements of Graham's style, where almost every move was an exclamation of concentrated emotion, Cunningham's style was like a patter of witty, lateral conversation. Movements entered and left his dancers' bodies with an almost anarchic unpredictability. In a single step one woman might make a slow circle of her leg, while her head turned this way and that like an anxious bird, and her bent arms rotated like propellers. A bunch of dancers might all be performing the same quick stitchwork of jumps but be constantly shifting direction like a swarm of insects.

Cunningham actually performed for several years with Graham's company, but he was liberated from the hard seriousness of her style by his ranging curiosity about the possibilities of dance. Unusually for one of her select band, he'd taken regular ballet classes and, though he had no ambition to become a Prince in tights, he was impressed by how lively ballet was on its feet, how fast it could move and how many rhythms it could play with.

In his own dances he began to work with the high legs and fast rhythmic footwork of ballet, while keeping the free curving torso of modern dance. He also retained the frank power and thrust of Graham's dance; his dancers never pretended that their bodies were weightless or that dance was not work. But his choreography was much less burdened by gravity. His dancers were rarely wrenched to the ground by the earth's pull or had to struggle with opposing forces. In fact, with their lightly pointed feet, strong legs, easy torsos and brisk jumps they hardly ever got down to the floor at all.

But Cunningham's dances also weren't about struggle, for the simple reason that they weren't about anything. If Cunningham had a creed, it was that his movement couldn't lie because it wasn't being asked to say anything. Dance, he argued, was about moving 'in space and time'. There were no plots, characters, messages or symbols in his work. With a lifetime's ingenuousness that irritated some and delighted others he always invited his public to make whatever sense or nonsense of his works they chose. Cunningham's dancers were the exact opposite of the towering tormented archetypes of Graham's work who jousted with unseen forces. They were like scientists, engaged in a scrupulous but very passionate exploration of what the body could do.

The choreography didn't come together solely from a union between classical and early modern dance. It was coloured by observations of the way people and animals behaved. Sometimes – inspired by John Cage's belief that any sound might be heard as music – Cunningham put 'found' movements and gestures into his work. In *Variations V* (1965) he danced a solo in which he pulled the leaves off a plastic plant and rode a bicycle, and in *Borst Park* (1972) he lay down and read a newspaper. Cunningham's favourite adjective was always 'interesting'. Without prejudice about high or low art, without intent to shock or preach, his dances were made out of what fascinated his quizzical curiosity.

The way Cunningham put his dances together was also new. Classical ballet had always followed the laws of Renaissance perspective in its design, the main action taking place at the centre of the stage with everything else acting as a receding frame. Graham's work similarly tended to place the main action, usually herself, at the focal point of the stage. But Cunningham argued that it was more interesting to have several things happening on stage at once, so that viewers had to decide for themselves what part of the dance they'd watch. The performers as a result often seemed to be pursuing their own private activities – when they paired up or formed groups, it seemed like an accident or a special moment of convergence in the infinitely complex laws of the dance.

Cunningham's logic was based on the idea that dance should reflect the dense information overload that we're used to processing every day in the modern world – that it should be the equivalent of channel hopping. It was influenced by modern theories of relativity (there are no fixed points in space) and by a larger artistic movement that prized contingency over order. Cunningham was artistic kin to John Cage, junking the traditional principles of harmony, and to Jasper Johns and Robert Rauschenberg, turning their canvases into non-hierarchical space, where every form, colour and image competed equally for the viewer's attention.

These artists were part of the select group that Cunningham used to contribute the music and design to his dances, collaborations that were themselves influenced by a kind of limited-chaos theory. The sound, sets and costumes created by Cage, Johns *et al.* were added after Cunningham had made his choreography, so that any connections that emerged between them were largely spontaneous. This was a way for dance to declare its independence. Cunningham believed that movement should be governed by its own timing rather than by the phrasing of a score, so he rehearsed his dancers with stop watches, often not adding the music until the first performance. Similarly he believed that dance generated its own design and didn't actually require the support of a backdrop or set. Cunningham simply added designs, just as he added music, to make the event richer.

Rainforest

In *Rainforest* (1968) Cunningham used an installation by Andy Warhol of bobbing helium-filled balloons which were allowed to interfere freely with the already-choreographed movement – colliding with the dancers, scudding across their path or disappearing out of the wings. Though the movement was also made independently of David Tudor's score (from which the work takes its title), *Rainforest* was one of Cunningham's pieces where the dramatic alchemy worked by the separate elements was profound. Watching it, no one knew if it was the music and set that were making them 'read' images into the movement or vice versa. The connections occurring on stage may have been accidental, but they seemed like sparks of meaning that the audience discovered for itself, linking up into a story that it wrote as it watched.

The stage in *Rainforest* certainly looked to many people like some primitive animal space. David Tudor's music, with its insistent pulse, twittering cries and electronic roars, sounded like the clamour of jungle life. And Cunningham himself admitted that Warhol's silver balloons did create 'the sense of a rainforest [where] there is always something overhead, the sense of something up there from which the rain is dripping'. Shining brightly against the black backdrop, they scattered throughout the piece like a forest murmuring with life.

The choreography itself was alive with mysterious but vivid detail. An intimate duet began with the dancers' feet pattering in tiny steps, then it exploded into hard, wide-stepping lunges, the dancers kicking aside stray balloons like beasts crashing through undergrowth. Some of the movement seemed to have deliberate animal references – a gesture like a cat washing its face, a man crawling beetle-wise across the floor with a woman draped across his back, a crouch held with the intent listening stillness of a leopard. But there was never a sense that the dancers were actually imitating animals – rather, some essence of animal motion seemed to have been distilled into their steps.

Part of the accidental quality of Cunningham's style was generated by his use of chance in the actual choreographic process, the way he would put certain aspects of its organization up for grabs. In *Suite for Five in Space and Time* (1956) he marked the imperfections on a piece of paper to decide the path of a dancer across the stage, and in *Suite by Chance* (1953) he worked out fifteen different leaps, then tossed coins to decide how they'd appear in the piece. By allowing chance to enter his choreography Cunningham believed he was not only tapping into the mysterious operations of the universe, but also, more pragmatically, discovering combinations of movements he might not have thought of himself. He was warding off habit. In 1955 he wrote, 'The feeling I have when I compose in this way is that I am in touch with natural resources far greater than my own personal inventiveness could ever be.'

Another of Cunningham's favourite ways of courting accident was the staging of Events. These were programmes of dance made out of extracts of past works which were performed as a seamless whole and often accompanied by an improvised score. The order in which the extracts were danced could change any day. By putting his works in this reinvented context Cunningham gave himself the fun of seeing new connections between them. Referring to one three-day run of Events in 1990, he said, 'It goes on from day to day, some things repeat, some things change. You never see the same performance twice. Events are actually about a way of looking and not thinking that what you're seeing should be something else. They're a bit like watching people in the street.'

Yet though an Event may be a quintessential Cunningham experience – a kind of Zen choreography which you simply contemplate as it passes in front of you – some of his later works have felt much more emotionally loaded. This is particularly true of those where Cunningham himself has danced. It's rare to see a man in his seventies performing with a dance company, particularly when his joints are as ravaged by arthritis as Cunningham's have become, his toes clawed and his hips stiff. It's also rare to see a performer projecting such an intense physical and mental intelligence on stage. Cunningham's eyes actively sweep the space; his head twitches as if it had antennae pricked to catch ideas floating by; his straightened movements communicate astonishingly clear decisions about their placing, rhythm and energy. For these reasons Cunningham can have the mesmerizing powers of a mercurial wizard. And the contrast with his other much younger dancers is always of extreme poignancy and interest. Against their strong burnished movements and radiating energy, Cunningham obviously looks old and stiff. But he looks like their master. In the activity of his brain and in his own moves you seem to discern the origins of their beautiful dancing. It's as if he were sketching what they will go on to paint.

Pictures

In this 1984 work Cunningham seemed to be tenderly in control of his dance company, checking and helping his dancers, and the warmth of this relationship was consecrated by moments of stillness in the work where dancers froze unexpectedly in some perfect image, thrown into silhouette by the lighting. In one of these 'pictures' a busy group dispersed to leave a single woman standing with her leg lifted at a high angle. She didn't move a muscle, but simply folded her hands and waited. The 'picturing' of this moment through the change of lighting made us marvel at the woman's control even as she stirred us strangely by her quietness.

Cunningham moved in and out of the piece, and at its close partnered a woman in a brief dance which ended with him cradling her horizontally across his body. The fragile triumph of Cunningham's strength (he looked too old and frail to support her weight) and their declaration of mutual trust made this moment wrenchingly poignant. But so too did the simplicity of the lift which seemed to state purely one person's considerateness in holding another.

Images like those created in *Pictures* point to a paradox that has always been at the heart of Cunningham's work, which is that the rigour with which he has stripped dance of its dramatic rhetoric and focused on its physical detail hasn't resulted in dance that is purely abstract. Rather, the process seems to get at some expressive core within the movement. By freeing dancers from the business of story-telling Cunningham has actually maximized their powers of communication.

Chapter Three: READING POST-MODERN DANCE

Between them Cunningham and Graham established the two major axes of modern dance. Their works added up to a huge and influential mainstream of choreography, while their style crystallized into training systems that have schooled dancers all over the world. However, by the 60s a new generation was poised to rebel against them.

EARLY POST-MODERNISM

THE MINIMALISTS

Dressed in T-shirts, jeans and sneakers rather than the supple jersey dresses of Graham's company or the leotards and tights of Cunningham's, a hip new breed of dancers began diligently subverting the glamour and gymnastics attached to dance. Not only did they refuse to be anyone other than themselves on stage – neither the fairies and princesses of classical ballet, nor the intense mythic protagonists of Graham's work – they also firmly disassociated themselves from the highly trained athletes that were Cunningham's dancers. Presenting themselves as defiantly ordinary and unbeautiful, they went about the business of reclaiming everyday human activities as the material for dance.

This didn't just mean incorporating a few 'found' movements into their choreography, as Cunningham had done. It meant making whole pieces out of running, walking or crawling. Anyone who danced steps did so in such a low-key manner as to deny the fact. They didn't point their feet, or stylize their bodies in any obvious way; they erased the whole history of academic dance from the stage – except as a point of negation. It was a back-to-basics campaign for choreography. As composer Steve Reich drily recalled, 'For a long time during the 1960s one would go to the dance concert where no one danced, followed by the party where everyone danced.' Critic Arlene Croce was one of many dance lovers who felt under siege, writing swingeingly that the principle of 'non dance' had 'captured – and paralysed – a whole generation'.

Yvonne Rainer, one of the most influential members of this generation, summed up its principles in a 1965 manifesto:

NO to spectacle no to virtuosity no to transformations and magic and make-believe no to the glamour and transcendency of the star image no to the heroic no to the anti-heroic no to trash imagery no to involvement of performer or spectator no to style no to camp no to seduction of spectator by the wiles of the performer no to eccentricity no to moving or being moved.

Of course, the aesthetic behind this was more complex than it seemed. Firstly, though Rainer's own works might have looked as if anyone off the street could do them, the choreography wasn't that simple to dance. The moves in her *Trio A* (1966) (which included arm swings to the front and back and kicks punctuated by a crouch and a lunge) involved a professional mustering of co-ordination, while their studiedly neutral style (the energy flowing evenly through each movement like very mild and logical speech) demanded a strict control of dynamics and breath.

Rainer also constructed complex theoretical structures to support her apparently modest work, comparing it point by point with the minimalist school of painting and sculpture that emerged during the 60s. Deploying the jargon of art critics, she argued that the latter's 'elimination' of 'hierarchical relationship of parts' was the same as her own rejection of 'development and climax'; that its substitution of 'unitary forms, modules' could be compared to her own insistence on 'the equality of parts, repetition'.

Just as Carl André might lay out a ton of bricks in a simple oblong pattern and call it 'non-priapic sculpture', so Rainer tried to abstract dance into a pure and non-expressive art of motion.

The point of this new school of choreography was also to find a language outside the established schools of dance – as choreographer Lucinda Childs said, 'It gave us a new recipe.' It provided an escape from the monumental shadows cast by Graham and Cunningham. In their quest for simplicity and subversion, some choreographers even included non-dancers in their work so that they could study the quirks of the untrained body in performance. (Rainer herself performed a shaky version of *Trio A* when she was recovering from a long illness and retitled it *Convalescent Dance*.)

Many other works were organized around simple tasks and structures, avoiding the need for story-telling or complex pattern-making. Trisha Brown has spoken of how her interest in 'the vocabulary of ordinary behaviour ... was in answer to the kind of puffed-up, embellished dancing of that day, the kind that yearned for something off stage right'.

In her piece *Rule Game 5* (1964), for instance, a group of dancers was simply instructed to move along a series of parallel lines and adopt a stance that would make them taller or shorter than their neighbour. Thus the dancer who was travelling along one line might crawl in order to be at a lower level than the dancer moving in a crouching waddle along the line next to them, or the bent-leg walk of the dancer further along. The piece was deliberately banal and practical in its groundwork (Brown once famously referred to herself as a 'bricklayer with a sense of humour') and the fun of seeing it lay in spotting the dancers' ingenuity in finding moves that fitted the rules.

To emphasize their 'ordinariness', certain dances were made for non-theatre spaces like parks, streets and rooftops. In Lucinda Childs's *Street Dance* (1964) an area of the street was marked off and two dancers moved among the crowd, gesturing towards various buildings. The audience, watching from an upper-storey window, listened to a taped commentary on the architecture and the weather.

Other works by Childs embraced the major aesthetic obsession of the period: repetition. In her 'white-on-white' choreography a simple sequence of runs, turns or walks would be recycled by one or more dancers along a strict geometric floor pattern, gradually accumulating variations in speed, rhythm and direction. Like all dancers of this period they assumed an expression of neutral concentration as they danced, attempting to bleach personal idiosyncrasy and expression from their bodies. It was the dance equivalent of the geometric, abstract art of Sol LeWitt (visual artists in fact formed the most enthusiastic support group of this work) and it induced a trance state similar to that generated by the music of minimalist composers like Steve Reich or Philip Glass (whose scores were frequently used).

While some choreographers devoted themselves scrupulously to this dance fundamentalism, others began to blend dance with other ingredients – the performers enacting obsessional games, miming, singing, playing instruments and sharing the stage with art installations or film. Certain performances were like parties with musicians, film makers and artists included.

Accounts of Meredith Monk's three-part *Juice* (1969) suggest it was a monumental classic of the genre – performed in several parts in New York's Guggenheim Museum and various districts of Manhattan. In part of the first instalment the spectators walked up the Guggenheim's spiral ramp past tableaux of dancers posing in front of an exhibition of Roy Lichtenstein's paintings. Three weeks later, the second part of the performance took place at a theatre where four fictional 'characters' regaled the audience with their life stories while frying chops and mixing chemicals. Monk herself whirled around like a dervish and sang; a log cabin was gradually dismantled to reveal a violinist surrounded by some artfully positioned books, a quart of milk and a print of a Lichtenstein painting. In part three, a week later, the audience assembled in Monk's own loft where they wandered through an exhibition of artefacts from the previous two instalments and watched four dancers on video discussing their involvement with the piece.

Part of the fun of this work was the polarization of views it generated, the ripe opportunities for argument. Never had there been so much high moral ground to occupy in the debate over what dance should or shouldn't be, about the professionalism or otherwise of the performers, about the seriousness of the content.

IMPROVISATION

Another ripe area for provocation was the new vogue for improvised dance. In some quarters choreographed movement came to be regarded as politically suspect – reducing dance to a trained-dog act and audiences to passive consumers. Improvisation, by contrast, liberated performers into discovering their own movement. It allowed them to take charge of their own bodies and it allowed audiences to share in the process of creation – watching art being made, riskily, out of the present moment.

Of course, the interest of improvised dance was still dependent on non-democratic values like expertise and talent. Dana Reitz, who became a highly skilled improviser during the 70s, perfected a Zen-like focus on the here-and-now in her dancing; and her astonishingly detailed moves and quick responses could, and still can, sustain a charismatic, hour-long solo.

Another 'star' of the improvisation scene was Steve Paxton, who danced for several years with Cunningham and went on to evolve the popular dance sport 'contact improvisation'. (This is basically a duet form of improvisation where two dancers try and maintain unbroken contact with each other as they surf over each other's bodies, balance on each other's backs, hoist each other through the air or nestle in each other's arms.)

At the time contact was politically and symbolically important to the avant-garde, because it stripped the *pas de deux* of its traditional physical sexism – its free-for-all manoeuvres enabling women to lift both men and women, and small men to lift large men. It also stripped the duet form of its old images of glamour and sex. Watching two people of any gender grunting, grappling and giggling through the search for bodily contact was very different from seeing a ballerina floating in splendid, unassailable grace on her partner's shoulders.

But in performance, contact has proved to be heartstopping. Experts in the art achieve a flying joint momentum as they duck and dive around each other; they can seem to be unnervingly in tune with each other's reflexes as their bodies tumble and feint. There is a unique excitement to be got from seeing moments of perfect beauty, balance or trust suddenly emerge out of a way-ward tangle of bodies, and from seeing highly intelligent minds and bodies turn a possible disaster into a triumphantly graceful move.

To achieve such moments the dancers have to be able to release all the tension from their muscles. Where classical ballet requires them to sustain positions by hard physical effort, contact impro-visation demands that they go with the flow of the movement, the two dancers engaged in a constant give-and-take. (Also see Chapter Nine: Improvisation.)

RELEASE

This concept of release, of letting movement eddy through the body like water, became an important aesthetic during the 70s. Some dancers at this point rejected the idea of putting their bodies into set positions that had to be corrected in the studio mirror. They chose instead to dance from the inside out, 'listening' to their bodies, letting them move in the most relaxed and economi-cal ways possible. The result was a style of liquid movement quite unlike the defined shapes of other dance forms. It could be slow and serene – dance as physical meditation – or it could be fast – a flurry of activity.

Another stylistic innovation of the 70s and early 80s was the reclaiming of humble parts of the dancer's body – the fingers, the little movement of the joints, the facial muscles. Dance didn't just have to be about explosions of power in the legs and torso. It could be a miniature play of detail. During the 80s small hand gestures and quirky facial expressions became new staples of the dance repertoire as choreographers found a language akin to classical Indian dance, where a gracefully extended finger or lifted brow might carry huge rhythmic or dramatic impact in the context of the dance.

The sum effect of these decades of deglamorizing, demystifying and redefining the boundaries of dance was to democratize the body. The big stunts – the balances, jumps, falls, sweeping legs and complex steps that were the traditional highlights of dance

– no longer held a monopoly. Any movement, however tiny, unexpected or awkward, could become a major choreographic event.

POST-MODERNISM PROPER

But once all the parts of the body had been reoccupied, choreographers no longer had to be so puritanical about throwing out the old dance values. Music and colour, story and character, complex steps and lavish lines became permissible again. Around the late 70s and early 80s the body started to dance full out. Yet it did so in a way that flouted every category in the book. For in the new age of cultural post-modernism, where styles were thrown into a global melting pot, choreographers became open to an extreme range of influences.

New dance forms have always been born out of the past clashing with the present, or out of one migrating culture transforming another. During the nineteenth century tap dance was created by African dance rhythms meeting the Irish jig in the ethnic Babel of North America. In the same way Spanish flamenco was influenced by the Moors, classical ballet by indigenous folk dance, Martha Graham by North American Indian dance. But in the late twentieth century – the age of video, cheap travel and historical reclamation – choreographers could surf the whole history and geography of dance at will, their contact with different styles both more instant and more simultaneous.

A random view of choreographers around the world during the last twenty-five years would thus show Twyla Tharp putting together rock and roll and ballet steps for a classical company and setting them to the music of the Beach Boys; Laurie Booth mixing the manoeuvres of contact improvisation with the Brazilian martial art Capoeria; Mark Morris combining the expressionist gestures of the early moderns with sign language and folk steps in his danced version of Purcell's opera *Dido and Aeneas*; and Shobana Jeyasingh deconstructing the classical Indian dance Bharatha Natyam, applying Western ideas of weight and energy to it, and collaborating with a mix of Western and Indian composers.

Never before have dancers had to be so multilingual.

PAUL TAYLOR

But history doesn't come in tidy packages. The American choreographer Paul Taylor (who danced with both Cunningham and Graham), for instance, anticipated the severest tenets of 60s choreography in the dances he made in New York during the late 50s. (In *Epic* (1957) he wore a business suit and, accompanied by a telephone talking clock, simply paced around, sat and waited. The response from Louis Horst in *Dance Observer* was a review without words – a column of blank space.) But then in 1962 Taylor broke with the Manhattan avant-garde entirely and made *Aureole*, which, with its stageful of dancers running and leaping to the music of Handel, came as a complete shock to both the establishment and the minimalists. The latter, as Twyla Tharp recalls, were 'embarrassed . . . threatened by his raw heat and power'.

Aureole

This work and the series of sunny lyrical dances it engendered were a unique mix of classical, modern and pedestrian movement. In these works Taylor's dancers performed steps that were recognizable from ballet – *jetés*, turns in *attitude*, lifts – but they did them also with the weight of modern dancers, and with the free and easy casualness of real people. They weren't too particular about pointing their toes, nor did they rigorously turn out their legs. Taylor – a big-boned, powerful dancer over six foot tall – picked his dancers for their physical juice rather than their dancerly shape. Though they were wonderful movers, none of them looked as if they'd spent years obsessively finessing their technique in a studio.

And these familiar steps were utterly changed by Taylor's rhythm and wit. In a string of *jetés* his dancers would bound along the ground rather than float in space, their speed facilitated by energetically swinging arms. *Pirouettes* could be spun on a dancer's knee. A woman might be hoisted up on to her partner's shoulders, but, instead of gazing serenely into the distance, she'd be looking cheerfully around the stage as if enjoying the view. And, instead of the sharp, intricate rhythms of ballet footwork, Taylor let his steps flood the stage, one step melting or bouncing into another as the dance rode the tide of Taylor's favourite baroque composers.

These works harked back to Duncan's vision of a leaping, dancing America – the body liberated into a child-like freedom and grace. But there was also a darker, more surreal side to Taylor's work which wrestled with the duality of human nature – the gap between body and mind – and man's capacity for evil, despair and folly.

Cloven Kingdom

Made in 1976, this was a witty, unsettling piece that made dance out of the beast lurking inside civilized man. Its range of reference was also unmistakably late twentieth century. Taylor used a baroque score but had it infiltrated, almost beaten up, by passages of aggressive jazz percussion. The dancers wore evening dress and moved with a serene gravity. But as the piece progressed their elegant façade began to disintegrate. A slouch, a waggled hip, a mischievous pouncing jump instigated some wanton boogying, and this in turn mutated into pure animal movement as four men suddenly somersaulted over each other like chimpanzees or lumbered across the stage like a herd of elephants. Gradually the entire cast donned extraordinary silvered head-dresses that looked simultaneously like space wear, carnival disguise and haloes from a Renaissance painting. These strangely attired creatures seemed to contain all aspects of human nature – its equal parts of animal instinct, abstract brain power and angelic grace.

TWYLA THARP

As a child Twyla Tharp studied a variety of dance – tap, ballet, baton twirling and ballroom dance – and as an adult she danced in Paul Taylor's company during the early 60s. When she first started making dance she appeared to turn her back on the variety of her background, making starkly stripped-down choreography. But in the early 70s she began raiding all the languages she knew, making choreography that could contain an entire encyclopaedia of dance within a single phrase.

The mix of ballet, jazz, ballroom, tap, street dance and rock and roll has varied in every piece but it is always virtuoso and intense.

Sextet

In this 1993 piece Tharp created her own version of the *pas de deux* – a dance form she has often equated very directly with sex. Three couples – clearly ballet-trained – moved through the dignified manoeuvres of the classical *pas de deux*. But their lifts and supported *pirouettes* were constantly invaded by jive, rock and roll, and tango – so that a *pirouette* ended up with the man and woman in a flashy, flick-knife exchange of Latin American leg work or with the woman's legs straddling her partner's waist. As the dancers spun through their increasingly ingenious repertoire of turns, they enacted a drama of erotic invitation and retreat. Exhausted, they finally slumped into an artless grope – a reminder that the piece was only, ever, about sex.

The Upper Room

Made in 1986 this pitted the power and energy of modern dance against classical speed and dexterity on a mass scale. Two dancers, dubbed the 'power women' by Tharp, led a group of men and women in sneakers who punched the air, shrugged and shimmied with a raw force and a relentless energy. The rest of the women were on points and darted across the stage like a flight of virtuoso jet planes, performing hair-raisingly fast and inverted ballet steps or cutting through the air in the arms of their male partners.

The contrasting beat and energy of these two styles set up their own dazzling complexity. But Tharp was also displaying all the variations it's possible to make on a dance phrase – reversing it so that it goes to the right rather than the left, condensing it, disrupting it with an input of new material, while all through the work Philip Glass's score kept winding the dancers to a higher and higher pitch of adrenalin.

TRISHA BROWN

In the late 70s Trisha Brown left behind the spare choreographic formulae of her early work. Gripped by what she's described as a 'rapture ... to move', she began to make intricate sensuous dance in which plain functional moves blossomed into lyrical spurts of dance. In this new style, the energy generated by a rippling spine could send a leg arcing into space, while a jump might end with the dancer poised, breathtakingly, on someone else's shoulders.

But though Brown and her dancers began to fly, balance and lope around the stage with remarkable virtuosity, they did so with the casualness of people doing nothing remarkable at all, almost as if the movement was happening to them. Certainly they didn't turn out their legs or point their feet. Yet what made their movement seem dramatic and mysterious dance was the structure and the timing of the choreography. Brown knew how a gravely focused gesture, completing a luxurious tumble of movement, could create a potent moment of silence. She knew how a woman leaping out from the wings to be caught mid-flight by a passing dancer could seem to dare the universe. As for structure, though the surface of the dance might seem like beautiful anarchy, an underlying logic could always be glimpsed. Out of a tangle of bodies three dancers might suddenly emerge, twisting and bending in unison, or one dancer close to the wings might echo the sequence of movements of another one centre stage. Phrases would recur but speeded up, reversed, slowed down or danced inside out – each piece setting puzzles for the viewers.

Set and Reset

In this beautiful 1983 piece both the dance and the designs (by Robert Rauschenberg) were a visual tease. Black and white gauze drapes hung at the side of the stage so that the dancing close to the wings was often half concealed. Large silver shapes hung from the ceiling on which a collage of film images was projected, filling the normally empty upper air with dense activity. Laurie Anderson's sound tape mixed voices, a striking gong and mysterious noises into the brew. And Brown's own movement played riddles. The piece began with a dancer walking along the length of the back wall (actually supported discreetly by other dancers) and it then launched into intense activity, with dancers constantly flying in and out of the wings. Yet, however random the movement appeared, the focus of the piece was actually being steadily shifted from one side of the stage to the other. First-time viewers often didn't spot this until it reached the halfway point and the dancers suddenly gathered into a formal line centre stage. Having made the point, they then peeled off, one by one, to continue their ecstatic dancing.

MARK MORRIS

Mark Morris had a quintessentially post-modern grounding in dance. Though born in Seattle, he developed a childhood yen to become a flamenco star and started taking classes in both Spanish dance and ballet. As a teenager, he joined an Eastern European folk troupe, and as an adult performed with both modern and classical companies. Thus, when he began making his own dances these eccentrically varied influences became the raw material for a unique style – which softened and complicated the feisty rhythms of Spanish dance, added *arabesques* and *pirouettes* to the skips and runs of folk dance and then threw in the expressionist gestures of modern dance plus a whole range of 'non-dance' moves.

Morris may quote dance steps from Bombay and the Balkans, from Balanchine and Broadway, but he's not academic about his sources. In fact, he has always insisted on the broad humanity of his dancers, finding interest in any part of their bodies and in any activity they might perform. (He might happily finish a phrase with the dancers up-ended, so that their bottoms confront the audience.) Also, being a post-70s choreographer, he doesn't aim for a uniform image of perfection, even though his works are so full of 'dancing'. His dancers look how ordinary people might look when they've been struck by a moment of inspiration.

The reasons for this are complex. First, like Taylor before him, Morris chooses the members of his company for their intelligence and personality rather than their conformity to a dancerly look. They don't have a honed, delicately muscled finish but are hard-working bodies that come in a normal range of shapes and sizes. Some of the women are bigger and tougher-looking than the men and the mix of racial types in the company reflects the make-up of any urban crowd.

Second, he's not interested just in moments of beauty in his choreography; he likes to see 'how the dancers got there', to explore the gritty mechanics of the movement. (He's said that what he hates most is 'people dancing in my face like "Watch me I can do this and you can't"'.) To avoid this impression of arrogant ease he often casts his dancers against type, deliberately denying them the steps that would come most naturally to them. The dancers are not allowed to 'fake' the movement, to do it automatically – they have to think and work hard at it. Third, he also tends to make things difficult. 'I choreograph steps on the wrong leg, in the wrong direction, too fast or too slow.' So what excites us in a Morris work is not so much the triumphantly finished position or the perfectly executed manoeuvre, it is the energy, the emotion, the motive and the rhythm that are the forces behind it.

Some audiences find this unsettling. They don't know if these are good dancers or bad. A typical example of this is described by Morris's biographer Joan Acocella. In *The Hard Nut* (1991), his version of *The Nutcracker*, he puts a whole group of dancers on stage, performing the same, very demanding move. This is a *pirouette à la seconde*, a staple of the male ballet dancer's repertoire, in which one leg is held straight to the side as the dancer turns round and round on the spot. The challenge is to keep spinning evenly, to stop the stretched leg sagging from strain and to avoid grinding to a halt before the music is finished. Morris's dancers are not ballet dancers, so this step is hard for some of them. And while one dancer may just get away with fudging it, a whole group of them, visibly forcing their bodies through the same stunt, becomes an image of fallible human endeavour – comic, brave and touching.

Because of the struggle that goes into Morris choreography the dancers' moments of beauty and triumph seem extra-miraculous when they do arrive. Audiences respond to them because they give us affordable images of how we too might transcend ourselves. (The very real skills demanded by the movement are less 'in your face'. They require an ability to count unpredictable rhythms, to capture subtleties of tone – Morris can flip from brutality to tragedy in seconds – and to achieve the clarity-within-casualness that makes his movement look both spontaneous and inevitable.)

Morris communicates his own taste, fantasy and humour more directly in his work than many of his contemporaries. Some of his dances tell stories; some of them evoke atmospheres; nearly all of them are about music. Unlike many post-Cunningham choreographers, Morris sets most of his dances intimately to scores, taking from them the structure, rhythms and colours of his movement. He's said that he learnt more about choreography from his favourite composer Handel than from anyone else – 'All that stuff that's going on in his music, the recapitulations, retrogrades, canons . . . they're beautiful, beautiful things that are just automatically interesting dance.' Whether he's using country and western music, Purcell, Schoenberg, or Indian film music, we see the score take physical shape as Morris's steps spring from its measures, as his dancers mimic its melodic counterpoint and as its energy feeds the drama of the movement.

L'Allegro, il Penseroso ed il Moderato

In this setting of Handel's dramatic oratorio, made in 1988, the movement closely reflects not only the music but the lyrics – two pastoral poems by Milton. The latter contrast a sanguine world view with a melancholic, and Morris's thirty short dances revolve around the same theme, invoking a densely populated world of gods and goddesses, shepherds and aristocrats, animals and flowers. It sounds an extraordinarily classical, even regressive, piece for a choreographer to make in the 80s and Morris admits cheerfully to being old-fashioned in certain ways. But the candour, sexuality and comedy of the movement are completely modern.

Sometimes Morris is disarmingly literal. He paints a jolly hunting scene in which some of the dancers snuffle around the stage like hounds, 'peeing' on some other dancers who've bunched up to make a hedgerow. At other moments, where there's a reference to climbing hills, two women clamber gleefully up the backs of their fellows; where there's a mention of birds, the dancers brace their arms like wings; where there are flowers in the text, their fingers frame their faces like petals; where there's a reference to birth, three women squat and open their legs. In a section referred to by the company as the 'stupid men's dance' all the men in the company form a group where they stamp their feet, slap their thighs and kick each other's butts in a tightly rhythmic sequence.

Certain gestures gather resonance every time we see them, like one haunting leap where the dancer's arm is curved like a sickle moon, an intimation of night. And literal or narrative phrases constantly dissolve back into pure dance pattern. As phrases are inverted, performed in canon or repeated, we see movement building into an intricate human clockwork. The dancers form circles, lines, pyramids and squares, a profusion of patterns that reflects the changing geometries of the score. Towards the end of the dance, to the triumphal chorus 'Mirth with thee I mean to live', Morris simply sends wave after wave of running and leaping dancers breasting the stage on a tide of energy. The simplicity of their movement is made gorgeous by the reckless speed of the dancers as they cross each other's paths with split-second timing. Finally on Handel's closing chord the dancers are knitted into three concentric circles spinning tirelessly round and round in the oldest and most universal dance form in the world. A simple statement of community, of dance as a human chain.

RICHARD ALSTON

The styles that fed into British modern dance in the 70s were as varied as those in the States. Richard Alston's early work, for instance, was rooted in the cool aesthetic of minimalism, in the easy, weighted approach of release and in the style of Merce Cunningham, with its plain arms, quick rhythmic footwork and taut legs. But almost from the beginning he set his dances to music which gave them a more lyric flow. Plus he had a love for English classicism, particularly Ashton's, which added a round-edness to some of the movements, a more lavish sensuousness as well as certain recognizable classical steps. Out of this emerged dancing that could be almost cerebral in its attention to composition and detail but capable of an extreme range, from sexy exuberance to ferocious energy.

Wildlife

This 1984 work was one of the strongest examples of Alston's interest in dance as a total aesthetic. Like Diaghilev he's always been fascinated by the way that music, movement and design connect to make a single world – and has often commissioned composers and painters to collaborate with him. For this piece Alston wanted to 'create a kind of non-specific culture, a place which somehow had its own logic, rituals, sound world and animal life'. Nigel Osborne's score brought together a bright, clamorous mix of sounds where jagged brass fanfares and driving percussion enclosed suspended meditative chords. Richard Smith's designs created a secret world of shadows and colour with three huge suspended, iridescent kites that rotated, rose and fell during the work – sometimes concealing much of the stage. Alston's own movement gave the dancers an urgent and non-human energy. At times they seemed like a watchful group of animals as they moved through the 'undergrowth' of the kites or else stood alert in the luminous spaces of a suddenly empty stage. Their bodies were sculpted into geometric patterns that echoed the shapes of the kites and they moved with odd extremes of force. Fast flurries of steps ended in abrupt falls or dangerous balances; a nervous quivering stillness would erupt into a wild leap – Alston himself has said he wasn't sure 'where the movement came from'.

MICHAEL CLARK

Clark also made a language by crossing classical ballet with Cunningham (for two years he worked as a dancer for Alston). But his own unique catalyst was neo-punk music and fashion – and the club culture that went with them. The effect of the music's brutal rhythms was to harden the edges of Clark's movement, intensify its force and disrupt it with confrontational gestures. A dancer standing in a classical turned-out position might thus have his or her hips thrust sluttishly to one side. Deft beaten jumps might be accompanied by pumping disco arms. A movement might suddenly seem to snag on itself and start viciously repeating as on some scratched record, or a lyrical flow be interrupted by a provocative V sign or a fascist salute.

Clark has always seen dance as an extension of his own life, and much of his choreography has been infiltrated by his non-dancing friends, who've joked and posed through performances of his work or even tried to dance themselves. His works have jumbled football, pop and ballet culture. He and his dancers have bared their bottoms, worn Nazi uniforms, or simply defied sartorial definition. Clark himself has sported a bubble wig, a frilly apron and dildo, a ballerina's tutu and a dragon's tail, and has appeared naked save for a fur muff.

During the 80s Clark made the dancing body a site of contradiction and subversion. Exquisitely achieved choreography was mixed with amateurish or unseemly gesture; sensuality was celebrated to the point of blatant eroticism. (Clark and his partner Stephen Petronio once performed a fifteen-minute duet in a bed that was essentially lovers' foreplay.) Classical beauty degenerated into trashy vulgarity. And Clark, one of the most talented dancers of his generation, refused to let anyone ogle his gifts.

Though he never expressed a coherent political view in his dances, the body had rarely been so contentious.

But in the 90s Clark started to strip away the camp and the confrontation, and to bare the body's most raw, tender and expressive elements. Returning to his ballet heritage, he used two of the great Stravinsky scores to discover his own kind of classicism. In *Mmm* (1992) he created a version of *Rite of Spring* – splicing the original score with sections of punk music in ways that actually intensified the churning energy of Stravinsky rhythms. Sourcing the power of his dance in the pelvis, the movements in this piece were heavy and implosive, resonating with dark energy. They often began as spasms in the groin that sent limbs ricocheting outwards or bodies into crazy spirals. At moments (harking back to Nijinsky) the brute force of the choreography would leave the dancers quivering in helplessly knock-kneed poses.

O

In this 1994 work Clark revisited *Apollo*, the great Stravinsky score used by Balanchine in 1928. Some of the choreography again recalled Nijinsky's primitivism – particularly the flattened profile and startled leap of his Faun. But, like Balanchine's ballet, *O* was about the birth of dance. With characteristic Clark mischief, it opened with a joke birth as a male dancer wriggled out from under the duvet covering Clark's own real-life mother Bessie (who has appeared in several of his works). Then Clark as the Apollo figure was seen in his own womb – foetally crouched in a cube of mirrored glass.

He stretched his body, accompanied by four beautiful reflections of himself, and as his limbs discovered their grace, they pushed their way out on to a stage that was all white space and dancing. His skewed, awkward limbs breathed into gracious curves, while three female muses demonstrated what these simple lines might become in lyrical dancing where classical balances were cantilevered off centre and where the lines of the movements were made baroque by proud circles of the head, by sensuous curves of the hips and by hieratic commands of the arms. This was choreography in which all Clark's earlier abrasiveness had been disciplined but not tamed – its energy held within the dancer's taut lines and lyric power.

However far post-modern choreographers might stray from the mainstream schools of dance – ballet, Cunningham, Graham – these styles are still the reference points from which we measure invention and deviation. But movement from non-Western cultures imposes very different images and values on the body, and over the last couple of decades dances from around the world have been migrating and cross-fertilizing at increasing speed. In Britain, for instance, the steady flow of Asians settling in the country since the Second World War has given a high-profile presence to Indian classical dance, not only in its own right, but as an important influence on other dance. Just as Punjabi folk traditions have mixed with British club music to produce the unique Anglo-Asian Bhangra sound, so the lines and rhythms of classical Indian dance forms like Bharatha Natyam and Kathak have become absorbed into the language of British theatre dance.

SHOBANA JEYASINGH

The career of Shobana Jeyasingh is a classic instance of this kind of migration. She was born in Madras, where she trained in Bharatha Natyam, and she first made her name as a dancer and choreographer in London performing that style. Yet her identity as an artist living in Britain was obviously no longer that of a South Asian dancer and she began to think of herself and her work as the products of a global culture. (As she has argued, these days we think there is nothing remarkable about eating Indian food, drinking Belgian beer, listening to African music and watching American films within the space of a single evening.)

Jeyasingh started the long process of rewriting her inherited dance language by working with Western composers like postminimalist Michael Nyman, whose music made her feel the rhythms and expressiveness of her movement differently.

Indian dance is very much about isolated movements of the eyes, hands and arms, which is what creates its body-popping effect. Normally these movements are put together in a very strict way, but after listening to Michael's music I changed them a little. One section of the score has a very lyrical quality . . . and I made the arm movements much more fluent to go with it. Someone told me it looked completely balletic, like an Indian Dying Swan.

Jeyasingh also began to apply more Western notions of form to her dancing, unravelling the complex language of Bharatha Natyam to create more austere shapes and structures. Traditionally the dance concentrates a multiplicity of detail within a single dancer's body. Its stamping footwork is measured out in mathematical combinations whose rhythms are further complicated by the jangling of bells from the dancer's anklets. The arms and legs are angled through triangular geometries which are embellished by *mudras* or hand gestures where fingers curl and splay in hieroglyphic shapes, by sharp tiltings of the head, by sliding glances of the eyes and by the dancer's gorgeous attire – richly coloured fabrics, flowers and jewels (see illus. 3).

Jeyasingh dismantled this dense play of activity into starker movements which were often performed simultaneously by several dancers grouped in circles, wedges or lines. She would have two groups performing different sequences to create a visual and rhythmic counterpoint; or have different dancers perform the same steps facing different directions so that they were presented, cubist-style, from several angles.

During this process the whole character of the dance style was changed. Where classical Bharatha Natyam revolves around a vertical axis, the body tall, the bent legs pressing down into the ground, Jeyasingh pushed her movements out of line. Her dancers' erect poise was thrown off balance as their upper bodies swooped in curves, or as gracious balances toppled into a fall or powerful lunge. The characteristically neat, startle-footed jump of Indian dance became higher and wilder; movements were repeated at aggressive speed, or suspended into extreme slow motion.

The Making of Maps

This 1992 piece was a statement of how Jeyasingh had redrawn the boundaries of her world, charting an artistic territory where East and West were no longer separate cultures. It was set to two scores; one for voice and classical Indian instruments by R. A. Ramamani and one for computer-mixed urban sounds by Alistair Macdonald, and with them Jeyasingh took her dance language on a journey across centuries and continents in its discovery of new lines and forms. With their plain costumes, their calm, intent faces, their austerity and their power, the dancers moved in a style whose basic grammar was recognizably Indian – but they no longer looked like Indian dancers.

BUTOH

The Japanese physical art form Butoh (originally called *ankoku butoh* or dark soul dance) began in the 60s as a very deliberate marriage of forms, as two dancers Kazuo Ohno and Tatsumi Hijikata brought together the intense, often grotesque language of early European expressionist dance and the stillness and pared-down symbolism of Japanese theatre. The result was a kind of body sculpture where the performers deliberately abnegated their performing egos and where movement didn't so much tell stories as distil extreme states of being. Butoh dancers still often wear thick white paint on their faces and bodies to blur their identity, even their humanity, and their movements disdain conventional dancerly skills as they progress, in nerve-screamingly slow motion, from one contorted position to another. Frequently props and special lighting effects intensify the sense of ritual through which the dancers give shape to their most primitive emotions.

EIKO AND KOMA

This Japanese duo studied with Kazuo Ohno and later with Manja Chmiel, a disciple of Mary Wigman. Their 1987 duet *Grain* was centred around the basic human cycle of sowing, eating and copulating, but its subject was also the first painful stirrings of human consciousness. At its opening the dancers scarcely looked like people – Koma was huddled on his back like a huge foetus, while Eiko's naked body was scrunched and up-ended so all that could be seen were her buttocks swaying in a slow arc. As they tried to move, Eiko had painful trouble placing her twisted feet securely on the floor, and the first time Koma stood he crashed top-heavily backwards on to the ground. After this they began to explore their senses as she rubbed her flesh lingeringly with handfuls of rice, while he caressed her foot. But when he tried to draw Eiko into a sexual embrace, she simply persisted in ramming handfuls of grain into her mouth.

On paper these actions sound little more than the play of kindergarten children, but the control which they demanded was intense. In this dance language of pain and extremity the dancers' falls, their cramped and twisted positions may never appear like the tricks of acrobats but like trauma, trance or terror that is genuinely experienced. In great Butoh performances we recognize a language that is both atavistically familiar and profoundly, unsettlingly strange.

AFRICAN AND AFRO-AMERICAN DANCE

The enormous, complex traditions of black African dance have been a huge influence on Western choreography throughout the twentieth century – not surprisingly since the centuries-old trafficking of African slaves represents one of the most enormous disseminations of people and culture in history. The various characteristics of African movement – syncopated rhythms, vividly articulate hips, rippling spines, free, shimmying shoulders, percussive feet and tiny jointed moves – have fed into tap, jazz and most of the social dance crazes from the charleston through to disco and break dance. For Westerners black dance has offered a liberation from the strict upright demeanour of its own traditions, from the metaphorically corseted spine. It has meant a style of dance where movement doesn't pump only through the arms, legs and feet but right through the body. It has meant a much more subtle, expressive and percussive range of rhythms for the dancer to play with.

These elements certainly fed into Martha Graham's style as into that of many other early modernists. And jazz dance, which is probably still the definitive Afro-American dance form, has influenced the work of most classical and modern choreographers. Balanchine is the obvious example. A jazz flavour is evident not only in blatant borrowings, like his pin-up-girl poses and shimmying shoulders, but in more pervasive influences like the isolating of small movements, the free activity of the dancers' hips, the use of syncopated rhythm, and the speed and force which send his dancers' legs kicking into the air.

Black choreographers have also made very conscious attempts to forge new languages out of their inherited traditions. Some, like Katherine Dunham and Pearl Primus, trained with white choreographers before creating their own modern interpretations of African movement and ritual. Dance Theatre of Harlem have been pioneers in evolving a black classicism. And post-modern dance groups like the American all-women group Urban Bush Women have drawn loosely on African dance traditions and rituals in the fierce, chaotic mix of movement and text with which they articulate the reality of black women living in late-twentieth-century inner cities.

Liberated from local traditions by technology and travel, today's dancing body might have more options than ever before. But whatever wealth of rhythms, lines and images is available to it, dance still falls short of the verbal precision and physical concreteness of theatre. In Europe, however, many choreographers have tried to overcome this gap, and the most iconic and influential of these theatre-oriented dance makers has been Pina Bausch.

PINA BAUSCH

Bausch began with a conventional dance training, studying with classical choreographers Kurt Jooss and Antony Tudor as well as American artists Paul Taylor and José Limón during the 60s. But all of these had a strong narrative instinct in common, as well as a dark streak, which possibly helped to launch Bausch into the creation of her own surreal and tormented spectacles.

In these works dance was only one element along with text, song, mime and stage designs of an epic, nightmarish scale. Individual works could last up to four hours and, though none featured literal stories, they revolved around a series of confrontations, confessions, ritualized actions and obsessive dance sequences which seemed to draw directly on the lives of the actual performers. Bausch has never chosen her dancers for pure technique, or even for stage skills. They have to be willing to dig deep into their own dreams and neuroses to provide Bausch with the raw material for her particular brand of theatrical psychotherapy.

The body becomes in these works much more than the medium for choreographic form; it actually seems to experience genuine pleasure or pain, its flesh physically caressed or more often bruised by the strenuousness of the movement, its lungs and heart literally heaving with exhaustion.

Nelken

The mix of gut actuality with surreal symbolism was acute in this huge 1982 work. Visually it was one of the most astonishing in the repertoire, with the stage covered by a carpet of several thousand pink and white artificial flowers. But the audience's pleasure in its pastoral excess was blocked by the fact that it was patrolled by a group of uniformed guards with Alsatians. These were not actors but the real thing, and their stolid professional presence made them distressingly threatening. During one section several male dancers began leapfrogging crazily over each other and their activities drove the dogs, straining at their leads, into a frenzy of barking. The audience was tense with the fear of a lead breaking and a dog sinking its teeth into the men's bare and foolish flesh.

The dancers' vulnerability was made even more shocking by the fact that they were all wearing badly fitting women's frocks. They were social deviants, natural victims in a police state, and while they were playing, a man in a black suit started chasing them. He caught one and demanded to see his passport. At this moment the subject of harassment was a man, but it's significant that he was dressed as a woman, because most of Bausch's victims are female. Over and over again her work reports back from the front line of a grim and sometimes comic sexual war – revealing how pitifully over-programmed both genders seem to be in their mutually antagonistic behaviour. The men abuse the women while the women goad the men to further cruelty. (Bausch's theatre has been attacked by its critics as a pornography of pain.)

In many of Bausch's works her dancers often seem caught in a choreographic trap – repeating the same moves over and over again. These are often violent, so that repetition doesn't create a state of contemplative trance as in some minimalist works but causes real discomfort. In Bausch's *Café Müller* (1978) repetition reached an almost unbearable pitch as a woman threw herself over and over again into a man's arms. He refused to catch her and let her fall to the floor, but she didn't give up and her actions became wilder until she was simply dashing herself against his feet – standing up and then throwing herself down as fast as she could.

ANNE TERESA DE KEERSMAEKER

The Belgian choreographer Anne Teresa De Keersmaeker was initially drawn to the rigorous pattern-making of American minimalists like Lucinda Childs in her work. But increasingly the repetitive base of her movement acquired more neurotic, dangerous qualities and her work moved closer to dance theatre, incorporating speech, film and surreal stage imagery. Many of her works have been performed solely by women, and as in Bausch's work we see them trying out roles and enacting their anxieties through punishingly recycled movement.

Bartók/Aantekeningen

In this 1986 work the stage was lined with wall bars, and two forbiddingly high shut doors; in the corner was a stuffed deer. The four women dancers seemed trapped in a room that was something between a nursery, a gym and an asylum, while the choreography also suggested that they were trapped in a male society where women could only occupy marginalized roles like children, lunatics or sirens.

The dancers appeared first in tight black dresses and high heels, standing round the stage in attitudes of passive exhaustion. They then broke out into a shockingly epileptic kind of skittering so wild that it threw them on to the floor, even though they still performed every move in precision-perfect unison. Sometimes their dancing softened into lilting, rhythmic steps or a cycle of dreamy turns, but without warning it would break into wild spinning where the dancers' limbs scythed through the air and their heads whipped round like crazed rag dolls. To recover they performed obsessive little dances where they fiddled with their hair and their clothes or else recited fragments of text, babbling a stream of mad imagery.

The way in which such choreographic extremes present De Keersmaeker's dancers is unsettling. As in Bausch's work, we admire their speed and dexterity, even though they seem to be dancing without personal volition, victims of the movement's lacerating repetition. As in Bausch's work, we see grown-up, beautiful women transformed into helpless little girls.

During the late 80s much of European dance had whipped itself into a frenzy of repetitive violence – dubbed by some as 'Euro-crash'. Stages were turned into assault courses as dancers, often wearing boots or heavy Doc Martens shoes, presented their bodies both as missiles and targets of abuse. In an atmosphere that fused sexual violence with generalized urban aggression dancers pushed themselves to extremes of daring: hurtling through the air to be caught (or not) by a partner; barrelling across the floor in bruising commando rolls; dashing themselves against the ground with the reckless force of their movements and sometimes even throwing objects. At times the dancers might be ducking and weaving to escape each other's violent intent; at others they might be offering a temporarily friendly shoulder to break another's fall; at others again they might be grappling in hungry lust. But all this physical trauma was generally bathed in glamour as the dancers, wearing black designer outfits, were flatteringly and stylishly lit and drowned in maximum-impact scores (ranging from rock to opera). This was dance designed for instant effect – hitting its audience in the gut, screwing the energy level to its highest pitch.

DV8

Rather like the low-key pedestrian dance of the 60s, 'Eurocrash' functioned partly as a blood-letting exercise – a pushing to see how far dance could be taken in one direction. And, like pedestrian movement, it has subsequently evolved to become just one more option in the choreographer's palette.

The British DV8 Physical Theatre, for instance, has always used aspects of this gruelling vocabulary since its first work in the mid-80s. But their work also shares the depth of research, the mental and physical honesty and the sophisticatedly surreal imagery of Bausch's theatre. Its politics are however more upfront. Lloyd Newson, the group's director, abandoned a successful dancing career out of the conviction that conventional dance was 'a form in crisis'. He believed that its techniques presented the audience with a decorative and false view of human relations, expressing nothing about the world outside the studio. He thought they also encouraged outdated and dangerous power structures in which the choreographer used the dancers as malleable raw material for his or her ideas rather than allowing them to become involved, democratically, in the making of the piece.

Newson has thus created his own works out of intense periods of improvisation where, Bausch-style, the performers excavate their own experiences for raw material and where they search for the movement that will give it shape. He has never spurned pure dance as one aspect of his physical vocabulary, but he and his dancers also use direct theatrical gesture, stylized violence, ritual movement and text. For him as for Graham it's crucial to do whatever's needed to tell the truth.

Newson is a high-profile gay artist, and his first early projects dealt directly with his own sexuality. He's said that the theatre has licensed him to do things he wouldn't do in real life. 'My anger comes out. It allows me to fight and yell, and maybe that's why I get so passionate about the work. It is inextricably linked to, you know, feeling oppressed.' But his work has also explored issues of power, abuse, love and loneliness on a more universal level.

Dead Dreams of Monochrome Men

This 1988 work was based on the story of the mass murderer Dennis Nilsen. Yet though parts of the choreography presented specifically gay images of desire and dread, narcissism and distrust, others created larger metaphors of the fear and power that inhibit all human relations. The question of trust between two male lovers, for instance, became intensified into a suicidal battle of wills as one dancer climbed repeatedly to the top of a high wall, then plummeted, without warning, into his partner's arms. With each fall he seemed to be taunting the latter not to be there for the catch, not to become too bored, too disgusted or too weak to bother.

The four men didn't touch each other except by stealth or in the guise of violence – they seemed terrified of admitting to tenderness or desire. And the piece showed with haunting logic how a thwarting of male gentleness and eroticism leads to violence. Nielsen killed because he was comfortable with his lovers only when they were dead, and the work closed with a weeping Nielsen cradling the motionless body of one of his victims in an anguished *pietà*. Then, with the callousness that was the flip side of his love, he took the body and strung it up by its feet, leaving it dangling for what seemed like minutes.

This moment created an image of appalling, authoritative

catharsis within the work, but it also stood as a potent example of the extreme range that is now open to dancers. Using all his powers of muscle and breath control and all his stoical endurance, the dancer here willed himself into the total antithesis of the glamorous, aristocratic athlete of popular image – allowing himself to be slung upside-down like so many kilos of butchered meat.

EARTH AND AIR

1 (*left*) Classical ballet aspires to the air. Marie Taglioni's revolutionary point work in *La Sylphide* (1832) created the illusion of flight.

2 (*below left*) In *Strike* (1927) Martha Graham based her radical dance philosophy on the pull of gravity.

3 (*below right*) Bharatha Natyam is grounded in the earth. Dancer Subathra Subramaniam moves with a powerful downward thrust.

DANCE AS PATTERN

4 (*above*) The symmetrical classical lines of the Kirov *corps de ballet* in a 1993 performance of *Swan Lake*.

5 (*below*) Constructivist body sculpture in Bronislava Nijinska's *Les Noces* (1923).

VIEWING THE DANCERS

6 (*left*) Margot Fonteyn as Aurora in a 1946 performance of *The Sleeping Beauty*.

7 (*below*) Martha Graham dancing as Medea in *Cave of the Heart* (1946), her horrifying study of jealousy.

8 Mark Morris as Dido in his danced version of Purcell's *Dido and Aeneas* (1989).

9 (*right*) Vaslav Nijinsky as the faun in his impressionistic interpretation of Debussy's *L'Après-midi d'un faune* (1912).

10 (*below*) Sylvie Guillem and Adam Cooper in a 1993 production of William Forsythe's *Hermann Schmerman* (1992).

COURTING COUPLES

11 (*above*) Fairy marriage. Antoinette Sibley and Anthony Dowell in Frederick Ashton's *The Dream* (1964).

12 (*below*) Erotic contest. Darcey Bussell and Eddie Shellman in a 1991 production of George Balanchine's *Agon* (1957).

LOOKING AT THE FRAME

13 (*above*) Carolyn Brown navigates a path through Jasper Johns's set in Merce Cunningham's *Walkaround Time* (1968).

14 (*below*) Dancers as moving sculpture in Oskar Schlemmer's *Triadic Ballet* (1922).

READING DANCE

15 (*above*) Comic lovelies. Les Ballets Trockadero de Monte Carlo's all-male *Swan Lake* (1995).

16 (*below*) Images of mortality. Merce Cunningham and his dancers in the stark choreography of *Quartet* (1982).

Part Two: **READING THE COMPONENT PARTS**

When we're sitting in the theatre, watching pure white circles of swans *bourréeing* by the lakeside, or seeing Cunningham's dancers scattering in streaks of elegant movement, or flinching as Pina Bausch's protagonists ritually berate their bodies, we may be mystified as to how all this activity came into being. Where did the steps come from? How were they made to fit the music? Why do the dancers look so right for the movement? How, we wonder, did it all come together? How does dance get made?

Writers hunch over their typewriters or word-processors; painters assemble their sketchbooks, canvases and colours. But although there are systems for notating dance (using a musical-style stave and line figures), choreographers don't sit down with pen and paper to compose their dances. Usually they spend weeks or months pacing round a studio trying to extract some physical beauty or meaning from the bodies of their dancers.

Like all artists, different choreographers work from very different motives. Some may be trying to tell a story; others may have a piece of music they want to interpret; others may simply be creating a pure formal composition. But what sets them apart is the raw material unique to dance – the mix of shapes and rhythms made by the human body, the space in which the dance moves, the music that accompanies it, the design in which it's set, and of course the dancers themselves. When we look at any piece of choreography these components are usually so intimately fused that we can't read them separately. Why would we want to wrench them apart and vandalize the perfect moment of the theatre?

Yet, to understand what makes the perfect moment in Bharatha Natyam so different from the perfect moment in Balanchine, we need to be able to compare the different ways in which they handle the elements of dance – and to do that we obviously need to understand what those elements are. So Part Two of *Reading Dance* takes a step-by-step view of how dances are made, looking at story-telling, music, structure, patterns, rhythms, dancers, and so on, as if each component existed in isolation from the others. It also sketches out how these components have been handled through history and the different roles they have played. This is an artificial, even ungainly, method of talking about dance, and the logic of this half of the book has to be ungainly too. But Chapter Four starts at the beginning, which is to question where the steps come from and how choreographers go to work.

Chapter Four: **WHERE THE STEPS COME FROM**

TRADITION

Anyone making a dance starts out with some style of moving – whether it's a style they've been trained in, a style that comes naturally to their bodies, or some hunch they've had about a new system for moving limbs around.

Most stage choreographers have been trained as dancers and have spent years disciplining their bodies in one or more dance techniques. The lessons they've learnt in class, in studio and on stage are obviously bred deep in their minds and muscles. They're the choreographer's physical database. But whether they stick to familiar steps in their own work or consciously invent a new language depends not just on individual choice but on when and where they work.

Where dance is part of a vernacular culture – as in most folk, ballroom or club dancing – people may invent new dances, but they won't expect to be recorded as choreographers. Even in nine-teenth-century Russian ballet a master-artist like Petipa would have viewed his work more as a synthesis of traditions than a statement of his own artistic vision. Certainly he possessed no copyright over his work, so his ballets could be performed or hacked about by anyone who wanted. Yet Martha Graham's situation only four decades on was completely different. Working in a culture that celebrated uniqueness and innovation, she believed herself to be inventing a new dance out of her own body and soul. Her works were hers alone, fiercely prized and defended.

In the late twentieth century the pressure to reinvent the language is still strong. But most choreographers have a much wider background than Petipa's as local traditions have been swallowed into a global culture that holds past and present, East and West, classical and popular in simultaneous suspension. Today a choreographer may have sources as diverse as break dancing, ballet and Bharatha Natyam to play with when he or she sets out to explore a new style.

THE GERM OF THE WORK

The individual styles that choreographers forge from their backgrounds aren't static – they change and discover themselves through the course of their careers. One of the pressures that produce change may be the starting point, or motive, for each new piece. The keys that unlock these vary from choreographer to choreographer and from work to work.

For Mark Morris, it's often a musical score that, as he says, 'takes' him 'by the collar' – or rather something tiny within it: 'a particular false cadence, a rhythmic displacement, or a strange solo instrument or a tiny rhythmic thing that only I think is interesting'. It seems as if he hears some tiny gap opening in the music that lets his dance imagination in.

For choreographers of narrative ballets it's more straightforwardly a character or plot that motors the dance – MacMillan's *Mayerling* and *Manon*, David Bintley's *Hobson's Choice* (1985) are story-driven dances where even the music is specially arranged or commissioned to suit the narrative.

For some choreographers it may be a physical challenge. When Trisha Brown began making *M.O.* (1955), one of the concerns that motivated her was inventing movements for her dancers' legs that were as rich and as interesting as those she normally gave to the arms: 'I became interested in the fact that legs are involved with both transportation and support, so they don't have the level of freedom of the arms.'

For some choreographers it may be an outside commission that shapes the process. When Siobhan Davies and Emilyn Claid were both asked in 1994 to create dances for the British company CandoCo they were faced with extraordinary limitations and extraordinary possibilities, since two of the company's dancers were in wheelchairs and one had no legs at all. Both choreographers made work that was recognizably within their own style but also explored elements they'd otherwise never have touched.

Such as wheelchairs. Not only could CandoCo's dancers balance on wheelchairs, but they could ride them and make patterns with them at a speed more hair-raising than that of any wheel-less performer. One dancer, David Poole, was also a virtuoso by any standard. Though he was born without legs, he could, while balancing on his hands, angle and lift his torso in amazing ways, as well as run, jump and leap with immense riskiness and grace. For Claid the taboos that surround the disabled also provided rich material for a piece that explored anger and sex (asking questions like, Do you have sex? How do you have sex?, etc.).

Many choreographers are inspired by dancers. Ashton's *Rhapsody* (1980) was created as a shameless showstopper for Baryshnikov, while Jonathan Burrows's minimal *Blue Yellow* (1995) was a more surprising vehicle for ballerina Sylvie Guillem. Lloyd Newson often uses the individual qualities of his performers as a starting point – their personal histories, the quirks of their bodies. William Forsythe makes work collaboratively with his dancers and says that the inspiration for each new piece simply 'comes from the decision to work together'.

When the young British choreographer Matthew Hart tried to explain what makes him begin the choreographic process over and over again, he said it can be anything, 'an atmosphere, the image of a leaf blowing, a gesture', that seems to insist on being turned into dance. Choreography is no more or less mysterious than any other art form, it just uses movement to make a statement, tell a story, compose a picture – to create something that wasn't there before.

THE EVOLUTION OF THE STEPS

Unless the work choreographed is a solo, making dance is always a collective activity. Somehow the dance has to grow from the nebula of hunches, images, memories, patterns and rhythms that's obsessing the choreographer into movements that can be danced by others. How does that process work? Do choreographers imagine the movements in their heads, make them up on their own bodies, write them down – and then teach them to the wait-ing dancers? Do they have a few ideas that they develop once they are in the studio? Or do they walk into the first rehearsal with nothing in their heads at all – except the original inspiration for the dance?

Every choreographer is, of course, different. Some are fluent, some agonize. The ballerina Alexandra Danilova recalls that Bal-anchine 'always worked very fast in rehearsals, the choreography would just pour out of him. But for Massine it was like having a baby: very hard and slow. He would pace back and forth trying to think what to do next. He never smiled or joked during rehearsals and he didn't like his dancers having a rest.'

Some choreographers go in for meticulous preparation – occasionally with idiosyncratic aids. Marius Petipa used to con-struct dances for his *corps de ballet* by pushing little figures around a table so that he had the patterns formed before he taught them to the dancers. Merce Cunningham now does much the same thing, only with the infinitely more versatile resources of a com-puter. Using a specially designed programme, he can call up a screen peopled by a dozen or so dancers who will move in step to his every command. (As he says, 'Petipa would have taken to this immediately.') Alternatively he can call up a single dancing figure and, using a cursor instead of the traditional dancing master's stick, he can nudge it into any shape or movement he chooses. These moves can then be programmed on to the multiple figures while a third function can make them dance to a variety of different rhythms.

The computer allows Cunningham to conjure up movements he's never imagined before, to make dance so rich in detail that he can't store it in his head. It allows him to work on his own when dancers aren't available and he doesn't have to waste their time by playing with moves that won't work out.

Yet the dancers are still the real instruments on which these two-dimensional flickering moves are transformed into fully formed choreography. In fact, Cunningham says the dancers always have an influence on how the movement ends up. 'It's always been a sharing, even if it might not always have seemed that way to them. Even if they do something, you know, odd, I try not to look at it as something wrong, but to see if there's something interesting to learn from it.'

Few choreographers actually use written notation as a way of composing dance, though many make notes and drawings. Martha Graham, for instance, used to brood lengthily over each new work, making copious, poetic notes about atmosphere and movement. She started with short scenarios that gradually became longer and more complex. But she rarely introduced the music till she'd reached a late stage in thinking about the movement, in order not to be distracted by another artist's rhythms and ideas.

Most of the choreography was composed on Graham's own body – while she was still mobile – with the result that idiosyncrasies of her own physique kept showing up in her choreography. For instance, the repeated left-sided split kick that made its way into many of her dances was a direct consequence of the fact that her left leg could extend higher than her right.

When Mark Morris first started making dances in the 80s, he too invented most of the material on his own body before he got to rehearsal – mostly because he couldn't afford much studio time. As a result he thinks his early work tended to be 'always about myself'. His more recent work is 'less of a *Weltschmerz* thing' because so much more of it is made on his dancers. 'I'll dance around on my own, sometimes get a gesture that goes with a particular motif. But the main body of work is done in the studio.'

Twyla Tharp is legendary for arriving with much of her choreography already either in her head or down on video, but Richard Alston says that whenever he prepares detailed movement in advance of rehearsals he ends up throwing most of it out, and that he has increasingly come to trust that

with the excitement of the dancers being there, one thing will lead to another. I'll throw out a rough movement idea like 'Go round to the back, throw that leg out in some kind of *attitude*, then bring one arm forward so that there's a pull through the body and then bring the head down.' I feel like I'm carving in space.

Frederick Ashton also used to make a habit of arriving at the studio without a single step to show, though, as Antoinette Sibley has said, he always had 'the music completely sunk in his whole body and the idea that he want[ed] to get over'. Sometimes he'd get his dancers to demonstrate what they'd just been doing in class in order to prompt a few ideas. Or he'd ask them to invent something, as in one rehearsal for *Dream* where he asked Sibley and Anthony Dowell to work out some manoeuvre that he'd dreamt in his sleep while he went away for a cup of coffee. 'It's that passing under his arm and coming up in the *pas de deux*,' says Sibley, 'and we didn't know how to do it other than cut my head off or cut an arm out.' But they solved it, and it's that kind of direct involvement in the choreography that makes Ashton's dancers feel particularly possessive about their roles – 'Fred actually makes the step on you, you make the step with him.'

Ashton was still the master of his own dances, however, unlike William Forsythe and Lloyd Newson who believe that the title 'choreographer' is inappropriate to their own more collaborative procedures. Forsythe has in fact developed a series of almost scientific systems that allow his dancers to choreograph 'Forsythe-style' dance even if he's out of the room. One of these systems might involve taking a shape made by one part of the body and then moving it around – a tiny bend in one finger, for instance, might expand into a sharply angled arm movement and then be amplified into an even bigger folding of the torso, while variations on the same movement may be soft or hard, fast or slow.

Once I asked Forsythe to demonstrate how one of his systems might look. He responded by holding out a bent finger which he suddenly stretched, thus torquing his hand into an asymmetrical gesture. The force of this move levered Forsythe's long body gracefully out of its chair, after which every joint in his body seemed to start sliding in all directions, his limbs angling and spiralling as in some hyperactive cartoon. It was beautiful and extraordinary to watch.

Forsythe generally has the last word in how this raw dance material gets put together, but he insists that the collaborative process produces movement that he could never have invented on his own. He cites a section of group choreography involving twenty-five dancers where each person danced their own phrase, but on every tenth beat, also connected with a movement danced by the others. 'No single choreographer could have made that piece; they couldn't have seen all the connections. It was amazing to watch. It sort of sparkled.'

Forsythe actually refused to say that he and his dancers invent the movement; rather he claims that 'it makes itself, we encounter it'. And even those choreographers who regard themselves as 'authors' of their work find it difficult to talk about the process of creation.

Mark Morris says that occasionally he will ask his dancers to do things for him such as 'There are six bars of music. I want everyone to get from here to here. Here are five moves. Do them in any order.' Or, 'I need a lift. He or she has to be way up here.' He thinks that 'dancers like to do that'. But most of the movement, he says, either comes from the music or 'just reveals itself': 'I surprise myself all the time. I think I want this to be a giant mob scene but it turns out to be a solo or duet or even an empty stage. When people say, "What's coming next?" I say, "I don't know, I haven't made it up yet."'

Choreographers usually have little explanation for the way that one step grows into another, the way that a new phrase of move-ment will alter the feel of an earlier phrase, the way that a struc-ture starts binding together passages of material. They can't account for how they know when a certain step, or rhythm or balance of forces, is right. But they know that at some point the work acquires a logic and an identity that shape their decisions. In some works that logic may be formal, purely to do with steps and the placing of bodies in space. In other works the logic may emerge from the music, the design – or the narrative.

One of the oldest motives for making theatre dance is telling a story – even though the slippery medium of movement doesn't naturally lend itself to detailed characterization or plot. Some choreographers (like Lloyd Newson) will use passages of text to say those things that dance finds literally unspeakable. But most still stick to the rich ambiguities of pure movement.

How, though, does dance tell stories if it can't label events, identify subconscious motives, or even move unambiguously from the present to the past or the future? (On stage the dancers' bodies exist in the present tense. Choreographers have to rely on lighting or some specially stylized movement to indicate that the action has shifted in time – and it's often not clear to audiences when they do so.) As I argued in the Introduction, there are some stories dance does best to avoid. But even in those narratives which suit dance (intense physical and emotional relationships, symbolic or fantastic scenarios) the precision with which it can express itself varies widely. At one extreme are the standard mime gestures of classical ballet, which can be decoded into clear objective statements (I love you, you will die, etc.). At the other are pure dance steps, which accumulate vaguer but much richer meanings simply through the way they're danced, through the music and design that accompany them and through their place in the choreography.

Certainly all movement can communicate. When Paul Taylor worked on one of his early minimalist pieces he thought that he was making 'an abstract dance out of natural postures and walking'. In fact, he realized that the body language of the dancers and their relation in space was also telling a basic plot: 'When one woman finally walks away across the stage, she isn't just walking, she's leaving the others. I learnt from this that posture and gesture are inseparable.'

But, as in any art form, context is everything, and steps or gestures acquire their meaning through their position in the work as a whole. A split *jeté* (flying leap) that registers heroism in one dance may suggest sexual ecstasy in another and ruthlessness in a third – or be a pure physical stunt in a fourth. (It's hard, though, to imagine it successfully conveying timidity or apathy.) An *arabesque* too can mean a thousand things – in fact, the only dance movements that have consistent symbolic meaning are the mime gestures of certain classical forms.

In Indian dance, for instance, there are hundreds of different hand and wrist movements that refer to gods and goddesses, or mimic the shapes of eagles, fish, flowers, peacocks and shells. When these gestures, or *mudras*, are accompanied by stylized expressions of the face, a single dancer can tell a whole story. In the mime of classical ballet, though, the facts we learn are more basic.

In the nineteenth century choreographers actually employed quite elaborate passages of mime, confident that the balletomanes in the audience would be able to follow their meaning. But though Odette still gestures to the Prince in modern stagings of *Swan Lake* the complex mime that means 'Yonder lies the lake of my mother's tears', and explains, in dumb show, the curse that's imprisoned her in the body of a swan, few of today's audiences will have much clue what she's doing. In general ballet mime now tends to be stripped down to simpler gestures. A circling movement of the arms above the head, for instance, always signifies dancing; the tracing of a circle round the face means beauty; two fingers raised high above the head with the other hand placed on the heart is an oath of love; clenched fists pointed to the floor mean death. These are usually used at crucial moments when a character has to recount his or her story or where a critical passage in the drama is reached.

But there's also a whole vocabulary of ballet gestures that sits between normal body language and codified mime. An outstretched arm, gracefully bent at the elbow with the palm questioningly lifted, typically signals the hero or heroine searching for their Beloved, hands clasped to the side of the head generally characterize confusion or despair. Like more codified mime, these movements are choreographed to the music and performed 'in style' so that they flow gracefully with the rest of the dance. (Giselle doesn't scratch her head in confusion when she's looking for Albrecht; courtiers do not greet each other with a 'gimme five' slap of hands.)

Twentieth-century story ballets do, though, incorporate more ordinary human gesture – partly because their scenarios tend to be too complex to rely on the black and white gestures of classical mime. With proficient dancers, these gestures can read as clearly as the body language of a straight actor – whether it be a shiver of lust, a tremor of nerves or the brutally explicit thrust of the jailor's buttocks in MacMillan's *Manon* when he forces the heroine to perform fellatio.

Often such gestures are woven deep into the dancing and can be hard to distinguish from choreography which expresses character and emotion by pure dance steps and where drama moves from the literal to the metaphoric. In *Manon*, for instance, Des Grieux's first love-struck solo is both mime and dance. The actual steps simply revolve around a slow turn in *arabesque*, a walk, a twist and arch in the back, yet the context of the dance – the fact that Manon and Des Grieux are mentally ripping off each other's clothes as they stare at each other on stage – and the rhythmic organization of these moves can make them a blatant declaration of feeling. When Irek Mukhamedov – a dancer of impressive intensity – first performed this role in 1991, the slow reach of his arm, the magnetized turning of his head, the sudden lavish arch of his back all registered with shocking acuteness the lover's helpless hunger, the racing of his pulse, the power of emotion to sock him in the gut.

(The non-literalness of dance movement, combined with its physical directness, makes choreography the perfect medium for expressing romantic or erotic relationships. Just as, in life, our bodies may deliver stingingly clear messages while our thoughts and feelings remain confused, so the skin-on-skin immediacy of dance can portray clear physical action while allowing emotion and poetry to play around the edges. One of the special virtues of dance narrative is that it can suggest complex feelings without having to nail them down with words.)

One of the great masters of body language was Antony Tudor. In *Pillar of Fire* (1942) his heroine Hagar is an unmarried woman in a small American town. She's in love with a man who seems indifferent to her and she aches with a sexual desire she believes to be immoral. Her isolation is highlighted by her female neighbours, who move in groups, linking arms, nodding their heads, dancing the same gossipy little steps. Hagar not only dances alone but her taut arms form a barrier against the rest of the world and her eyes never make contact with anyone else's.

When she finally has sex with the local Lothario, her hunger and her shame are vividly merged. Even in an embrace or a lift, she holds her body stiff with resistance and keeps her back turned to him. Later when this man rejects her, Hagar's humiliation is painfully registered by the retching heaves of her shoulders. Only when her real lover admits his feeling for her does Hagar look directly at another. As they embrace, the town's young girls pass across the back of the stage – feet shimmering in delicate *bourrées*, arms gently waving like some Proustian image of memory trembling across the years.

Balanchine's *Apollo* (1928) moves right across the narrative spectrum, from the literal gesture of its hero being unwound from his swaddling clothes to abstract pattern. Apollo's three Muses are characterized by the rhythms of their steps – the chatterboxy point work of Polyhymnia and the high, swinging, measured legs of Terpsichore. There are also many fleeting visual references that enlarge the theme. When Terpsichore and Apollo touch pointed fingers, like Adam and God in the Sistine Chapel, they are announcing their joint destinies. When the three Muses lean over Apollo's back, their lifted legs form a halo of *arabesques* that are the rays to his sun. Even in the patterns of the choreography, in the many triangles and circles that are formed by bodies and limbs, we see Apollo's association with order, symmetry and civilization. The movement mimes Alpha and Omega, the perfection of classical geometry.

Balanchine's *Serenade* (1934) is regarded as his first plotless ballet, yet even this tells a kind of story, showing how ordinary bodies become stylized into dancers. The stage opens on a whole company of standing women who, in grave unison, curve one stretched arm into the beginning of a fifth position, rotate their legs into turn-out and point one foot to the side. The women have become a *corps de ballet*. *Serenade* is also the story of how dance imagery can migrate from one ballet to another. There is one woman who always seems apart from the group, and who at one point runs on to the stage and falls. In some revisions she loosens her hair and briefly becomes Giselle embarking on her Mad Scene (the gesture almost mimics the old ballet), and we look at her with new eyes as a tragic victim, as every tragic victim in ballet.

Cunningham remains far more inscrutable than even Balanchine about motives and messages, but at times he can activate our imaginations even more busily. When (in old age) he dances with his company, the drama in his work is frequently focused around the contrast between his age and the rest of the dancers' youth. Most people looking at *Quartet* (1982), for instance, would see something like experience battling with mortality, the frustrations of the artist and the callousness of beauty and youth. The work almost looks like Cunningham's *King Lear* except that the movement is so very private, quirky and understated. There's no shaking of fists or beating of breasts; there's no rhetorical thunder or angst (see illus. 16).

But even though labels can't be pinned on the work's images, some appear unbearably bleak. Harsh sounds like high winds and sea birds dominate the score while four dancers work tightly together on a bare stage. In the back corner is Cunningham, a lone agitated watcher. At times he seems absorbed in his own restless movements; at others he becomes drawn into the orbit of the group, as if trying to control it. But he seems unable to get what he wants, shaking his head and hands in little gestures of frustration, and sometimes he's actually thrown out by the others, carted off like a difficult invalid or elderly troublemaker.

Whatever pure 'dance' ideas Cunningham may have been exploring in *Quartet*, his own performance always evokes the pain involved in his yielding ground to the younger dancers. And this introduces another crucial element in dance's power to communicate, which is how the individual dancer chooses to affect us.

The way that dancers perform steps, and the emotions they choose to project as they dance, can make all the difference between a movement that expresses something, and a movement that doesn't. Take, for instance, the spiralling backward fall beloved of Martha Graham. If a dancer is simply practising this most dramatic of body gestures, it may seem no more than a difficult manoeuvre. If she's been told that it's motivated by something specific, like despair, then she'll focus on its expressive possibilities (the nerve-screamingly slow corkscrewing of the upper body, the anguished opening of the chest and the reckless toppling to the floor). She's unlikely to be feeling real despair, but she'll be physically and even emotionally living in the image of despair created by the movement.

It may be that the fall has no actual motive, yet the dancer still feels it as a 'despairing kind of move' because of its drastic rhythm and action. Dancers may experience tenderness as they extend their hand to their partner even in a non-dramatic work, just as they may feel a sense of exhilaration as they jump. Emotions like these play around the edges of the movement, they are part of its rhythm, texture and colour. Some dancers may not consciously note them, but others may explore them as important clues to the choreography. They may develop them into an imaginary story as they dance.

Viewers too vary between meaning-hungry souls who flush out drama from every movement and those who focus more analytically on style and technique. Most of us are usually doing both most of the time. The question of how dance functions as a language is one of the most complex bits of philosophical baggage carried by the art form and it can't be properly unpacked here. But the anecdotes of dancers and choreographers give some clues as to the practical issues involved in the way dance does or doesn't tell stories.

The American ballerina Gelsey Kirkland, for instance, always liked her steps to mean something, but when she was dancing with the New York City Ballet she found that her quest for drama clashed with what Balanchine appeared to want from her – which was to get on with his choreography and not attempt to interpret it. He told her that her energy and intelligence were sufficient to animate his ballets; he didn't need her to invest them with a secret story of character. She, however, felt she could only dance her best if she was allowed to express emotion. 'Motivation and psychological depth, emotional and dramatic intensity – these were qualities Balanchine attempted to repress in his dancers and in his ballets,' she claims in her autobiography *Dancing on My Grave.*

Kirkland's view of Balanchine's mechanical conception of dance is actually exaggerated, since Edward Villella, another dancer with NYCB, recalls the choreographer scolding him for concentrating too much on steps and counts when he was learning the role of Apollo and ignoring drama: '"Dancers," said Mr B, "are poets of gesture."' Though Balanchine's instructions may not have been emotional enough to suit Kirkland, strong images did in fact colour many of his moves. In *Apollo's* opening solo the dancer's arms are braced in a manner that Balanchine liked to describe as an 'eagle on a crag'. He also has to stand like 'a matador with the bull rushing past' then to kick 'like a footballer'. Balanchine gave Villella these images as clues not only to how he should move, but also to how to project the classical/modern ideals of male strength that are crucial to the role.

Some choreographers do, however, go out of their way to instruct their dancers not to emote, and expect them to suppress the feelings that they experience as they dance. From their position the dance material is pure and complete in itself. The British choreographer Siobhan Davies, on the other hand, has devoted an entire work to exploring the emotional subtext of movement, trying to understand how a mere arrangement of arms and legs can communicate ideas and emotions.

Her starting point for *Wanting to Tell Stories* (1993) was 'the rich set of feelings that dancers get as they make a dance'. Though she had no plot or theme in mind, she wanted to force these underlying feelings into focus. So, as she made the movement, she asked her dancers to examine how it made them feel, what possible stories it might tell. As the piece progressed, the company developed the choreography in two directions – as pure dance (what movement came interestingly or inevitably next) and as drama. Sometimes it was the choreographic logic that dominated, sometimes the narrative.

At no point in the finished dance did a fixed cast of characters emerge, or a single plot, but it was full of small dramatic moments. It seemed to lift a curtain on long-running scenarios, to give us glimpses into dozens of private rooms. On a stage that was divided into separate spaces by screens one woman ran in a wide repeating circle and she kept looking anxiously over her shoulder, as if she was being pursued and looking for escape. In another area a man and a woman danced, touching easily. The rhythms of their movements were lazy, their movements relaxed, like a conversation between familiar lovers. In another space a man scooped up a woman's foot and cradled it in his hand, so that she was standing, stork-like, on one leg. This simple passing gesture spoke volumes about the nature of their intimacy – its erotic charge (the sensuous caress of his hand on her foot), its jokiness (the quirky, unromantic nature of their position), and its vulnerability to shifts in the balance of power between them (she was standing above him, but he was sustaining her balance).

Davies's work was almost like a dance version of Hitchcock's *Rear Window* except that there was no mystery to solve. None of the narrative clues could be taken out of the dance that held them. Davies tried to describe the logic that determined the work's evolution. 'You get a very clear taste for what you are heading towards, there's no other way of expressing it. These aren't stories that can be told in any other way than through this dance.'

Chapter Six: **HEARING MUSIC**

Just as some choreographers set out to tell stories while others very definitely do not, so some choreographers set their dances to music, while others shut their ears to anything other than the sound of their own movement.

George Balanchine claimed that 'music is the ground on which dance walks', and the inventiveness with which he made steps dance to the rhythms, melodies, structures and colours of his scores has become a benchmark for musicality.

But at the other extreme Merce Cunningham has always believed that dance loses its independence when it relies too closely on music. Movement has its own timing, rhythms and phrasing which can be diminished when it dances attendance on a score. Why should a choreographer be tied to a composer's ideas?

THE CHOREOGRAPHER'S RECORD COLLECTION: A BRIEF HISTORY OF DANCE AND MUSIC

Centuries ago no one could have made Cunningham's intellectual separation between music and dance. Most of the earliest formal Western dances had the same name and structure as the music that accompanied them, so that a danced minuet was always performed to a musical minuet, a danced saraband to a musical saraband, and so on.

Baroque composers like Handel and Purcell used these dance music forms as the base for longer compositions, which is one reason why choreographers still return so enthusiastically to their scores. The rhythms of a Purcell opera or a Handel oratorio are ready-made for dancers since they retain a dance scale and pace, and their patterns are so buoyantly legible.

But as baroque dance suites developed into sonatas and symphonies, and as orchestral forces expanded, so music for dance also outgrew its early models. Waltzes, polkas, polonaises and marches could still be heard within these larger scores, but as ballet narratives became more sophisticated, music had to develop more complex strategies for furthering the plot. Composers became adept at using motifs to highlight character and at scoring atmospheric effects, as Adolphe Adam did in his specially commissioned music for *Giselle* (1841). This was one of the first ballet scores to use leitmotifs for characters, giving sweetly melodic love music to Giselle and Albrecht, chilling chords to the Wilis and a threatening stabbing motif to Hilarion (who punctures Giselle's happiness). There are also passages when the orchestra almost soundpaints the action. At the climax of the Mad Scene the music rises to a harrowing crescendo of pain as Giselle runs to her mother and falls dead at her feet.

During the nineteenth century composers who wrote specifically for dance were often a jobbing crew. Minkus, Glazunov and others had to be able to respond minutely to their choreographers' specifications – a *corps de ballet* entrance followed by a ballerina variation; 120 bars of a cheerful waltz followed by a rousing march number or three minutes of a mazurka. The structure of the music was as formulaic as the structure of the ballets, and the seams between numbers were often so crudely exposed that a 'single' score sounded like a medley of different tunes. The extent to which numbers could be taken out or added to meant that certain scores ended up as a shameless musical patchwork. The score for Petipa's final version of *Le Corsaire* (1899) was actually pasted together out of music by five different composers.

Not surprisingly these scores were sneered at by the musical establishment, although some had their moments of poetry. In Minkus's music for *Bayadère* there may be laughable oddities, like waltz music for Indian temple dancers and creakily rum-te-tum numbers for the ensemble dances. But there are also passages of genuinely infectious dance music and a shimmeringly atmospheric setting for the lovely Shades Act.

Yet, as the *Oxford Dictionary of Music* bluntly puts it, Minkus had the 'misfortune to be a contemporary of Tchaikovsky'. And it was the latter who succeeded in turning the pragmatic, worka-day craft of ballet composition into great art (though Delibes, who composed exquisitely coloured ballet scores for *Sylvia* and *Coppelia* in the 1870s, ran a close second and his music was greatly admired by Tchaikovsky).

Not that Tchaikovsky, when he composed his own ballet music, had total artistic licence compared to Minkus *et al.* When he and Petipa began work on *Sleeping Beauty* (arguably the greatest col-laboration between them), the latter made many of the usual stipulations about length, expression, tempo, etc., before Tchai-kovsky went to work, and would occasionally interfere in the writing process. (When Tchaikovsky was beginning work on Aurora's variation in Act II, Petipa wrote to him, 'For the moment do not compose it, I must speak to the *danseuse*.')

But still Tchaikovsky had more liberty than most professional dance composers. Not only did he write whole tracts of the music without any instructions, he'd also disobey some of the ones Pet-ipa gave. It was certainly freedom enough to produce music that's now regarded as almost Mozartian in its fluency. (Though the score of *Sleeping Beauty* was coolly received by some critics at its première, and thirty years later, when Lytton Strachey first saw the ballet in 1921, he reported to Sacheverell Sitwell, 'It made me feel sick. The whole thing was so degraded, especially the music.')

Despite Strachey's fastidious queasiness, what Tchaikovsky had actually succeeded in composing was a highly danceable score whose soaring thematic and harmonic structure was vividly studied with musical evocations of character and mood. (Musi-cally he created the equivalent of King Florestan's palace with its furnishings and occupants in place.) Much of the music for the Fairies in the Prologue, for instance, is based on standard dance numbers like the galop or the waltz. But what we hear are melody, instrumentation and rhythm, creating character in exactly the same way that Petipa twisted ballet steps to make individual dance languages. In the Breadcrumb Variation the violins play pizzicato notes to suggest the crumbs falling through the air, which are echoed by the double basses to suggest the crumbs reaching the ground. In the Canary Variation, piccolos and flutes twitter their accompaniment and when the Lilac Fairy concludes this section, the music has a slow, spacious grandeur, its sound is rich and voluptuous.

But despite Tchaikovsky's achievement dance music was still widely regarded, in the musical establishment, as second-division stuff. It was considered beneath the talents of great composers to write for dance, and choreographers were bound by an unwritten law forbidding them to lay hands on scores not written for them. To set a ballet to Chopin, Mozart or Brahms was artistic trespass and damage. (When Kenneth MacMillan wanted to choreograph to Mahler's *Song of the Earth*, as late as in the 60s, he was refused permission by the Royal Opera House, though he went on to make the work for Stuttgart Ballet.)

Consequently when Isadora Duncan launched her personal dance revolution round the Western world, it wasn't just her bare feet and occasionally bare breasts that startled her audience – it was also her barefaced cheek in using the classical music repertoire. She waltzed to Brahms; she rippled her arms to Schubert; she choreographed her own spring to Mendelssohn's *Spring Song*. If dance was great art, she claimed, then it should be accompanied by only the best music.

She didn't persuade everyone, and some of the more monumental classic scores are still considered sacrosanct. (Béjart's version of Wagner's *Ring* was met with screeches of outrage by many critics.) But twentieth-century composers are generally eager to write for dance and this has much to do with Diaghilev's influence. In his search for the ultimate drop-dead fashionable dance event, the impresario brokered many marriages between the hottest talents in music and choreography, and no sensible composer wanted to be left out.

Often these collaborations could be fraught. When Stravinsky composed the music for Nijinsky's *Rite of Spring* it was so jaggedly unlike ordinary dance music that Marie Rambert had to be brought in to help both choreographer and dancers puzzle out the counts. The composer wanted his music played very fast – 'Twice as fast,' recalls Rambert, 'as we could possibly dance' – and he professed a dislike of Nijinsky's final results (though near his death he claimed it was the best of all the versions he'd seen).

But to us both dance and music seem equal partners in a single radical vision. Both artists wrenched apart their inherited languages to discover forms that were as shockingly primitive as they were aesthetically revolutionary. Dance and music no longer followed the old-fashioned ballet structures that divided neatly between formal entrées and solo variations, but created dense, urgent textures of sound and movement. Both were fired by an image of a brutal precivilized world that prefigured, with awful clarity, the trauma of the impending world war.

One of the most harmonious of the Ballets Russes alliances was *Apollo*, an early Balanchine/Stravinsky coupling that helped to define the baseline of twentieth-century neo-classicism and that was considered by Balanchine to be the turning point in his life (though he wasn't strictly the first choreographer to use this score). For both artists it was a return to the past, conceived in terms of a radical future. Historically the ballet's title recalls not only the Greek god Apollo but also Louis XIV, who danced as the Sun King in his own court ballets, and Stravinsky's score contains measures from old court dance music like the saraband and pavan. Balanchine's choreography too is rooted on the classical-dance grammar that originated from the same court dances.

At the same time both movement and music have a modernist austerity which is all clean surfaces, white light and restraint – prefiguring another space-age Apollo. And they have too a very modernist range of reference. Like a T. S. Eliot poem that mixes Cockney slang with quotes from Shakespeare and the Greeks, Stravinsky's score moves from a variation (for Calliope) whose beat is based on the alexandrine metrics of a couplet by Boileau to a section of syncopated quasi jazz. Balanchine too will come out of a perfect classical *arabesque* into a jazzy quartet where you can almost see the dancers' canes and straw hats, or show a supported *pirouette* on point when the dancer is in a low-slung sitting position.

As Richard Buckle has described in his biography of Balanchine, Stravinsky's score also creates one of the most paradisical musical apotheoses ever written. The principal theme, first heard before the rise of the curtain, is repeated over and over as the ballet draws to a close, creating a sense of enlarging peace. A steady stepping rhythm is heard on the cellos and basses while the dancers slowly ascend the slope of Parnassus, and at the same time a persistent tremolo is heard on the violins and violas, enveloping the whole stage in a golden haze. At its London première, the theatre designer Gordon Craig went home as soon as the ballet finished in order not to dilute the feeling that he'd died and gone to heaven.

Since Diaghilev, ballet's record collection has expanded dramatically. While some choreographers have continued to stick with the more predictable rhythms and melodies of the pre-twentieth-century repertoire, others have ranged as widely as rock music, Philip Glass, electronic sound collage, or even silence. Yet, however divergent their choice of music, most ballet choreographers still have one thing in common, which is that they retain a dependent relationship with their music. Most of them still work to a finished score.

This is unlike many modern dance makers, who've tended to fear that their language would be compromised if it was pegged too closely to music. Martha Graham mapped out most of her choreography in silence, and the final work emerged out of a struggle between the patterns she'd already made and those she heard in the music. But she did always choose scores that reflected her style. She fastidiously avoided pre-twentieth-century music that might create a mood of familiarity or nostalgia, working instead with (then) unknowns like Paul Hindemith, Aaron Copland, Henry Cowell and her mentor Louis Horst. She also preferred her music to be percussive, without the lubricant of melody to soothe the choreography's edges. In music as in dance she wanted every moment to stand out sharp and plain.

It was Cunningham, though, who made the most radical break. First he refused to choreograph his dances to music at all, depending purely on a stop watch to set the timing of the movement. Secondly, although he allowed music to run alongside his dances during performance, the scores were unlike any that dance audiences had heard before. Most were composed from either treated 'natural' sound or electronic effects, creating an atmospheric sound world for the dance. Cunningham's long-term collaborator John Cage composed the bulk of them during his lifetime (along with his pupil David Tudor) – and it was his practice of using found noise instead of conventional instruments and his chance methods of composition that first helped to define Cunningham's dance aesthetic.

Certainly Cage's and Tudor's quirky squibs and brutal bolts of noise can be as startling as some of Cunningham's more extreme juxtapositions of movement, while their use of human or animal sound can mirror the tender natural images that sometimes crop up in the choreography. And, as we strain to make sense of their seemingly unmappable structures, we are confronted too by the apparent serendipity of Cunningham's own logic.

The genre originated by Cage has influenced a new breed of scores – or soundscapes – like those composed by Hans Peter Kuhn. Kuhn's meticulously structured collages, that might feature machine noise, bird song and musical scraps, are often used by virtuoso improviser Laurie Booth. They help, hauntingly, to define the world of the performance, giving rhythmic clues, colour and drama for the movement to feed off.

Another musical vogue that dates from the mid-80s is the post-modern pot-pourri dance score in which operatic arias might rub rhythms with rap, Bulgarian women's choir music and salsa. These musical collages can be a neat (sometimes too neat) way of injecting variety into a dance, of channel-hopping effortlessly between a range of cultures, moods and emotions. Some choreographers have turned to text instead of music, like Richard Alston in his 1980 *Rainbow Ripples.* This was set to some text by poet Charles Amirkhanian where the words were treated so that they became loops and splutters of rhythm with just the occasional phrase ('let's try something *new*'), sounding clear and colliding comically with the dance.

During the 70s and 80s, those avant-garde choreographers who still worked to a score were often strict minimalists and two of their favoured composers were Steve Reich and Philip Glass. To watch the austere geometries of a dance group stepping and whirling along repetitive tracks of movement while buoyed along by equally repetitive waves of sound was to enter, often thrillingly, into a double-locked trance state – an aurally and visually hypnotic chamber.

READING DANCE TO MUSIC

For some choreographers, both classical and modern, there are certain scores that just beg to be danced to. As British choreographer Mark Baldwin has said, 'They remind you of the basic instinct to move your butt around the room. Certain music, when you hear it, has legs.' Those choreographers who do set their dance closely to music will be getting a lot of input from the score – a ready-made length and structure for their choreography, a set of rhythms, phrases and melodies to respond to and a series of contrasts between fast and slow, loud and soft, large and small scale. They may also be getting style and mood.

When we watch such a dance, we may not register the relation between movement and music in much detail. But as we sense connections between choreography and score arising, we also start to sense a kind of inevitability about the work, a promise of things falling into place. It's like following a path that winds through a formal garden. We don't know where it's taking us, but we know we don't have to navigate for ourselves; we know that the views have been planned to please.

Structure

The length and structure of a piece of music will often provide the basic skeleton of a dance work, and with Morris's *L'Allegro, il Penseroso ed il Moderato*, for instance, it's pretty obvious how the dance follows Handel's score. With each new song there's a new dance (both movement and music reflecting the words of the libretto) and when the score changes mood and pace, so too does the choreography.

But choreographers also respond to much smaller structures and mechanisms in the music, and often where a composer uses canon, inverts a phrase or spins variations on a theme, the dance may do the same. The visual effect is the same as the aural – we get the pleasure of seeing movements repeated but with teasing differences. In a canon (like a round in singing) several dancers perform the same phrase, but each starts at a different moment so that the steps are staggered out in space and time. When a theme is varied we get to see the same basic material, but the steps are put together in different combinations, danced with varying kinds of attack, or performed by different numbers of dancers. (When Trisha Brown began to make a work to Bach's *Musical Offering* she was intrigued by how much compositional mileage Bach could get out of one musical theme. As she says, 'A theme is a spare and elegant sequence of notes that sets up possibilities for later use, to turn upside-down, sideways, embellish and reduce in every direction possible.' Her own *M.O.* was an attempt to mirror this fertile invention by finding dozens of ways of varying her own basic movement themes.)

Choreographers may respond not just to the structural detail of their score but to the instrumental colours and melodies. As critic Joan Acocella notes, in Morris's *Motorcade* (1990) the trumpet flourishes and big piano runs of Saint-Saëns's *Septet* are directly translated into big flourishing lifts and joyous runs. As dance music critic Stephanie Jordan has pointed out, during one section of Balanchine's *Ballet Imperial* (1941) a dancer precisely rises on point and then bends her knee to mirror a falling melodic line.

In such cases what we hear is also what we see – and our senses are simultaneously sharpened and clarified. But if a dance follows the score too slavishly, there's a danger that both cancel each other out. 'Micky Mousing' – where the movement trots along with the music step for note – is considered one of the deadly sins of choreography. Not only does the effect become irksomely predictable but the movement is made to look silly. It becomes like a machine obediently marching in time to the music's commands. It can seem to drag excessively when the music is slow and to scurry frantically when the music is fast.

(Paul Taylor has sometimes been accused of being too literal with his scores and it's certainly true that his dancers happily leap, step and turn in exact time to the music. But their movements have a muscular heft that sustains their independence. As they dive down into the beat of Handel, for example, and spring back

out, it's with an energy that suggests they are bouncing and striding by their own volition rather than acting on the instructions
of the music – like a virtuoso on a trampoline, a jockey on a horse.
Music and dance are equal forces, dashing along together.)

Wholesale music visualization aims to re-create every aspect of
the score in dance. When the music soars the dancers leap; when
it whispers the dancers tiptoe or creep. When violins play, so do
a group of designated violin dancers; when the brass play so the
brass dancers move. This genre of dance-making was voguish at
the beginning of the century, but apart from a couple of exceptions
(Massine's epic ballet *Choreartium* (1933) to Brahms's Fourth Symphony) it now looks old-fashioned to us.

Generally it's acknowledged that dance and music thrive best
when they retain some independence from each other. Dance may
use music to set up certain rules in its own construction, but it
should then have the fun of breaking them.

Take the case of Richard Alston. Alston sets most of his dances
to music and says that his choice of score is determined by a 'gut
response' to those that 'call forth something from me that I'll be
interested in exploring. Do I really want to live with this for
months? Can I really see people moving to it?'

He's particularly drawn to 'the energy and stridency' of contemporary composers like Peter Maxwell Davies and Harrison
Birtwistle as well as to music for wind instruments – since the
musicians' use of breath is so like dancing: 'the sound comes from
so deep inside the body'.

Having chosen his score, Alston listens to it over and over again
'waiting for a series of certainties of what I'd like to happen to
particular moments – like "Yes, there it should be just one person
dancing."' He says he's not an analytic listener, but when he sits
down to read the score he then starts to get a visual shape of it –
establishing how the music develops, how it divides into sections,
where passages repeat, and so on.

All of this basic structural information feeds into the way he
builds his own dance, so that he may repeat where the composer
repeats, transform musical pattern into physical dance shape, and
so on. But though he uses the music in detail, he says it's important 'to end up with a play between joining and leaving the music,

otherwise you just go to sleep'. So there are many passages where the dance obeys its own logic rather than that of the score. And even those passages which were originally close to the music get subtly prised apart during the final stages of the work. Where, for instance, Alston might initially have had a dancer bending her legs, then rising on her toes to a sequence of low and high notes, he might finally decide to take away the rise – a tiny detail but one that makes the dance–music relationship more lively. In performance too he encourages his dancers to play with the phrasing of the movement and not stick too obediently to the music, so that the movement creates 'its own silent score'.

The most musical choreographers may often be those who take the most interesting liberties with their scores. For instance, in the final *Allegro* of *Concerto Barocco* Balanchine has the *corps de ballet* drumming out the rhythms of the violins with their points, but he also has them moving their arms on a beat that goes completely against the music. In his 1981 work *Gloria* (set to Vivaldi's score) Mark Morris starts off with two women dancers following the melodic line of two women singers. But then he doubles up the women dancers so that there are two per singer, and later on the same dancers carry on moving when the singers have stopped – joining in with those dancers who've been following the orchestra. The dance increasingly leaves the music behind as it develops its own logic.

Ashton tended to have a less analytic approach to music than Balanchine, Alston or Morris – he could neither read nor play music, but conductor and arranger John Lanchberry insists he had a 'massive, inborn instinct for what is right'. Though at times he'd bind his steps to the exact rhythm of the score for sharpness or legibility, often he'd let the movement flow right over it, or seem to dance, cheekily, between the notes. His phrases are sometimes almost impossible to count, yet the effect of the dance coming and going with the music is highly sensual. It delays mutual climaxes, then brings them about with stunning force; it plays what we see against what we hear. As Stephanie Jordan has described, there's a moment in *Rhapsody* (1980) where the lead couple are dancing at a speed that seems quite contrary to the music (Rachmaninov's *Rhapsody on a Theme of Paganini*). Only when the piano part emerges clearly from the orchestra do we realize that their quick steps and jumps have been following its line. Something similar happens in *Monotones* (1965) where Ashton cuts across the almost static serenity of Satie's music with running passages and spacious patterns, countering the potential tedium of its sweet regularity.

Rhythm

The rhythms and melodies of a score can't strictly be separated from its structure, yet in some dances we're aware of them as unusually compelling elements in the dance–music relationship. When rhythm strikes us this way, it's because the movement isn't just riding along with the counts of the music but seems to be grappling with it, like some elemental force. The rhythm may bowl the movement along, threaten to engulf it, get straddled by the dance, then fight to break free again.

In flamenco and many classical Indian dance forms this turbulent relationship is often dramatized by having the musicians on stage with the dance. The dancer begins by obediently marking the musicians' rhythms with her feet, then as the music builds its own complicated counts so she complicates her own, sometimes playing ferociously difficult games with it (dancing six bars of six counts over the music's nine bars of four counts, then spinning more and more intricate numerical variations, for instance). Even as the music tries to impose its own order she has to find her own rhythmic freedom without losing track of the counts.

The music for Western dance used to be valued in terms of how discreetly and legibly '*dansant*' its rhythms were – lifting the dance along like a graceful, sympathetic partner. But *Rite of Spring* changed that, its complex rhythms creating an assault course for every new generation of dancers and choreographers as they've attempted to surf its crashing waves of sound. (American dancer and choreographer Sara Rudnor says to her students that 'everyone should experience the terror of making their own *Rite*'.) When American dancer Molissa Fenley danced solo to it she looked astonishingly vulnerable as she tried to survive its onslaught. Sometimes she'd kick and slash to stay on top of it, sometimes its rhythms would invade her, her small sturdy frame juddering with their force.

The impetuous rhythms of John Adams's *Fearful Symmetries* (1989) have made it another favourite with choreographers. The score makes us think of cityscapes, machinery and bright lights as it cruises through passages of densely textured repetition, builds to crashing dissonances, gentles back into delicate shimmers of sound, then roars up into top gear. In Ashley Page's setting for the Royal Ballet (1994) the music drives the dancers inexorably forward with its tension and energy. At times they seem an urban tribe moving in pouncing formations like runners in a rush-hour marathon, then their energy gets so heated that they launch into orbit, men whirling and leaping, women swinging limbs perilously out into space.

Melody

As Martha Graham was suspiciously aware, melody, a sweetly linked sequence of notes, can have a lubricating effect on dance. If sounds are joined into a clear and beautiful shape, then the steps which closely accompany them will also appear as a pleasing whole. Music and dance reinforce each other, so that what we hear tells us what to see. For this reason, melody often helps us to remember movement more clearly. By singing the notes in our heads we can often call up clear images of the dance that accompanies them.

But melody is more than a potent mental glue. Its joyous or tragic sounds can reinforce the movement's drama and unlock its poetry. In *Swan Lake*, for instance, when Odette first appears, shaking drops of water from her wings as she turns from bird to woman, she's accompanied by a melody on the oboe. It's as if she and the instrument are mingling their two private arias. The oboe's plangent melody, heard so clearly away from the rest of the orchestra, sets Odette apart in her own separate world of love and grief.

When Odette learns to trust Siegfried, the melody is taken first by the violin and then shared between violin and cello (always a vehicle for passion in Tchaikovsky). Even without this music

Odette's dancing would be gravely and nobly expressive. Her torso arches slowly backwards under the apparent burden of emotion; her head is bowed with remembered suffering; her leg stretches up in a sigh of ecstasy. But the music adds its own rich, dark sensuality of tone and the yearning lines of its melody seem to draw out Odette's movements into even longer, more exquisite lines. Finally, as the twin voices of the cello and violin combine, so we see the prince lift and embrace Odette with increasingly joyous freedom. (This section of the *pas de deux* music was originally written as a duet for soprano and baritone voice, which is one reason why its melody seems so intimately human, why its phrases seem to rise and fall with the lovers' breath.)

Atmosphere

In some works the music doesn't just reinforce what's already in the choreography, it creates its own meanings. In fact, in a passage like the *grand pas de deux* from Act II of *Nutcracker* I'd argue that we read the dance through what we hear in the score.

What we are seeing is the Sugar Plum Fairy and her Cavalier dancing together for the first, and last, time in the ballet. We know very little about them as characters, since they've done nothing but watch graciously from the sidelines as the ballet's heroine Clara is entertained by figures from the Kingdom of Sweet. Potentially these two characters are the dullest people in ballet. Yet their duet forms the work's emotional and physical climax; it is *Nutcracker's* heart. And what makes it so is not Ivanov's choreography (or subsequent versions of, grand though they may be). It is Tchaikovsky's music.

We now know that Tchaikovsky was in mourning after the death of his sister Sasha when he wrote this music and that he was afflicted by fierce homesickness, so it's not fanciful to read heartache and nostalgia into the lovely falling scales of the opening melody. The scoring is firstly for strings, with a sweet rippling of harp, but out of this intimacy develop scale, distance, and magnificence with the addition of brass and percussion. This combination of instruments gives a poignancy to the upward reaching of the dancers' arms and lends grandeur to their stately *arabesques*. It suggests a human fragility behind their triumphant lifts and behind their careful courtesies to each other. The *grand pas* becomes a metaphor for all classical ballet in which two beautiful dancers put a noble and civilized gloss on the heartache of the real world.

At another musical and choreographic extreme, Cunningham's *Winterbranch* (1964) has also affected its audience as high drama because of the input of its music (as well as its design). Cunningham has claimed that the work evolved out of a purely technical interest in choreographing falls, but his public insisted on interpreting it as a piece about a holocaust, a concentration camp or a storm at sea. These readings were motivated not only by the fact that we tend to view people falling down as dead or dying, but also by Robert Rauschenberg's brutal lighting, which suggested prison camps and the Apocalypse, and La Monte Young's score, which blasted piercing sound from two speakers into the audience's eardrums in a drastic physical assault.

Lucinda Childs was part of a generation even more fiercely opposed to sentiment in dance than Cunningham, and in *Available Light* (1983) her nine dancers moved as if governed by mathematical necessity, criss-crossing the stage in perfectly ordered lines, varying the same tight vocabulary of steps. Yet, despite the rigour of the choreography, the rich sonorities of brass and keyboard in John Adams's accompanying score put emotional flesh on the lean structure of the dance. Moments where it threw up some weirdly Wagnerian echoes caused the dance to resonate suddenly with a very unminimalist grandeur and passion.

Clinching the Style

Any choreographer who uses music knows that it will be one of the most immediately registered elements in their dance – creating instant mood and style. We have a pretty good idea what a piece will be like if it is set to a) Górecki, b) Chopin or c) the Sex Pistols, and we also get a clear message when choreographers subvert those expectations. When Taylor had his elegant dancers turn bestial to Corelli's music in *Cloven Kingdom* he used the gap between their exuberance and the music's civilized orderliness to make his point about contradictions in human nature.

For many choreographers – Balanchine, Alston, Morris, Ashton – the wide variety of their output owes a lot to the variety of their scores. Morris can move from profound religious emotion (Vivaldi's *Gloria*) to sweet and tart nostalgia (country swing), from utopian grandeur (Handel's *L'Allegro*) to *film noir* horror (Schoenberg) or kitsch orientalism (Bombay film music). Balanchine can move from tight acerbic rhythms (Stravinsky's *Agon*) to lush swathes of movement (Brahms's *Liebeslieder Walzer*) to parading monumental dance forces alongside the grand orchestration of Bizet's Symphony in C. Ashton can be jazzy to Richard Rodney Bennet, elegiac to Elgar, fantastical to Mendelssohn, witty to Walton's *Façade*.

For some choreographers that kind of musical range would be a distraction, even a betrayal, of their work's integrity. (Cunningham dancing to Sibelius just doesn't bear thinking about.) William Forsythe, for instance, nearly always uses the same composer, Thom Willems, to create the scores for his work – their minimal, abrasive sounds sharpening the edges of his own movement. He steers clear of the classical repertoire (unless it's treated or deformed in some way) because he feels it would be a spurious 'legitimizing' of his work.

Some choreographers like to rule out the interference of any kind of music, working and performing in silence. As Dana Reitz has said, 'The body has its own rhythms and patterns of sound that you can only hear if you're quiet.' In her improvised performances it's that innate musicality which she explores – the swish of her own feet, the pulse of her breath and heart – and all the idiosyncratic rhythms that make up her style of moving. Of course, no stage is entirely silent and stray sounds often affect Reitz as she improvises. 'If a plane passes overhead, you can't ignore it, you don't exactly dance to the plane but your reactions to it are part of your material – it all happens in a split second.' A typical instance of this occurred during one London performance when a sudden downpour of rain drumming outside provoked a passing gesture where her fingers vibrated their own silent accompanying tremolo. For Reitz the sound score is different every time she dances.

Chapter Seven: **STRUCTURE: THE BASIC ARCHITECTURE OF DANCE**

If choreographers are setting their work to music or telling a carefully plotted story, they will probably start with some clear sense of the structure and length that they're aiming for. If they've been commissioned to make a three-act ballet or a short duet, they'll also be working within certain structural limits. But often the internal structure of a work (how it gets from A to B) doesn't make itself plain to a choreographer until he or she is deep into the rehearsal process. As Twyla Tharp has written, 'When I go into a studio I know exactly what I want, but never quite how I'll get it. Each dance is a mystery story.'

However, even if the structure isn't always the starting point for a choreographer, the final format of the work will have a powerful influence on the way an audience views it. No one sits down to read a Dickens novel the way they would a poem by Wallace Stevens. The attention that we can beam on to a few lines is impossible to sustain over several marriages and a clutch of death scenes, and the kind of enjoyment we get is qualitatively different. In the same way, audiences expect very different things from a long ballet and a fifteen-minute solo.

CHANGES IN THE GRAND DESIGN: A BRIEF HISTORY OF STRUCTURE IN DANCE

When the public sits down to watch a sixteen-hour performance given by a troupe of Kathakali dance performers in South India they have to be mentally and physically prepared to pace themselves through a very long sitting. They have also to adjust to the show's many gear changes between fierce battle scenes, soothing love dramas and decorative interludes. The extreme contrasts of scale and focus involved make it seem less an entertainment than a self-contained world. To watch a full-scale Kathakali show is not to take time out for a brief diversion.

The nearest dance equivalent in the West is the three- or four-act classical ballet. Here the story also unfolds through alternations of dance and mime, energetic spectacle and leisurely, plot-suspending *divertissements*. Time is concentrated, then expanded; reality crosses over into dreams or visions; lovers meet in a private world and are then sucked back into the public forum.

During Petipa's reign in St Petersburg the structure of these ballets rarely varied, with the basic dance plot being padded out with vision scenes of white-frocked dream-women as well as national dances, storms and battles. The order and the setting might vary but the mix had to be the same. Yet in some of the great ballets of the period this formula transcended its own clichés to become pure poetic logic. In *Swan Lake*, for instance, the structure is perfectly tuned to telling the ballet's story.

Act I opens with a full stage. The court is partying, though Siegfried is already having to face the fact that his laddish spirits don't chime with his responsibilities to marry. He goes off hunting with his friends – and so takes the ballet straight into its Act II Vision Scene, which is the white magical realm of the lakeside. Here Odette, unlike the revellers of Act I, dances by herself, and she mimes for Siegfried with a tragic intentness the story of her enchantment. When her company of sister swans dance they form a pure grieving frame around her. Time slows to a single embrace as she and Siegfried fall in love and dance their *pas de deux*. And nothing breaks the moment's spell until Odette is called off stage by the magician Rothbart.

When the ballet returns to the court in Act III the contrast is shocking. The bustle and colour confuse our senses as much as Siegfried's. Among so many courtiers and princesses it's not surprising that Odile can so easily pass herself off as Odette. After Siegfried's first dazed thrill at seeing her the proceedings are interrupted by the obligatory series of national dance *divertissements*. But these don't hold up the story. Partly thanks to the swirl and dash of Tchaikovsky's music they whip the ballet into a blur of swagger and sensuality, driving us further away from the purity of Odette's world and into chaos. By the time Siegfried and Odile come on to dance, everybody's blood is up. The near sexual climax of Odile's triumphal thirty-two *fouettés* has been well prepared for. No wonder Siegfried swears that he loves her.

Act IV returns to the hapless virginity of the lakeside where the swans are dancing an agitated storm. They flood the stage in circles and lines of anguished dance, while the betrayed Odette flutters in their centre. When Siegfried arrives the storm focuses around his *pas de deux* with Odette, a dance of private sorrow and forgiveness. Such is the intensity of the moment that even the final battle with Rothbart can't destroy its effect. Its authority allows us to believe in the apotheosis, where the dead lovers are flown away to heaven.

Fokine and his generation, however, regarded the formula of these ballets as creaky, over-upholstered excuses for display. In their search for choreographic truth they cut out the narrative padding and razzmatazz and concentrated their works into single acts. Although some later choreographers, notably Kenneth Mac-Millan, have made inventive efforts to sustain the three-act form (introducing more grittily realistic plots and psychological motive, experimenting with text and film to vary the dance language), the single-act work stands out as the definitive form of twentieth-century ballet – the equivalent of the tightly written, spatially and temporally compressed short story. It has spawned works as varied as the folkloric narratives of Fokine, the music realizations of Balanchine, the compressed one-act dramas of Ashton and the deconstructions of William Forsythe. Most last between 20 and 40 minutes – which seems to be the maximum length of time over which most choreographers can sustain a pure dance impetus without introducing diversions and distractions.

The structure might be generated by the music, the plot or the logic of the dance itself – most likely some combination of the three. Many of Fokine's works still have a nineteenth-century narrative solidity – ending as they often do with a marriage or a death. But Balanchine's *Apollo*, although beginning with the god's birth and ending with his ascent of Parnassus, is already far more formal in its pursuit of dance logic. We're interested in the rhythm and composition of the dances for the three Muses, not in which woman Apollo will choose as his mate. In the 90s William Forsythe creates ballets where there is rarely a story and where the music imposes no obvious beginning, middle and end. There may be encounters, suggestions and incidents woven into the movement, but it's the logic of the dance itself that decides where the ballet is going and for how long.

Modern choreographers have also veered towards compression. The American choreographer Doris Humphrey once remarked tartly that 'all dances are too long' and the early moderns often made extremely short, concentrated works. As in ballet, most of today's repertoire averages out at around 20–30 minutes, though choreographers who work in dance/physical theatre generally extend their range to around 60–90 minutes.

Many of these works aren't predetermined by a score or a pre-existing plot, but evolve out of a working process – the development of a theme using movement, speech and the manipulation of props. The pacing of the dance may move from the concentration of dance time into the less formal pace of real time when the dancers break off to speak or gesture. It may move from the rush of physical activity to the static contemplation of physical objects. Such works tend to need more time than the average pure-dance piece in order to furnish their imagined world and, rather like a Kathakali spectacle or an old classical ballet, the variety of their elements will sustain a longer span than pure movement does.

(Some of Pina Bausch's work, however, deliberately strains its own structure and the stamina of its audience to breaking point. The four-hour span of *1980*, for instance, puts the audience in the same position of endurance as the performers, and part of the exhilaration of the piece is the final, shared feeling of 'Look, we have come through!')

WHERE DANCE STRUCTURES COME FROM

A choreographer may decide on a one- or three-act ballet, a pure dance or theatre piece – but other elements may also influence how the work is structured.

Music

If a choreographer chooses to work with a score that has a strong shape and compelling momentum, then half their work may be done. But what makes good structural sense in music doesn't always make good structural sense in dance. Though we might listen absorbedly to a minutely exploratory section of music, we might find the same leisureliness tedious when it's yoked to dance. The ear can be more patient than the eye. Christopher Bruce's *Crossing* (1995), for instance, makes intense drama out of some of the dark colours in Górecki's Second String Quartet, but during its slow middle section the dance becomes trapped and enervated by the music's clotted rhythms. With Stravinsky's *Rite of Spring*, many choreographers often run out of dance to fill the music's sustained passages of ferocity. Though the musical structure holds, the dance structure sags.

Choreographers don't necessarily need a score to be influenced by musical structure. Some dances are composed on the basis of musical forms, so that a dance rondo, for instance, will, like the musical rondo, depart from and return to its basic material in the order AB, AC, AD, A. Many late-twentieth-century choreographers have also copied minimalist composers by creating their works in discrete sections, each of which exhausts one idea before moving on to the next. The dance is like a set of differently coloured movement vignettes strung like beads on a string.

Plot

A story is obviously a given like a score – providing a beginning, middle and end for a dance as well as important landmarks along the way. But a choreographer has to have the structural skills of a writer when it comes to pacing the narrative. Events and characters have to be established with care; tension and climax have to be stage-managed. Tudor is a master at revealing character and motivation with just a few concise signature moves. John Cranko too shows in seconds the fatal contrast between the bookish dreamy heroine of his ballet *Onegin* (1965) and her more wilful, flirtatious younger sister.

But choreographers can't handle detailed description or reflection as successfully as writers, and their stories can rapidly pall when they stray too far from intense action and emotion. Most of the *Romeo and Juliet*s that have been choreographed to the famous Prokofiev score suffer badly from a sagging Act II, for if they follow the original libretto, all the critical love and death interest takes place in Acts I and III and there's little other than sword fights and street life to fill the second. When David Bintley choreographed a ballet to Thomas Hardy's novel *Far From the Madding Crowd* in 1996, his source provided him with as much romance and tragedy as he could wish via the heroine's three love affairs – but also a lot of unwieldy background narrative and philosophy. It must be the first ballet in history to depict a sheep-shearing competition.

Graham was thus both bold and canny when she realized that dance narratives weren't always best served by sticking to chronological logic. By concertinaing background events and telescoping time, by moving freely between dream time and real time, she was able to cut out long-winded plotting and concentrate on what her movement did best – unravelling the soul, psyche and sexuality of her characters.

The Real World

Choreographers are presented with other givens that influence structure – such as the kind of slot their work is meant to fill. As with TV programmes and feature films, there are rules about the acceptable length of dances. If a large theatre or opera house isn't showing a two- or three-act ballet, it usually prefers to programme a trio of roughly 30-minute works. This format ensures that audiences are getting value for money for their tickets (and that there are two intervals where they can spend the rest on food and drink).

Theatres which regularly programme post-modern dance works are happier to accommodate the single 60–90-minute-format piece – which has the advantage of requiring no extensive set changes. The prevalence of this format can, though, have the negative effect of pressuring choreographers to double the natural length of a work simply to sell it to a venue.

The Choreography

But, of course, any good choreographer is making most of the important decisions about how the work is put together. The internal structure – the building-up of dance phrases, the evolution of pattern and imagery, the contrasts of speed and scale, the balancing of numbers and forces – is ultimately what we look at when we judge the design of a work.

When we do, however, there are few rules to go by. For it's an obvious truth that a design which holds one piece together might collapse in another. Even though four hours of slow ritual may be crucial to the intensity of Pina Bausch's *1980*, in lesser pieces it may be simply mind-numbing. Even though repetition may induce a deeply pleasurable trance in a piece by Lucinda Childs, it may in another context put us to sleep. Even though dense activity in one work may be thrilling, it may bring on a migraine in another; though extreme contrasts may be energizing, they may also seem unsatisfyingly restless. There are no certainties that determine what makes a good structure.

Balanchine, for instance, claimed that 'The structure of a ballet must be tight, like the structure of a building. Good ballets move in a measured space and time like the planets.' Yet he was describing the ideal pursued by his own works, and neither Bausch's *Nelken* nor Meredith Monk's *Juice* nor DV8's *Strange Fish* (1992) fit this bill. They are far more leisurely, crammed and chaotic – but there are many who consider them masterpieces.

And what about Cunningham's Events, where extracts from existing works are stitched together into a collage and performed as 90 minutes of seamless dance? Obviously there's no over-arching coherent structure here – yet in a really successful Event the structures that hold together the individual modules of dance act as an internal magnetic force that pulls the whole Event into some kind of shape.

Given the confusing range of contemporary dance aesthetics, is there any general conclusion to be drawn about the way we read a structure as successful or not? Probably we're more conscious of bad design – when we feel that a passage has gone on too long, or that a climax has been swamped in too much busyness; or that an ending has tailed away. In a work like MacMillan's *Mayerling* we're certainly aware that the ballet is straining at the seams to accommodate its sprawling narrative, taking in court intrigue, Rudolf's syphilis and drug addiction, his involvement with revolutionary politics as well as all his disintegrating relationships with women.

When we're conscious of a strong or pleasing structure in a work, it may feel like a shape – a series of sharp peaks and troughs, a high plateau or a symmetrical curve. Or as Edwin Denby often described it, a rhythm. By that I think he meant a pressure that not only binds individual phrases together but also sustains the piece as it moves through slow and fast sections and through contrasts of action – so that the work feels more than the sum of its parts.

A strong dance rhythm can also be felt as a tug on our expectations. Cunningham, for instance, has often dispensed with conventional notions of structure by having the curtain rise on a stageful of moving dancers and, after 20 minutes or so, lowering it while they're still busy. The work seems like a window opened on to some much longer event.

But if they have no beginnings, endings or climaxes, Cunningham's works do have an internal rhythm that's like an ebbing and flowing of energy. And there's often a moment towards the end which feels like the reverse of the stillness that falls just before a thunderstorm. Our eye suddenly takes in the fact that the dancers are massing on stage, like bees ready to swarm. The dance seems to be gathering all of its force together to focus on its last few images.

Great Endings

Whether a work ends on a question mark or a climax, it's crucial that the choreographer doesn't just seem to have run out of ideas, because it's the ending that sticks with us when we leave the theatre (especially as we can't return to certain passages, as we might with a book or record).

Composers have it easier than choreographers when it comes to producing their final thrills, since a large orchestra can make a great deal of noise for minutes on end and musical endings can carry on climaxing for ever. But all the big dance effects like jumps, turns, lifts, and so on, are over in seconds. It's hard for dance to sustain those same bombastic final gestures.

Some choreographers, though, have a talent for them. For instance it isn't easy to remain seated for the last moments of Mark Morris's *L'Allegro*, as the company of dancers sweep across the stage, and the close of his *Grand Duo* (1993) is also breathtaking. Fourteen dancers have been circling the stage, stamping their feet and slapping their bellies and thighs in a wild urgent ritual during which the build-up of force is phenomenal, and when the dancers suddenly stop the release leaves us shaking.

An equally unforgettable, if more distressing, *coup de théâtre* is Lloyd Newson's horrifying ending for *Dead Dreams* – where a murder victim is left hanging upside-down from a meat hook.

But nineteenth-century ballets are also good at endings. They put everyone in the ballet on stage for a huge procession or marriage, as in *Sleeping Beauty*; or they whisk lovers off to heaven in a magical bit of stage machinery as in *Swan Lake*. They have temples collapsing and bodies falling as in *Bayadère*; or they boldly strip the stage to one single anguished figure as in *Giselle*.

In this century Cranko mimicked this effect at the ending for his ballet *Onegin* where Tatiana is left contemplating the enormity of her loss after dismissing Onegin from her life for ever. Ashton did something similar when he had Natalia Petrovna gazing into her bleak future after the departure of Beliaev in *A Month in the Country*. For ever afterwards we remember these ballets through the simple, concentrated pain of their endings.

But the conclusion imposed by Prokofiev's score for *Romeo and Juliet* is a tough one to manage. The music unwinds with lovely but painful slowness to a cathartic close – yet all the choreographer has to play with is one corpse and a dying girl. In MacMillan's version Juliet has to drag her bleeding body most of the way round the stage before finally being allowed to die in a beautiful slow-motion backbend. A charismatic dance actress can invest this drawn-out finale with agonizing tension; a less powerful performance may be unable to quiet the small cynical voice in our heads that says this is a very long-winded and inefficient way to expire.

When a choreographer walks into the studio for the first rehearsal, he or she will have a group of dancers, possibly a plot or score, and possibly an outline structure to work with. Perhaps straight away, or perhaps after painful thought, a body will be sculpted into its first shape, or the first step or gesture will be demonstrated. Slowly (it takes on average an hour of studio time to create a minute of finished dance) the steps will get built into phrases, and the phrases will get built into patterns.

SHAPES

When Richard Alston speaks of sculpting his dancers' bodies into shapes it might seem that he's much more limited in the forms he can create than painters or sculptors, who can chisel or draw whatever enters their imagination. For although the bodies of individual dancers can vary from the knobbly to the curved, from the elongated to the squat, the basic design of men and women remains the same.

Yet every dance language stylizes the body so that its potential for creating different shapes is maximized. The turned-out positions of classical ballet can encompass a whole airy geometry of lines and curves. The scrunched-up rolls and thrusting angles of early modern dance can turn the body into hewn granite and beaten metal. The fleeting images in Cunningham's movement can make bodies look like birds, insects, animals or streaks of paint. The functional simplicity of 60s minimalism can make us look again at the ordinary mystery of the human form.

Not only can choreographers mould one dancer's limbs into stars, spirals and a variety of animal forms, they can also make more complex shapes by balancing one dancer on top of another or combining several dancers into huge body sculptures. The American company Pilobolus and its offshoot Momix, for instance, have evolved an entire choreographic genre by turning their dancers into shape-changers.

Their work demonstrates the variety of forms that a few bodies can create – particularly when aided by the magic of modern lighting and fabric. Joined at shoulder and hip, a couple of dancers can become a giant hermit crab emerging from its shell, sculpted in light, they can become an exquisite flower, and transformed by yards of billowing material, they become a jellyfish.

Moses Pendleton's *Bonsai* (1980) is a classic of the genre. The stage opens in darkness with the thin strains of Japanese flute music playing. As light slowly dawns, the audience sees two giant fungi on stage which only reveal themselves as two women crouching on the shoulders of two men when the dancers begin to move. From here the four performers stretch their arms into delicate curves like the branches of espaliered trees, their hands join and flutter to become the petals of an enormous flower, then they regroup again into something like a couple of hunch-backed giraffes.

This concentrated image-making takes to an extreme the body's magical power to transform itself. It's a brightly coloured version of the mystery of classical dance where a dancer can become purely an Arabesque, a Leap or a Turn. It's the reason why a tribal hunting dance can turn a man into either hunter or prey, or why a whirling dervish can spin his body into a conductor for the gods' power.

PHRASES

Most choreographers, though, aren't content with making static shapes – they set their bodies in complex motion with steps or movements. And just as few poets write in single-word sentences, or few composers present their listeners with a jumble of disparate notes, so most choreographers build steps into phrases.

A phrase essentially is what links separate moves so that they

form a logical, pleasing or expressive shape. It extends the possibilities of the individual step by combining it with others. It allows
the dance to move through space, enlarge its scale and complicate
its design.

A phrase begins with a movement impulse, like the first release
of a singer's breath, and ends when that impulse has run its
course.

A good dancer can display the shape of a dance phrase clearly.
A great dancer, like a great singer or actor, can illuminate the
phrase by adding a personal stress of his or her own (see Chapter
Ten: Viewing the Dancers).

Identifying the Dance Phrase

As a rule, we don't watch dance as a series of separate phrases.
But certain phrases may stick out sharply from the larger dance
pattern, and strike us in different ways. We may notice a phrase
as a pattern of rhythms (as in tap or flamenco), or as a sudden
acceleration of scale (like a series of little jumps that progresses
into an explosive leap). We may sometimes see a phrase as a
series of evolving shapes in a dancer's limbs, or we may see it as
pure energy – where we see a line of movement taking a walk
through the body.

Most often a phrase takes in all these elements. It's a small
journey that takes the body somewhere into space, gives it
rhythms and shapes to play with, then leaves it at a point where
another phrase can efficiently take over.

A good phrase will turn individual movements into images
or set up a chemistry between steps. But, of course, different
choreographers make phrases as variously as writers make sentences. Jiri Kylian, director and choreographer of Nederlands
Dans Theater, can spin his steps up into long, near-seamless skeins
of dance, so even where he uses a sharp gesture or a sudden shift
of direction, each action seems like an inevitable consequence
of what's gone before. This fluency flatters Kylian's dancers
immensely; their bodies rarely snag on awkward transitions or
get caught in clumsy shapes; their momentum neither drags nor
becomes hyperactive.

But the problem with extreme fluency is that ideas can drown in it. Bad choreographers who have the knack of spinning movements effortlessly out of each other can be as oily and dull as a glib rhetorician. So while we may love those choreographers who make dancers' bodies look beautiful and fluent, we also prize those who yoke their ideas together with violence, whose images fizz with the force of their contradictory energy. We're thrilled by the danger of Balanchine having a man slide to the floor and, from his precariously prone position, swivel his ballerina's leg as she turns in *arabesque*. We grin at the cheek of British choreographer Lea Anderson stitching her dancers' feet through a nifty Scottish jig even while their arms undulate with the passionate curves of flamenco. And we are awed by Graham, who in her finest works could seem to batter the human body with gestures that yanked and twisted it in different directions.

PATTERNS

Out of single phrases choreographers build the larger patterns that turn dance into architecture, geometry, landscape, image and music. Steps are distributed between different dancers, allowing the choreography to travel along more elaborate flight paths, while lines and shapes evolve into moving sculpture, and rhythms cross and multiply.

The kinds of patterns that dance can construct are infinite – from basic circles, squares, diagonals and daisy chains to closely twined groups and the intricate mechanisms beloved of a choreographer like Mark Morris.

A typical instance of the ingenuity that goes into Morris's dance construction occurs in *Behemoth* (1990). Fourteen dancers are divided into two groups on each side of the stage and all perform the same seven-beat phrase. They're all, however, moving out of sync with each other, and in little subgroups they're also travelling along different paths, like a loop or a zigzag. What we see is thus a symmetrical structure of 2×7 dancers that actually contains fourteen people doing completely different things. What we also see are fourteen lanky, plump, short or tall individuals bound briefly together within a perfect machine. The dance gives us a glimpse of an impossible unity, an ideal communion of ordinary bodies and souls.

In Act II of *Swan Lake* the *corps* moves in apparently simple patterns – double circles that spiral out to form parallel lines. But where different groups of dancers are performing different movements the effect is of a mass of tick-tocking shapes and rhythms, of richly textured surfaces reflecting light and shade. When the dancers flock back into unison it's like seeing the reflection on wind-ruffled water calming into a clear image.

Often dance patterns may parallel devices in musical composition. Choreographers may create visual counterpoint, where the movements of two or more dancers interweave like two melodies. They may set up a ground bass of repeating steps against which one or more soloists dance their own melodic line. They may create the equivalent of progressive key changes as the same phrase is danced facing different directions or with subtle alterations of scale.

The building of complex dance figures works a profound transformation on movement. While we still see individual steps clearly, they also become cogs in a larger puzzle, and as we try to work out the puzzle, we keep getting new views of the steps.

Paradoxically the more rigorous the patterns underpinning the dance are, the more random the finished result can look. When Twyla Tharp was making *After 'Suite'* in 1969 she recorded in a notebook all of the ambitiously schematic rules that she'd used to set her dancers in motion. For example: 'Canon, with two dancers moving at very quick tempo, the third doing the movement slow motion. The slow-motion dancer "bumps" one of the fast dancers and they reverse roles; the process repeats again and again as they pass the movement back and forth like a sort of relay baton.'

Though the entire dance was composed out of such complex mechanisms, the movement actually appeared to critics in the audience to be 'mysteriously arbitrary' and 'brilliantly irrational to the eye'.

DANCING WITH NUMBERS

Another system for building large dance structures is duplicating numbers. When only one dancer is moving we view that dancer as an individual, and we respond to the way his or her body and personality gel with the choreography. But when two or more dancers perform the same steps, then the dance becomes a force that binds them. The choreography becomes bigger than the dancer.

With small numbers, unison dancing can focus differences in the performers even as it unites them. In an early duet by Anne Teresa De Keersmaeker called *Fase* (1982) two women swung through identical dance patterns to a repeating score by Steve Reich. As they strode along geometric pathways, swinging their arms and twisting their bodies (the dance was hard physical work), they looked like twin prisoners of the movement's logic. Yet at the same time they emerged as individuals exhilarated by the choreography's challenge and competing with each other to outface its rigour – De Keersmaeker tense and apocalyptic, her partner Michelle Anne de Mey more buoyant and yielding.

With large numbers dancers become much more abstract. We see them less as people than as pumping legs, curving arms and bending bodies. Of course, within the group we may still zoom in on individuals either dancing their hearts out or getting things wrong. Yet we also remain conscious of the larger pattern, the collective act.

When dance becomes multiple its various elements, rhythm, shape and line, are distilled into powerful forces. And it's with these that choreographers often paint their boldest compositions, for bodies moving *en masse* can carry a huge dramatic and visual charge.

Nijinska's *Noces*, for instance, ranks as one of the great dance designs of the century, with the individuality of its dancers almost violently subdued into massed pyramids, wedges and staggered lines. Martha Graham's *Steps in the Street* drills its dancers into a collective social force. The hair-raising power of Morris's *Grand Duo* is achieved by fourteen dancers pounding the same rhythmic path, the choreography knitting them into a primitive tribe with a power far more terrifying than the sum of their individual selves. Béjart created one of the most massive *coups de théâtre* in the repertoire when in *Kabuki* (1986) he had forty-seven samurais commit ritual suicide in one collective stab. Tharp's *Upper Room* seems at its climax to be crammed with so many drumming, wheeling dancers that the space can barely contain them.

But in the nineteenth century Petipa could unleash an equally lethal energy in his *corps* of ghostly Wilis in *Giselle* as they crossed the stage in tiny, chugging hops, their arms and legs stretched in the drifting line of a Romantic *arabesque*. Generally this movement is used to register an airy beauty. But the force of their numbers here makes them a deadly army, ready to crush whatever lies in their path. When, mid-phrase, they all sweep in their extended legs and change weight, circling their arms and tilting their heads, it is a collective hiking-up of fury. And later, when doomed Hilarion and Albrecht separately beg for mercy, a gesture of refusal ripples down a diagonal of angry women, each one in rapid succession averting her face and pressing down her palms in a signal of death.

This is the *corps de ballet* knit into a single poetic image and a single visual design. But a magnificently schooled *corps* will also display its own technical greatness even as it collectively paints the lines and images of the ballet. When the Kirov dances *Swan Lake* on a good night, its *corps* can look like a single dancer reflected in a hall of mirrors. Because the dancers have been schooled from infancy in the same tradition, they appear to hear the music as one, phrase their movements as one, and even look as one – with their uniformly long, sway-backed legs, delicately braced arms, modestly sloping shoulders and tilted heads (see illus. 4).

In a Busby Berkeley chorus the dancers are a crowd of smiling, ruddy-cheeked chorus girls who've become identical cogs in a single dance machine. It's a marvellous optical illusion. But with the Kirov *corps*, as with any great ballet company, we see something more. We see history, tradition and continuity. We see the essence of Style.

Non-dancers are often bewildered by the accuracy with which thirty-two people can move in time with each other. Apart from intensive drilling in rehearsal, the trick in performance is for every dancer to follow the one in front; to make sure that each step is danced at exactly the right angle (for instance, facing front or diagonal right), and to keep an eye on the small taped crosses that mark out the geography of the stage.

Nothing, however, can prevent the occasional mistake, which always looks more disastrous in a group dance than a solo. Members of the Royal Ballet *corps* once shared some of their worst horror stories with me, which included the performance of *Giselle* where the Wilis were all *bourréeing* backwards off the stage, looking beautifully like blown mist, and the last dancer got her headdress stuck so that her head was left protruding out of the wings, tugging frantically to get free. Or the Swan who mistimed a cue and launched into the centre of the stage by herself and then had to make a panic dash for cover. Or the group dance in Act I of the same ballet where the women were meant to circle the men and be lifted by each in turn but got out of rhythm, so that some men ended up with four women to lift and some had none.

REPETITION

Where large numbers of dancers perform a steady recycling of the same few movements, then dance becomes a ritual, an incantation of forces. The most famous instance of this is the opening of the Shades Act in *Bayadère* where the vision of around three dozen dancers executing the same sequence of walks and *arabesques* over and over again can make a single moment expand in time and space until it seems to engulf us.

Contemporary minimalists have tried hard to achieve the same effect. In fact, ever since American choreographer Laura Dean set her dancers spinning serenely round and round the stage in the early 70s, trance has become one of the major experiences of modern dance.

Ideally, this is a trance that induces clarity. As the audience sees the same moves over and over, with only minute variations, it comes to know their shapes and stresses intensely. Choreographers who can keep the dance pressure constant and whose movements are essentially interesting can make this experience a revelation rather than a bore. For instance, in her 1986 piece *Typhoon*, the Hungarian choreographer Krisztina de Châtel achieved both calm clarity and intense drama.

In the work's opening section five dancers tracked back and forth across the stage, their arms swinging, their bodies arching and dropping with serene regularity. But variables were then introduced so that the dancers began moving at slightly different speeds and began to lag behind or overtake each other. And in the last section the work's calm was violently disrupted by three huge wind machines which sent howling torrents of air through the dance. As the performers struggled to maintain their patterns, their movement became alive with imagery, the lift of their bodies had the exhilaration of birds in flight, their arms became whirling propellers, their roles changed from efficient dancing machines into small people fighting the forces of nature.

In the work of Bausch or De Keersmaeker repetition often creates an overwhelming image of pain and imprisonment as dancers force their bodies through the same helpless falls or the same doomed embraces. But repetition can also be liberating. When a single dancer performs the same movement over and over again, it can translate into an image of perfect form and even endow him or her with a shamanistic power.

The obvious example of this is Odile when she spins through her thirty-two *fouettés* in Act III of *Swan Lake*. At one level the performing ballerina is no longer herself or the character but simply the movement (a supporting leg that pumps through each turn, a working leg that whips the foot in to the knee and out again). But at another level she is Odile endowed with magical potency – hypnotizing the court and Siegfried with each mesmerizing spin, transfixing us with the witchy smile and focused glare that keep whipping in and out of view. (Of course, the *fouettés* have to be near-perfect to sustain this illusion. When they are not, the ballerina is horribly herself, fighting to keep her turns from straying across the stage, fighting to stop her supporting leg from buckling with exhaustion, fighting to keep the working leg aloft – fighting for her dignity.)

Modern choreographers rarely use that kind of intense

repetition for show – but Graham in particular always loved its dramatic effect. Time and again her heroines slash through the same driving kick or huddle into the same anguished jump (torsos bent, arms thrust down between their thighs, legs splayed in a stiff V-shaped leap). The repetition of the steps winds the emotion up to an unbearable pitch.

STILLNESS, SPACE, RHYTHM AND TIME

The choreographer's raw material isn't, though, just the flesh and blood Plasticine of the dancers' bodies. The patterns made in a dance aren't simply created by the interlocking of moving limbs. Elements that are less tangible, like stillness, space, rhythm and time, are also vital to the drama and composition of dance.

Stillness

Without stillness the driving, brilliant, wayward, witty, sexual energy of dance would collapse in on itself. Despite being a physical art form, dance depends on stillness to create some of its most magical effects.

It's stillness, for instance, that defines most virtuoso dance moments: the leap that hangs in the air; the balance that extends for seconds beyond its natural limits; the turns that spin so fast the body seems to freeze; the lightning footwork which the dancer is able to execute with a divine calm. It's stillness too that gives extra resonance to a phrase – when we see a movement welling up from somewhere in the deep quiet of the body and then playing itself out into thin air.

It's stillness, finally, that defines a great performance. When we can feel the whole of the dancers' energy and imagination concentrated in their gaze and when the movement seems to come from a still centre, then performers most convince us that they are drawing on special forces.

Very different dancers confirm this. Indian classical dancer Unnikrishnan says, 'In my technique stillness is a statement of strength. You can create stillness with your eyes even when you're moving, just by looking at a particular point. If I'm dancing a god, I may hold a gesture or raise my leg and remain still, and that makes me very powerful. I'm completely in control.' Julyen Hamilton, a British dancer who improvises movement during performance, talks about stillness as a 'quality of the mind and the body that ideally you always carry with you ... if you can tap into that stillness, it seems to stimulate movement from a much deeper and more universal source.'

Stillness is also a way for choreographers to manipulate our attention. When Petipa masses the stage with densely patterned movements he always freezes the final picture, as if turning up the lights, so that his audience can marvel at his invention. Lea Anderson also regards the stillness between movement 'as much a tool as the movement itself'. It's an essential way of letting her audience register the designs in her choreography.

Anderson also plays with different effects in stillness. 'If you have one person who is still while everyone else is dancing [that dancer can either be] focused on the other dancers so you hardly notice them. Or they can charge their stillness with something that makes you have to look at them. That can make you very uncomfortable.'

That discomfort is one, among several, effects which Paul Taylor was aiming for when he made *Duet* in 1957. Following the Dadaist logic of John Cage's composition for silence *4'33"* Taylor made a dance where the performers hardly moved. By stripping them of complex movement and kinetic dazzle Taylor gave his audience little to look at other than the body's basic form.

Space

Space isn't simply a neutral area where the dance takes place. Like the stillness between movements, it's part of the dance itself. It's both the canvas and the paint; it's the air it breathes. In fact, choreographers talk as much about space as they do about the bodies that move around it.

Movement takes up room and it exists in relation to all the space around it. It dramatizes the air. So when dancers race across the stage, as at the end of Mark Morris's *L'Allegro*, the exhilaration of their movement isn't due just to the energy with which they spring off the music or cut across each other's path – it's also due to the fact that the space seems as turbulent and resistant as their bodies. We can almost see wind streaming through the dancers' hair, can feel them breast the air like swimmers ploughing through water.

Alternatively when a dancer hangs for several heartbeats in a high *jeté*, the space takes on a different character – it seems momentarily to become a cushion or a cloud on which the dancer rests. When Anne Teresa De Keersmaeker's women whip their limbs around in a collective fury, you feel they are slicing the surrounding air into tatters. When dancers become still, there can be a profound feeling of the air settling round them, forming a halo that both illuminates and resonates with their stillness.

Space is, of course, the background against which we see the movement's line and pattern – but ideally it is never inert. It is full of extensions and echoes of the choreography. One of the concepts basic to the Japanese martial art Ki Aikido is that strength comes from letting energy flow through and beyond each limb, not from tensing the muscles and short-circuiting their power. The fighter aims for a spot inches beyond his slicing foot.

In dance too a movement shouldn't stop at the fingertips or the toes but radiate beyond them. As it travels, it also leaves invisible trace lines hanging in the air. When a leg circles from front to back, we can almost see the curve it's travelled; when dancers whip through multiple turns we can nearly visualize the speed rings whizzing round their bodies. When a passage of fast footwork is executed, the tracery of invisible echoes may glitter among the visible movements. This play of invisible lines exaggerates the speed, the light and shade, the sculptural depth of movement. (It's one reason why, in the more inert space of film and television, dance looks so much tamer.)

Space also connects the dancers – it is the arena into which they project emotion and movement. Wary, fearful or resistant body language may make the air between dancers a solid wall, while dancing that is tender or yearning will make it hum. One of the most poignant aspects of Tudor's choreography for Hagar in *Pillar of Fire* is that she not only dances alone but also seems to move in a pocket of inviolate space. MacMillan's Manon, by extreme contrast, is aware with every pore of other people's eyes and bodies – the space between her and every man on stage is electric with desire and display.

Dancers talk of how they can project emotional responses even if they are standing with their backs turned – and once they turn to face us, their gaze can cut through distance as if it was butter. There is a moment in MacMillan's *Romeo and Juliet* where Juliet sits in the exposed centre of the stage playing a mandolin for her guests and for Romeo in particular. When Darcey Bussell performs this role, she can at this moment seem to shrink inside her (actually) very powerful body, looking tiny, startled and lost within the huge space. But at the same time the dark, hungry beam of her eyes gobbles up the distance between her and Romeo, in Juliet's unconscious anticipation of their embrace.

Obviously when dancers start to move they can vary the force of their dancing so that it projects a wide range of messages across space – a lifted leg might strike at the air between dancers, or it may yearn. Tudor creates a terrible image of loss in his *Dark Elegies* (1937), for instance, simply by having the women dancers gently cradle empty air with their arms, in anguished memory of the dead children lamented in Mahler's *Kindertotenlieder*.

Even when dancing has no dramatic motive it can charge the space by the power of its composition. When dancers connect in lively ways (picking up on each other's movements or forming compelling patterns) our watching eye travels busily between them, tracing a composition out of the bodies and the air between. If, however, they don't connect, or do so in predictable or awkward ways, our eye loses interest, we're more likely to watch just one dancer or to let our gaze drift. Space becomes dead air in the same way that dull background in a painting is no more than blank canvas.

Merce Cunningham is, however, a master at animating space. One of the most distinctive features of his work is that it has no central focus – the stage is filled with different competing activities. The space enclosing his dancers becomes peculiarly alive and elastic as it seems to contract around a single duet, then grow more spacious to accommodate a larger group, and then physically shift to where a flock of dancers is entering. Cunningham can do this because he draws our eyes around the stage so deftly. We think we are focusing intently on one activity, but some echo, some rhythm on the edge, cues us to look elsewhere. Our gaze is constantly tracking around the stage.

Cunningham's dancers can also, individually, appear to occupy a lot of space or very little. They can be doing small complicated steps on the spot, then suddenly launch into a long-distance flurry of jumps. In fact, the way that any dancer occupies space is an important key to his or her style. English classical dancers have always been contrasted with Russian or American dancers because they take up less room – their movements are smaller; they dance under themselves rather than striking out; they are brilliant rather than bold.

American dancers may often move with the exploratory thrust of pioneers, striding over the ground, pressing forward into space, taking it up by right. Baryshnikov in his prime, though, was the king of upper space, the air. His buoyant elevation and his ability to ornament and complicate his jumps mid-flight gave him the momentary look of a swallow diving and fluttering above the audience's heads.

Indian dance forms like Bharatha Natyam, by contrast, press down into the floor and though the dancer's limbs often stretch wide from the body, they rarely strike out into space like those of Western dancers. The movement is activated in the air immediately surrounding the body; the interest is focused on details in the hands, face and feet. These are miniature dance moments that would be lost if the movement had to travel huge distances.

Rhythm

Dance isn't just an art form composed in space, it also plays with rhythm and time. In fact, for many people it is rhythm – a juicy contrast of stress and release, a steady pulse, or sophisticated syncopation – that most excites them in dance. Sometimes the rhythm is created purely by the dancers' movements; sometimes it is a combination of music and dance. In an ensemble like Les Ballets Africains the rhythms of the thirty-two drummers and dancers can give audiences a near-overdose of adrenalin as the drummers' fusillade of percussion is pitted against lines of fiercely stamping, chugging dancers. So absolute is the resulting rhythm that our hearts pump and our bodies beat time. We are physically charged up to join in – which is why most social dances have such powerful basic rhythms. They are a call to arms and legs.

The rhythms of a dance may start out as the basic beat of the feet – the one-two-three step of the waltz; the shuffle-hop step of tap. But these 'time signature' rhythms are then amplified, given texture and variety by everything else that's happening in the body. In Black African dances the spine may be rippling, the pelvis rocking and the arms pumping in complicated cross rhythms, while the beat of the foot may vary from a flat shuffling against the floor to a heel lifted in a crisp upbeat.

In classical Indian dance the glances of the eyes, the poses of the arms and the gestures of the hands are all performed to strict counts so that the body is alive with rhythmic detail. In ballet the sharp accents of the feet are embellished by milder rhythms in the arms and by the over-arching climaxes of balances or jumps.

In Graham's choreography we may see rhythm simply as an elemental, emotional force that tugs at the dancer's body – as in her early solo *Lamentation*.

Often the rhythms in the dancer's body give a physical juice to the music that accompanies them, which would be lacking if the score was only heard. When we can actually *see* the downbeat of the music as a thrust of the dancer's leg, or an upbeat as a jump, then rhythm becomes a muscular force. (During the Ball Scene in MacMillan's *Romeo and Juliet*, Prokofiev's music acquires a brute menace as the Capulet family move to it in drilled forma-tion – their feet stamping down in tribal triumph on the first pummelling stress of every bar.)

When dance plays *against* the music it can also create visual and aural wit. A breezy jump seen against a heavy stress in the music becomes a passing paradox of lightness and weight. When a movement freezes instead of continuing its expected path through the score we almost see and hear a skipped heartbeat. It is the play of dance rhythm against music rhythm that breathes air and light into their relationship.

Rhythm also underlines important features of dance style. In minimalism it's the movement's hypnotic pulse that makes the choreography more than a dull recycling of steps. In Giselle's solos it's the light, upward lilt of her jumps and skips that makes them evoke vulnerability rather than empty prettiness. In Indian dance it's the complex maths of the footwork that generates much of the performance's visceral excitement. In Graham's *Steps in the Street* it's the brusque machine rhythms of the movement that clinch her vision of imprisoning social forces; while in Cunningham's choreography it's the witty, irregular beats of the steps that emphasize their sharpness.

Time

It is rhythm too that allows choreographers to play with Time – to drive it forward, freeze it or make it race. Generally dance performances compress time. A narrative ballet can encompass years within three acts, a 20-minute piece by Cunningham involves dancers in more physical activity than most people attempt in a week. But individual dance works also occupy their own distinctive time. Much of Tudor's *Jardin aux lilas*, for instance, occupies the solid 'present tense' of a formal garden party. But this public time also stalls, freezes and harks backwards when the focus shifts to the characters' inner time and reveals their fantasies, fears and desires.

In Graham's *Deaths and Entrances* time is elastic, so that past and present can exist simultaneously or rapidly alternate, while in Ashton's *Scènes de Ballet* (1948) the ballet occupies a continuous present that is formal time rather than narrative time. When the dance rhythm is fast, actual clock time flies, while at other moments it seems to be stilled within the calm geometries of the choreography.

During the 60s and 70s choreographers like Trisha Brown and British minimalist Rosemary Butcher started to try and put dance back into real time. They performed their movements without artificial dance stress, so that a walk might amble across the stage just as it would across a street; a roll might tumble with comfortable slowness; a gesture might be the most unemphatic of shrugs.

This was all part of their larger commitment to de-stylizing the dancing body, making movement look functional and ordinary. But the real time they sought wasn't quite the result. Butcher's works were so beautifully contemplative that they moved into 'art-gallery time' where viewers could gaze at gently moving bodies, then stray into their own thoughts, secure that the work wouldn't advance far without them.

But if sustained real time is impossible in the theatre, the use of momentary real time remains an important option for a choreographer who needs to puncture an illusion or shift the tone of the work. In DV8's *Strange Fish*, dancer Wendy Houstoun expressed her character's anguish by thrashing her body painfully among a heap of white stones. She couldn't hurry her actions but had to negotiate the stones' hardness for real. It looked, and probably was, excruciating.

In Bill T. Jones's *Still Here* (1994), a work about life lived under the threat of terminal illness, there were sections where real patients appeared on video screens talking about their experiences. What defined their realness was the fact that within the work's artfully patterned surface of dance and music their hesitant, chuckling or panicky testimonies moved with the stop–start rhythms of actual life.

Moments like these highlight the fact that even apparently naturalistic dance movements, like mimed gestures, are usually performed in dance time rather than real time, usually to create maximum eloquence. In Bausch's *Nelken* we're given a comic and definitive insight into the role that timing plays on gesture. The piece opens with a man reciting the lyrics of the song 'I'm Looking For The Man I Love' and also 'signing' the words. His gestures are performed in the semi-mime, semi-speech rhythms of sign language and their shapely beauty is haunting. But when the song itself is heard, he has to speed up his gestures to the music. Drilled into a regular beat, the gestures suddenly turn into a comic and rather foolish little hand jive. They dance but they can no longer speak.

Chapter Nine: **IMPROVISATION**

Usually decisions about steps, rhythm, phrasing, structure, and so on, are made in the studio and the dance is finalized into a choreographic 'text' that is learnt by the dancers. When the public go to see the work in the theatre they expect it to look pretty much the same from one performance to the next. Certainly if Romeo and Juliet decided to skip the balcony scene one night, or the dancers in Balanchine's *Agon* got in the mood for some slow waltzing, we'd feel something was seriously wrong.

In the 60s and 70s, though, many choreographers and dancers began to argue that the nightly performance of routine steps drained their art of its creativity. Where, they questioned, was the input from the performers, where was the excitement for the audience? Where was the freshness of the dance? If, on the other hand, they improvised rather than recycled the same familiar steps, both dancers and audience might be launched on an interesting if risky voyage of discovery. Their relationship would no longer be that of product and consumer but of fellow travellers.

Within a generation the idea of dancers being their own choreographers became current. Performers became hooked on inventing their own movement – not simply developing a personal style, but discovering techniques for spontaneously generating one movement out of the next. A British handbook published in 1990 by Miranda Tufnell and Chris Crickmay called *Body Space Image* describes improvisation as 'a means to excavating layers of experience, sensation, character and feeling that we normally rush through or suppress'. And its authors outline several exercises or 'Bone Meditations' through which dancers can sensitize themselves to the range of movement within their bodies – 'imagining a liquid space in each of the joints . . . a brightness at the breast bone'.

Exercises in improvisation can be a wonderful discipline for dancers – giving them an alert understanding of their bodies and also making them responsive when working with choreographers. (Dancers who can only follow set routines may be less confident about contributing ideas to new work.) But physical meditation doesn't necessarily make interesting dance. As the British improviser Laurie Booth readily admits, 'There are people who can make dances out of their kidney and liver, but in the theatre all they do is raise burning issues of boredom.'

So when does improvisation become a solitary descent into physical narcissism and when does it spark into a performance? Obviously a performer with an arresting body, a versatile technique and a compelling personality has a significant advantage. But these need to be harnessed to quick wits, a steady nerve and an ability, as Booth says, to 'thrive on insecurity'.

Like many improvisers, Booth himself tends to perform within a previously established structure, which might be created by a score, a lighting plan or a scheme of ideas. There is a work, in the sense that a run of performances share the same aim, personality and a history. But unlike a choreographed dance, the moment-by-moment material is spun out of nowhere, so that every time the work is performed its details will vary.

Nancy Stark Smith, who's been revered as a guru within the American improvisation scene, refers to this nowhere as 'the Gap'. It is 'where you are when you don't know where you are and it is one of the most precious spots offered by improvisation'. It's through the Gap that 'you find the unexpected, sought-after original material'.

British dancer Julyen Hamilton refers to this Gap as a stillness. It's a combination of centredness and heightened awareness in which artists make themselves open to all the surrounding stimuli – their own body, the audience, the lighting, the sounds on stage, the actions of other dancers – and which simultaneously feeds them into dance.

In Booth's performances we may often see the movements that spurt round his body as an intense physical tussle between gravity and energy – balancing in a handstand, he'll twist like an eel back on to his feet and plunge into a wide, deep lunge, then, as if arrested by a sudden idea or emotion, he'll switch down the voltage of the movement, his body collecting itself into a pool of calm, the energy ebbing away through a gentle scrolling of one hand. In a good performance the workings of both his mind and his body have been laid in front of us, and we feel that we've entered an intimate relationship. We know who this dancer is, what choices he's making, what risks he's taking, what mood he's in.

When Booth performs with a group, then their collective skills can pitch the thrill of improvisation to an even higher level, though, of course, the potential for mistakes is also increased. If the dancers don't read each other's moves quickly enough, then one may try to fly into space just as another reaches out to pin him in a hold; or a couple may launch into some mutual rolypoly manoeuvre that just ends in a tangle of arms and legs.

But as any professional risk taker knows, whether they be trapeze artists or jugglers, it's the possibility of failure that makes success look so chancily perfect. For audiences it is very pleasurable to see bodies tumble riotously together and somehow resolve into a pure balance, to see mass energy suddenly shaped into clear form, to see a passing brushing of a limb turn into a frankly tender embrace. We know that what we are seeing is unique. It is dance as the perfect unrepeatable moment.

Of course, improvisers can't always sustain a perfect spontaneity. As Booth acknowledges, there are moments when it's impossible not to give in to the temptation of showing off – taking risks for their own sake, finding movements that work and milking them for the audience and basically 'being a cocky bastard'. There are also moments when cheating is inevitable – falling back on to moves that have worked in the past, lapsing into a semi-set routine. Going on to automatic pilot seems particularly attractive / necessary when 'the venue is freezing and there's only three men and a dog in the audience', or in those nightmare moments when you suddenly realize (as Booth did) that your trousers have 'split from the waist to the arse'.

Improvisers are the adrenalin junkies of dance.

Whether a work is set or improvised, it exists only through the dancers who perform it. And for many in the audience, assessing the dancers (their technical triumphs and their personal peculiarities, their glories and their goofs) may give more of a buzz than looking closely at the choreography. When the susceptible ballerina-fancier Théophile Gautier reviewed Fanny Elssler in *The Tempest* in 1837 he unabashedly admitted that the woman herself was of far greater interest than the choreography. 'The literature of legs,' he wrote, 'is hardly a subject for discussion; let us come at once to Fanny Elssler.'

Yet performer and role aren't so easily separated and there's a basic paradox involved in making any dance judgement. Is the dancer good, or is the choreography making them look better than they really are? Is the choreography bad, or the dancer simply inept? How do we tell the dancer from the dance?

Obviously a dancer who can't get his or her body round the choreography (who fudges the lines, blurs the rhythms and fails to capture the poetry of the role) may blind viewers to the choreography's virtues. And a 'star' dancer who appropriates a role as a vehicle for private glory can be just as pernicious. Writing in the 1940s about the virtuoso ballerina Irina Baronova, critic Edwin Denby despaired, brilliantly, of the way she mugged every performance. 'Of her present style I can find nothing good to say. She hams with a heartlessness that is frightening. She ogles, flounces, capers and cuddles, jumps, turns and stands, slamming down each effect like a virago operating a cash register.'

The ideal viewing conditions for a dance may be when it's actually performed by its creator – since so many choreographers either make the movement on themselves or else feed their personal style into it. (Several of Martha Graham's dancers suffered badly from the fact that her technique was constructed around her own wide pelvis and mobile hip joints. Many of her falls, floor exercises and leg movements were and are painful to more narrowly and tightly knit performers.)

Graham herself was the undisputed star exponent of her work. Not only had she forged her entire technique around her body but her work was, until the last stage in her career, fuelled by the hell fires and happinesses of her own life. She thus had the unique emotional and physical intensity to sustain its dramas on stage. In our own time Michael Clark, for instance, remains the only completely satisfying exponent of his choreography – its peculiar languid grace, its mixture of wantonness and abstract purity, all become limpidly clear when he dances.

Mark Morris too brings a completely personal quality to his work when he dances it himself. In terms of pure physique it's hard to imagine someone else with the same voluptuous mix of bulk and delicacy, with the same instinct for the grand gesture and the casual shrug. It's also hard to imagine anyone else with the same maraudingly contradictory personality – able to convey sweetness and violence, abandon and subtlety, rudeness and ecstasy in the span of one short dance.

In 1989 I watched Morris rehearsing Mikhail Baryshnikov in the creation of *Wonderland*. Baryshnikov is one of the most powerful dance intelligences of our time – a star by virtue of his instinctive grasp of whatever style he's dancing and his ability to show it beautifully plain. But though, in this dark Hitchcockian piece, Baryshnikov was latching on to the choreography fast, there were qualities that even he didn't naturally reproduce. Morris was working on a phrase in which Baryshnikov's 'character' had to arch back his head as if about to have his throat slit. When Baryshnikov performed the move it seemed right – a tense, nervous baring of the neck. But when Morris did it, it became something more, a sensuous stretch that seemed an invitation to violence, bringing an unsettling note of depravity and complicity to the moment.

But choreographers may work so intimately with performers that the latter become ideal exponents of their style. Ballets Russes dancer Lydia Sokolova claimed that she responded to the choreography of Leonid Massine in a way that she never did to anyone else's 'because the whole system of it seemed to be part of me'. The same was also true for her colleagues Lydia Lopokova, Leon Woizikovsky and Stanislas Idzikovsky. Sokolova believed they were so well suited to Massine's work that their interpretations 'could never be repeated by anyone else. That is why these perfect ballets, although they are still done, are in a way, *lost*, and when Massine ceased inventing his extraordinary movements for [us] we were lost too, and never did anything so great again.'

Some dancers rise to the status of muses for their choreographers (Margot Fonteyn for Ashton, Lynn Seymour for MacMillan, Suzanne Farrell for Balanchine) – as do whole companies (the Royal Ballet under Ashton's direction, the New York City Ballet during Balanchine's lifetime, Twyla Tharp's company during the late 70s and early 80s). One of the eeriest phenomena that can occur in dance is when we watch one dancer perform a role that was first created intimately on another. Because the choreographer went so deep into the original dancer's style and personality to make the movement (as when Ashton choreographed Titania on Antoinette Sibley), subsequent performers may almost morph back into their predecessor as they dance it – a transmigration of body and soul.

Where a very close relationship exists between choreographer and dancer the performer and the movement can seem to be in each other's spell – encouraging each other to greater invention and lucidity. Sometimes the magic occurs when choreographers are pushing dancers against the natural grain of their training. When Twyla Tharp choreographed the ballet *Push Comes to Shove* (1976) for Baryshnikov it was a love letter from a modern-dance choreographer to a great classical dancer. Describing the process in her autobiography, Tharp tells how she raided Baryshnikov's technique for its virtuoso jumps and turns and then forced him to dance them in a new way, so that the moves 'twisted or lay far back from his supporting leg'. She wove in non-classical elements like syncopated timing and parallel feet. And as Baryshnikov tried to find his way through these physical puzzles, she recalls, 'His solutions were breathtaking. He was learning to manoeuvre round an ever tighter base and the precision and audacity of his leaps and *pirouettes* astonished me.' Baryshnikov cheerfully described the intensive rehearsal process demanded by this as 'a cross between the perfect vacation and being in church'.

Nureyev too was avid for new challenges – the Kirov-trained Prince trying to get his body round the harsh angularities of Graham's style or the bouncing casual grace of Taylor. A different kind of chemistry occurred when Bolshoi-trained Irek Mukhamedov created the lead in *Fearful Symmetries*, choreographed by Royal Ballet-trained Ashley Page. Mukhamedov, renowned for his dramatic eloquence and heroic dancing, may initially have seemed an odd choice of star for a choreographer with no interest in high drama, and with an austere, asymmetrical, speedy style. Yet Mukhamedov brought to Page's choreography a dark and dangerous power, while he himself was galvanized to move in an unusually acerbic and angular manner – his characteristic plushy Soviet jump skewed off centre, his limbs punching ferociously through the air.

All the dancers mentioned above are generally acknowledged to be 'great' artists – but even so there have been Baryshnikov-fanciers who've dismissed the ecstasies of Nureyev fans, just as once balletomanes fought in the streets over the rival claims of Taglioni and Elssler. So what is it that defines a major talent in dance? Where some see grace, others see a pretty pair of legs; where some see technique, others see ego. Taste in dancers can be as subjective as taste in lovers, food or art.

Inescapably, it's a dancer's appearance – his or her physical personality – that impacts first on an audience. A beautiful or extraordinary body attracts as much attention on the stage as in real life, just as a forced smile or a bizarre hairstyle can distract us from a dancer's talent. There are uncomfortable moments when critics and fans suspect themselves of judging dancers like contestants in a beauty competition – lovely legs, shame about the feet; terrible rib cage, but gorgeous arms; smashing mover, but must do something about that flashy grin. We may not sink to the level of those members of the Jockey Club in nineteenth-century Paris who used to scan the *corps de ballet* avidly for new mistress material. But even when the discussion moves to aspects of style or technique, it can still operate close to the level of assessing horse flesh – amazing jump, flexible back and lovely balances, but can't *pirouette* to save her life.

Some dancers become identified with a single aspect of their technique: for instance, Nijinsky with his jump; Taglioni with her point work, and in our own time Sylvie Guillem with her sky-high leg extensions. The public expects to see these stunts at every performance, whatever the work. But great dancers are more than pretty faces and flashy effects. They are performers who make dancing appear a natural form of expression, who make the body look articulate and extraordinary, who can move or startle us with the images they form and above all who make us see the dance clearly. In all of these things it's hard to disentangle a lucky genetic inheritance from a special dance intelligence.

A dancer's line, for instance – the way the body looks, the kind of shapes it naturally makes – is a question both of brute physique and of an instinct for the contours of movement. On the basic physical level, the drastic angles and thrilling verticals of Sylvie Guillem's line are produced by her very long limbs, flexible joints and considerable strength (see illus. 10). From her highly arched feet through to her hyper-extended knee (which sways back slightly rather than jutting forward, so emphasizing the clean line of the leg), to the lean curves of her thighs, her long slender torso, long neck and long, elegant face, Guillem seems almost like an abstract of a human body – totally streamlined for efficiency and clarity. In addition, the near-unfettered movement of her leg in its hip socket, which allows her foot to graze her ear when she lifts it to the side, and the flexibility of her lower back, which almost enables her to fold her body in two as she lifts her leg to the back, make her seem utterly indifferent to the forces of gravity. People gasp when they see her dancing because she seems to have been granted a special exemption from the normal rules of movement.

Less genetically favoured dancers have a harder time creating an illusion of divine ease. A large head or short neck can detract from the image of the dancer floating serenely above a hard-working body; they can make the movements of the head look clumsy, and they can also make the shoulders look strained. Even a jawline that naturally thrusts forward can introduce a discordant angle into the dancer's line.

And so it goes down the body. A barrel chest or jutting ribcage can suggest too much mortal bulk; short legs or an over-long back bring the centre of the body too close to the ground and tip the line of an *arabesque* out of proportion (the leg can't sweep upwards so grandly). Overdeveloped leg muscles make the line less sharp and sweet, and if the foot doesn't have a high, strong arch, the leg also loses that extra quivering length when it's pointed.

And flesh? For many of today's dancers the voluptuous curves favoured by the nineteenth century are out of the question. The struggle towards a streamlined technique combined with a fashionable, androgynous aesthetic, requires bodies that look as if they feed on air and have been purified into mere energy and line.

This image holds much more sway over female classical dancers, where the whole point of the language is to idealize the body and to maximize its lightness and grace. The language of modern dance has traditionally brought dancers back to earth, has emphasized struggle and mortality. It has also celebrated individuality, and the body image of modern dancers has been not only more realistic but also more diverse. Graham's dancers were often sturdily muscled young women; Cunningham's dancers, though often as lean and light as any ballet troupe, have also included older, heavier and more quirkily constructed bodies – Cunningham, after all, still performs in his seventies. And one of the axioms of post-modern dance has been that beauty and grace reside in the most street-ordinary of bodies – gangly, plump, square, short or bald. Mark Morris positively avoids dancers who are ideally skinny (what he calls the 'dead virgin look'), preferring not only the strength but the colourful stage personality of bodies whose individual contours haven't been dieted into conformity. Michael Clark had the magnificently plump Leigh Bowery perform in his works, as well as his own mother Bessie. And for some companies body shape, age and colour are a political as well as an aesthetic issue – the line-up of dancers reflects a conscious decision to feature, say, large women, black dancers or performers over forty, groups who've traditionally been excluded from Western classic dance.

(Age can hone dance to its purest elements. Cunningham's late performances are made luminous by the refinement of rhythm, shape and motive in his movement, and when NYCB dancer Edward Villella was first being coached by Balanchine for the role of *Apollo* he saw the same distillation of style in the latter's steps. Balanchine stopped Villella. 'That's not Apollo, I'll dance it for you.' Then, Villella recalls, 'This man of sixty danced it for me in his suit, wearing loafers and a cowboy tie. He looked regal, like there was an American imperialism in his background, and I was stunned because he wore style. It permeated from his mind; his musicality was extraordinary.')

Even in ballet, which doesn't theoretically favour deviations from the ideal, imperfections can add to, rather than detract from, the dancer's line. In real life the performers we cherish are very individual, and it's often the physical limitations they've had to overcome which force them to develop a unique style – the grit produces the technical pearls. Antoinette Sibley acknowledges that she was never able to equal the dazzlingly high leg extensions of today's dancers. yet even in the 1980s, during the last years of her career, she was still able to produce the rippling, swooning, dipping brilliance of her upper body that had always been her special gift.

Nureyev had a relatively stiff back, but he could still appear to dance with the loose-knit grace of a wild animal because of the easy open carriage of his torso and the peculiarly cushioned power of his jumps. Baryshnikov's teachers feared he was too short to make an ideal classical Prince, but he made up for his literal lack of height with the astonishing airiness, deftness and versatility of his jumps.

One of the most miraculous shape-changers of all time was Vaslav Nijinsky. His body was admittedly blessed with two great advantages. The first was his legs, which were, as his sister Bronislava remarked, 'like a grasshopper's' – very powerful and perfectly constructed for jumping. The second was his arresting stage face – the long slanted eyes and high sculpted cheekbones which facilitated his transformations into the half-human, exotic characters for which he was famous.

But as a physiological arrangement of muscle, bone and flesh, Nijinsky's body was not generally prepossessing for a dancer. His neck was thick, his torso quite bulky and his legs neither long nor slim. Photographs of Nijinsky in street clothes show a rather stocky, even awkward, young man. Yet when he's posing in character, the line of the dance movement animates and transforms his body.

A photograph of him posing next to Tamara Karsavina in *Spectre de la rose* shows him deep in a role in which, as he once said, he had to appear like a 'half-shaped dream' with 'no sex, nor form'. While the energy that presses his tightly crossed legs down into the ground hints at the formidable jumping power of Nijinsky's muscles, his upper body tilts with extreme softness towards the kneeling Karsavina, giving an androgynous look to his stance. This is exaggerated by the expression of eerie sweetness on his elegantly inclined face and by the delicacy with which his arms are angled over his head, his fingers curling as softly and defencelessly as a baby's.

Later photographs of Nijinsky as the Faun show by contrast a fierce tension running through his body, torquing it into flat two-dimensional planes – though even here there is a childlike vulnerability hovering over the back of his bent neck, and a frank sensuality in his opened palms, which suggest the Faun's primitive emotions and his animal naïvety.

The world's greatest dancers – whether they be Fred Astaire or Margot Fonteyn – seem to have an intuitive sense of the right movement. They don't rely on a mirror to judge whether their limbs are in the correct position – they can feel their body's shape. They can judge what kind of tension a phrase requires – where their muscles should be stretched and where they should be softened, where they should suggest repose or where they should look ready for flight. They also seem to occupy space very clearly. Like actors who can throw their voices accurately, they know exactly how and when to project the movement a long way, and when to keep it close and quiet. They dance from the inside out, and it's usually very easy to identify which dancers have this kinaesthetic sixth sense and which don't, whether they are performing ballet, Bharatha Natyam or jazz. Like those rare people who never look bad in photos, these dancers seem unable to strike a false position.

But dance isn't just about the shapes made by the body. It's about rhythm, speed, stillness and attack. And what people gloat over in great dance performances isn't just line, but also phrasing.

Of course, it's the choreographer who creates the basic phrase structure. But it's the dancer's job to show it clearly and also to reveal fresh nuances within it – and some, simply, do this much better than others. Even quite technically proficient dancers can be like awkward drivers who make you jarringly conscious of their every manoeuvre, so that you see every preparation and step as a separate endeavour, rather than as part of a larger effect.

A routine jump, for instance, may become a brief, breathtaking miracle if a dancer is able to speed extra fast through the steps leading to it, prolong the jump itself mid-air (the trick is to breathe in at the apex of the jump and stretch the chest and limbs, so that the body seems to grow and freeze simultaneously), and then extend the dying fall of the phrase by cushioning the landing and letting the body's remaining energy unravel through some gentle grace note – like a slowly lengthening arm or bowed torso.

The drama of a harsh staccato phrase becomes much more emphatic when a dancer is bold enough to hurl his or her energy at each move, then abruptly stall it. A phrase of fleet, fast movements becomes brilliant when a dancer can show each step clearly without blurring or haste – as if there was all the time in the world. In the relaxed, liquid style of release the dancer has to let the movement ripple its way through the body unchecked by tension or strain, like water finding its way through channels in the sand. In every case it's the dancers' facility for controlling their energy which creates the effect – revealing the contrasts of taut and relaxed movement, of active and passive, of acceleration and delay.

The way dancers phrase movement is often intimately connected to the way they hear music. At a basic level a dancer's musicality is a talent for keeping time, which a surprising number find difficult to do. Alexandra Danilova claims that the ballerina Olga Spessivtseva had to have someone standing in the wings to count the music for her, while Marie Rambert has written that Ashton's greatest difficulty during his brief dancing career 'lay in keeping time with music. Eagerness and intense nervous energy . . . made him deaf to sound.'

Some works, of course, are harder to count than others. Danilova admitted to having problems with Nijinska's *Noces* 'because her dance phrase didn't finish with the musical phrase'. And during any performance with live music the orchestra's conductor can either soothe or savage a dancer's relationship with the score. A sympathetic one may speed up or slow down to stay with the dancer (Russians expect this). An unsympathetic one may simply ignore the stage. Julian Braunsweg recalled Stravinsky conducting three performances of *Petrushka* 'with his eyes glued to the score, not once looking at the dancers'. When the latter complained that he was going so fast they were afraid of breaking a leg, he told them they 'had to learn to dance to my timing. I wrote the score.' When the stage director added his own request that the conductor slow down, he replied with apparent astonishment, 'You're paying me by the minute, aren't you, what are you worried about?'

Classical dancers are actually trained to listen to music in different ways. Russians, for instance, are taught not to rely on counts but to listen for the shape of the phrase – they tend to sing when they're learning the music. During a performance they will often slow down to emphasize a moment of climax, expecting the orchestra to accommodate them. French dancers tend to play over the top of the music – sometimes skittering slightly ahead, then slowing down to wait for it to catch up. Balanchine-trained American dancers are expected to keep much stricter time.

But even within these national variations the genuinely musical dancer achieves the same effect, which is to make vivid physical drama out of the music. Such dancers seem to hear the movement so far inside their bodies it's as if the notes are singing through their veins. Paradoxically they also look as if they are moving *inside* the music, pushing and pulling it into the shapes of the dance. The sound appears to well up somewhere deep within them and to play its melodies out through their limbs.

One of the most profoundly musical dancers of our time is the Kirov-trained Altynai Asylmuratova, who seems to dig right into the music to find the key to each role. In Act II of *Giselle*, when she lifts a leg slowly to the side, it seems to drift up on the music's rising melody. As the flirtatious Kitri in Petipa's *Don Quixote* (1869), her hands and feet snap through the score's rhythms so brilliantly and freely that you can almost see her gathering the music up and tossing it around.

At certain moments the stress of her phrases can respond so deeply to the stress of the music that their combined force is breathtaking. When as Odette she throws back her head on an anguished chord, a simple gesture becomes a terrible cry of hope and pain. In dancing like this the pressure of the music becomes impossible to distinguish from the pressure of emotion.

Like other great dance actors, Asylmuratova makes dancing look like a spontaneous release of feeling – as if each move has to happen because of what the character is experiencing. Of course, there's a basic acting technique involved in this, projecting clear gestures and facial expressions, and finding the character's distinctive rhythm and stance. (The Danish ballerina Toni Lander has said that when she was performing Odette's mime passages in *Swan Lake*, 'I found that I was doing a lot of it up on half-pointe. She's working herself up. When you get excited you cannot stand down.')

But dancing can play just as important a part in characterization as acting. Critic Arlene Croce once noted how the unusually fluid dancing of French ballerina Magali Messac made her a fearsomely insinuating Odile – the softness of her moves exaggerating the dangerous subtext of the choreography. 'Odile is soft, so soft that the twisting, violent *en-dedans* spins between her partner's hands stand out as near-naked moments of force, a baring of fangs rather than a display of technique.'

With some rare dancers characterization goes beyond dance and acting technique, as if they have somehow acquired their character's heart, brain and nervous system, and this ability to project a complete imaginative world can also mark out dancers who don't have characters to portray. Laurie Booth, for instance, seems to have a film playing in his head as he improvises on stage. The beam of his dark gaze changes focus as if he's dancing through a landscape none of us can see. His gestures signal wariness, serenity or wit and the quick changes that ricochet through his body seem like responses to invisible, dramatic events.

Merce Cunningham too can suggest intense mental and emotional activity through the smallest gesture or the most flickering change of expression. And what's mesmerizing about performers like these is that they persuade us that the world projected by their bodies and imaginations is unique. They do this not by thrusting their ego on us, but by asserting the force of their individuality. In fact, throughout the history of dance, whenever writers have celebrated the stars of their age, it's been the mystery of the artists' personalities, their singleness of presence, which their prose has struggled to articulate.

When Théophile Gautier tried to define the difference between Taglioni and Elssler he produced the following, famous, metaphorical distinction:

Mlle Taglioni is a Christian dancer . . . she flies like a spirit in the midst of transparent clouds of white muslin with which she loves to surround herself; she resembles a happy angel who scarcely bends the petals of celestial flowers with the tips of her pink toes. Fanny is a quite pagan dancer; she reminds one of the muses, Terpsichore, tambourine in hand, her tunic exposing her thigh, caught up with a golden clasp, when she bends freely from her hips, throwing back her swooning voluptuous arms, we seem to see one of those beautiful figures from Herculaneum or Pompeii.

When Russian critic André Levinson tried to sum up Anna Pavlova's mystique he did so in a single, poetic image: 'In the curve of Pavlova's insteps are expressed all the yearnings of the Russian soul.'

When Edwin Denby made a brave attempt to analyse the special virtue of Alicia Markova's dancing he too landed up in the realm of the mystical:

Miss Markova's delicacy in lightness . . . the quickness in the thighs, the arrowy flexibility of the instep, her responsiveness in the torso, the poise of the arms, the sweetness of the wrists, the grace of neck and head – all this is extraordinary. But her dancing is based on a rarer virtue. It is the quiet she moves in, an instinct for the melody of movement as it deploys and subsides in the silence of time . . . the sense of serenity in animation she creates is as touching as that of a Mozart melody. She is a completely objective artist. Who Markova is, nobody knows.

And Denby's wonderful description of Martha Graham also concluded with a frank acknowledgement of mystery:

What holds the piece together is the lucid concentration of Miss Graham in the central role, a personage to whom all the events on stage are completely real. They are images she contemplates within herself and also sees independently active outside her; and her mobile face lights up at the objective impressions. She is adolescently tender, dancing with her two beloveds at once; she is terrifying and horrible in her mad scene; her final gesture is adult, like tragedy. Very strange too is the mysterious elegance which never leaves her.

Even American critic Hubert Saal's vigorous no-nonsense description of Baryshnikov ended up on a cosmic note: 'He blasted off with the hesitation and majesty of a space ship. He turned – once, twice – and every thread on his costume was plainly visible as he soared high above the audience like an astronaut looking back to earth.' And Twyla Tharp – often the most pragmatic of choreographers – has also said that it's the divinity of certain dancers that makes her fall in love with them: 'My bodies need to be intelligent, beautiful and sophisticated, capable of the amazing, possessing the great and simple ease that makes you believe one thing: God lives here too.'

Twyla Tharp has written that, 'For the longest time I could not understand duets between men and women. "Why aren't they just in bed together?" I asked myself.' But these days, when it comes to sex, she drags her dancer out of the bedroom, and she has become famous for making some of the most intricately constructed and lusty duets in the business. Like many choreographers, Tharp acknowledges that the chemistry that sparks between two dancers is one of the most fundamental pleasures of dance.

Simply as physical raw material, two bodies offer much more scope to the choreographer than one. Eight limbs, two torsos and four feet can be sculpted into a far greater variety of shapes, and they can perform manoeuvres like lifts and supported balances that are physically impossible for the single dancer. Added to these are all the possibilities of duplication, syncopation, and contrast that come with partner work, as well as the space that lies between two bodies, which can be charged with the passage of their emotion and energy.

As drama, the *pas de deux* is also the ultimate vehicle of sex. Any two people dancing together can evoke the whole history of couple dancing – from the courtship of the waltz to the seductive danger of the tango. Tharp herself knows well the potency of these forms. In *Sextet* she has three couples performing decorous classical *pas de deux*, the steps of which are invaded by fast and dirty jive or tango moves – blatant sexual metaphors.

The range of dance movements that actually mimic sex is huge. MacMillan's Juliet arches orgasmically as she's lifted over Romeo's prone body, while Ashton's Natalia Petrovna beats her foot in a terrified ecstatic heartbeat in Beliaev's embrace. The couples in Mark Morris's *New Love Song Waltzes* (1982) grope their way through mundanely familiar embraces, then suddenly extend their limbs in an ecstatic star burst that images love as poignance and splendour – unlike the women in much post-modern European dance who lash their bodies angrily against their partners as if they have to hurt in order to feel.

But the skin-against-skin immediacy of dance can evoke other human relationships with equal vividness. In Ashton's *Enigma Variations* (1968) a small vocabulary of quiet, reticent gestures portrays unexpectedly subtle nuances of friendship and intellectual sympathy, while in DV8's *Enter Achilles* (1995) a playful, rolling tussle between men can flip with deadly speed from friendly ragging to murderous aggression.

From the exquisitely refined poetry of Odette and Siegfried's Act II *pas de deux* to the flying off-the-cuff balances of contact improvisation, a duet can distil a whole relationship into minutes of dance.

Yet, just as an individual dancer can make a choreographic moment either mediocre or magical, so partnerships can make or break a duet. It's not just individual stars in dance that get spoken of in the hushed tones of legend, but also the great partnerships, like Fonteyn and Nureyev, Sibley and Dowell, Fred and Ginger, and the ice-skaters Torvill and Dean. When some extravagant chemistry works between two performers we see them combining into a personality larger than themselves, see them scaling technical and dramatic precipices that are beyond them as individuals. Like vigilant dating agencies, dance fans and PR agents are always trying to match the next perfect couple. (Though Ginger Rogers always claimed that, 'So-called chemistry is an invention of casting directors and publicity people. We worked together, and worked well, because that is what professionals do, honey.')

But fans of one of the most famously combustive dancing couples in recent history would have had no truck with Rogers's cynicism, even though no computer would ever have paired them for a date. When Margot Fonteyn and Rudolf Nureyev first danced together, Fonteyn was in her forties and seriously considering retirement, while Nureyev was only twenty-three, with his whole career at stake. She was a dancer who epitomized the elegant purity of English classicism (see illus. 6) – he moved with the physical flamboyance of the Russian school. She was an icon of decorum and grace – he was everybody's image of wild-boy genius.

Fonteyn has written with frank humour about the problems of their age gap. When she was first asked to dance with Nureyev she admits she panicked comprehensively about 'mutton dancing with lamb', and before their partnership became a household image she had to endure wincing moments, as when a fan gushed all over Nureyev at a party and then enquiringly gestured at Fonteyn, 'Is that your mother?' When Nureyev himself got uppity and tried to change too many details in their performance she'd put him down by remarking sarkily, 'Rudolf, I have been doing this ballet since 1938. I suppose that was before you were born.' His reply would be, devastatingly, 'No, just exact year.'

But even while Nureyev was still learning to speak English it seems they developed a mutually protective understanding, and both admitted to learning a lot from each other. While Fonteyn had years of experience to share, Nureyev's more analytic approach to dancing forced Fonteyn to examine the nuts and bolts of her technique in ways she'd never considered. Above all, the differences in their trainings, physiques and temperaments seemed to react like an extreme genetic mix – producing an unexpectedly exotic offspring.

They looked good together, of course – his feral, muscular grace adding rawness, energy and heft to her more delicate line. But it was also the fact that the feistiness of his temperament seemed to break through some deep reserve in her, releasing what dance critic David Vaughn has described as a 'new rhapsodic freedom of movement, and uninhibited ecstasy in her acting'. Until Ashton created a special vehicle for the partnership in his version of *La Dame aux camélias*, *Marguerite and Armand* (1963), audiences had never seen Fonteyn fly to such extremes. Vaughn describes her as ranging from coquettish romance to a despairing 'tottering, trembling walk on point', while her final *pas de deux* with Nureyev expressed 'raw passion and desperation so real one [was] almost embarrassed to watch'.

Even in familiar classics like *Giselle* the drama of their bodies and personalities was potent. In their Act II *pas de deux* the real-life fragility of Fonteyn's older body made her seem an even more ethereal spirit, even more unpossessable by this ardent young man. And even when they produced the inevitable dud performance, the public were so wooed by the romance of their partnership that they tended to see the dancing through its afterglow. Two stars are far more blinding than one.

The attraction of opposites was just as powerful in the Astaire–Rogers combination – of which Katharine Hepburn famously said, 'He gave her class and she gave him sex.' As screen personalities alone, they were an unlikely pair. He was all dapper elegance, witty self-containment and sexual detachment – a man hard to imagine without at least a pair of tailored pyjamas on. She was inclined to gauche outbursts and wry jokes, while her glamour was blatant – bright lips, dyed blonde hair and a tough, rounded body that knew what it wanted.

As dancers, their contrasts of style were similarly extreme but also mutually accommodating. Astaire's slender, almost dangling limbs seemed to dance of their own accord – as if the rhythms just rattled around him – while Rogers's body, with its old-fashioned plastique, had a more solid quality. She took up space, and her movements were sensuous curves. Yet just as he brought speed, dexterity and wit to their joint moves, she made them tactile and weighty. She earthed the partnership; he made it fizz.

But there is no formula to determine what makes a partnership work or not. Sibley and Dowell achieved mutual glory not because of their differences but because of their similarities. Both were small, slender and delicately blond; they were physically cut from the same cloth – and to veteran Royal Ballet dancer Leslie Edwards this was the essential factor. 'You need the right material ... you can't put a calico hem on some satin – it looks ghastly. You need two satins.'

They were also both trained from childhood in the English style – so that they shared the same understanding of classicism and the same dramatic approach. And limb for limb, curve for curve, their bodies slotted together well. Dowell found Sibley the perfect partner to handle. 'Proportions did a lot to make us fit. She was exactly the right height and weight for me.' Sibley also says their similar construction made it simple for them to look good. 'We just echoed each other, we didn't have to think about our arms and our legs being at the same angle.' Equally importantly they heard the music the same way, which, as they once said, meant that 'there's never any doubt as to how we're going to move'. Given that a sudden hesitation, an inconsistency in timing can be fatal to a lift or balance, their joint instinct for phrasing gave them an unusual confidence.

As they matured together, Sibley and Dowell also projected a sense that both inhabited the same world during a performance. In a ballet like *The Dream* they knew the choreographer and the characters so well their dancing was like a spontaneous exchange. Sibley seemed to feel under her skin the sharp-tempered pride that made Titania bait Oberon, the sensual hunger that always drew her back to him, while Dowell showed precisely how Oberon's ruthless arrogance was tempered by his tender uxoriousness (see illus. 11).

Nothing is more frustrating or absurd in a *pas de deux* than two dancers with blatantly different views about a work – one who finds its comedy amusing and one who doesn't; one who's prepared to believe in magic and one who isn't. A fragilely Romantic ballet like *Giselle* can be ruined if the ballerina is dancing a peasant heroine with a defenceless heart but her lover appears not to have left the twentieth century. It can also be ruined if the dancers are shamelessly competing. Hard though it is for an energetic male ego, there are whole passages of classical dance where the man's job is basically to make sure that his ballerina doesn't fall over. He has to partner her dextrously; he has to create a glowing space around her; his gaze has to focus the audience's love for her. He can't be milking their applause for himself, and looking as if he's champing to get on with his own solo. Equally she has to look entranced by his attentions, stay in role and, even as she shows herself off, avoid making things difficult for him.

Unique artist though she was, Alicia Markova could, apparently, be a trial to dance with during her long career, and one of her partners from the 1930s and 40s, Igor Youskevitch, claimed that she possessed some outrageous tricks for upstaging her man. During the season of *Giselle*s he realized that every time he arrived at the big moment where Albrecht declares his love for the heroine, Markova had engineered things so that he was standing with his back uncharismatically turned to the audience while she still faced front. Basically Markova had been moving backwards during the scene instead of remaining opposite him, so that he was forced to turn round to face her as he mimed. So the next performance he started moving backwards with her, and because she refused to give up her trick they 'wound up together all the way at the backdrop'.

Youskevitch also says Markova didn't like to jump in order to help her partner in a lift, preferring serenely to rely on the fact that she was so slender. But, as he says, 'Lifting even 90 pounds is not that simple.'

In Jeffrey Taylor's biography of Irek Mukhamedov the latter recalls the distracting nightmare of dancing with the Bolshoi ballerina Ludmila Semenyaka who, for all her ease and brilliance, was an incessant chatterbox on stage. During one of their few performances together she maintained a running commentary – 'I'm off balance. I'm too high. I'm too low' – until her most exasperating comment, 'Put me down. You're hurting my liver', goaded Mukhamedov (normally a conscientiously committed dancer) to growl, 'One more word and I'll drop you in the orchestra pit.'

It's not just ballerinas who are troublemakers either. Danilova recalls that when she danced with Massine, 'if [he] was annoyed with me, he would pinch me . . . while I sat on his knee or while he supported me in *arabesque*'.

Modern dance has a less glitzy star system, which is one reason why it boasts fewer famous partnerships. Its repertory also has a shorter shelf life and its companies are less stable. Because of this we rarely see two people dancing together consistently, and when we do the roles themselves are less likely to be shouting, 'Look at this couple, how romantic and glamorous they are.' When we watch modern dance we tend to be looking more at the choreography than the dancers.

But even if couples don't tend to become household names, a few have become remembered icons. Those who watched Cunningham's company in the days when Carolyn Brown was one of its prized dancers talk of the emotional and physical gravity she added to Cunningham's own mercurial presence. In several of the works that American choreographer David Gordon has made over the last decade, his own appearances with his wife Valda Setterfield have seemed directly charged by their joint emotional history. At one point in *Nine Lives* (1985) Gordon sat Setterfield on his knee with a cosiness that suggested years of sitting by the same fireside, while in *Offenbach Suite* (1985) he created a romantic duet for them in which he, solid and bearlike, held her tiny quixotic body in a simple lift and turned her dreamily round and round.

During the 1980s British New Dance audiences were inclined to treasure the partnership between Kirstie Simson and Julyen Hamilton. There was an almost Astaire-and-Rogers disparity in their bodies – he compact, freckled and elusive, she blonde, rounded and centred – that made them look extraordinary together. But the fact that they were also an off-stage couple fed into the intimacy of their dancing. Many of their duets possessed an almost baiting rivalry – 'I dare you to walk away; I might just throw myself at you' – while their close knowledge of each other also allowed them to risk beautiful feats of daring.

But analysing the logic of a partnership is, in the end, as fuzzy as analysing the logic of a love affair – it's a fluky reaction between bodies and personalities that either works or doesn't. It may, in fact, be easier to pin down the reasons why partnerships *don't* work. During the early 90s, the marriage brokers of British ballet were furiously trying to establish a permanent partnership between the very young Darcey Bussell and the ex-Bolshoi star Irek Mukhamedov, who'd recently joined the Royal. The two had created together the lead roles in MacMillan's *Winter Dreams* (1991) and the signs for a successful coupling looked good. His intensity and air of adult knowledge sparked in her a deeper, darker expressiveness, while she was one of the few British women dancers who could match his physical power and scale. When Bussell and Mukhamedov jumped across the stage together it not only caused an exhilarating explosion of energy, it also put interesting pressure on traditional male and female roles.

The two were subsequently cast to dance the lovers in Mac-Millan's *Manon*. These were roles originally created on Dowell and Sibley (with the equally tiny Jennifer Penney standing in for

Sibley when she was injured) and certain lifts which had been relatively simple for them turned out to be hazardous for Mukhamedov and Bussell to perform together. While he is not especially tall for a man, she has very long limbs and stands at 5'7" which makes her 6'2" on points. In *Winter Dreams* this wasn't a problem because all of the choreography had been tailored to them. But for some manoeuvres in *Manon* it must have been treacherous. At one point in the ballet the man has to duck down beneath the ballerina's outstretched leg while she is in mid-*pirouette*; then, while she is still turning, get his shoulder under her groin and lift her up. It's hard enough for a partner to judge the height of the woman's leg and the force of her turn accurately for the lift, but even harder for a man of average height to then contain and balance a tall woman. During another passage the man is running while holding the woman's body at arm's length above his head. Then, still running, he has to lower her to the ground and almost simultaneously fall down at her side. Fluently danced, this is a recklessly passionate moment – but for Bussell and Mukhamedov the mechanics would be terrifying. Both dancers went on to dance the ballet very successfully with other partners.

Changing from an accustomed partner to a new one can be equally treacherous. Lynn Seymour, for instance, recalls a performance of John Cranko's *Taming of the Shrew* (1969) which she once danced with David Wall. Wall was used to dancing this ballet with the much lighter ballerina Merle Park, while Seymour herself was used to dancing with Wayne Eagling, who was not as strong as Wall. Disaster hit with

a simple thing, a little throw into the air from a lying position which David and I had never actually rehearsed. I'd found a way of helping Wayne with it, but Merle hadn't had to help David . . . So when we came to that bit . . . I pushed and David pushed and I went waaaaay up, right behind him and crash landed, flat on my back. And he lost me . . . He was looking all over and I was looking the wrong way myself because I should have landed in front . . . Well, the whole audience stood up and gasped.

So difficult are some of the accommodations and risks involved, it's not surprising that many dancers prefer performing solo. New York City Ballet dancer Merrill Ashley has said that for years she was 'more comfortable dancing alone'. She found it hard to trust her partners. 'You have to learn to relax . . . my tendency was to try and help my partner do everything . . . and that actually makes it harder for him. If he's a good partner he can fix it, whether you're helping him or not.' But the way Ashley describes the experience of being partnered, she makes it sound like one part terror to three parts bliss. Interviewed at a time when she was still dancing the Sanguinic *pas de deux* in Balanchine's *Four Temperaments* (1946), she said, 'I don't even see the man. I feel like I'm just riding around on top of the world, just floating. You're hardly even aware that there's somebody behind you grabbing you and taking you there.'

In dance as in life, the kinds of roles available to men and women have, historically, been strictly prescribed, and it's in the *pas de deux* of nineteenth-century classical ballet that the differences between male and female dance can often seem most sharply opposed. The man lifts the woman, who perches with serene elegance on his shoulder; he steadies and supports while she displays her charms. The *pas de deux* of *Swan Lake* and *Sleeping Beauty* are dances of male strength set against female lightness, of male power against female grace, and when they're performed by today's dancers they put twentieth-century feminism into suspension, in a way that feels even more extreme than a reading of *The Old Curiosity Shop* or a performance of *Traviata*.

This is partly because the roles available to the sexes were even more codified in the simplified fantasies of nineteenth-century ballet than in the literature or opera of the period. The men dominating the classical repertoire were heroes striving to right the wrongs wrought by evil villains, while the women tended to be either princesses awaiting rescue or unattainable ghosts. The only women with real power were the bad ones, the witches and the whores.

But gender differences were also written into every move the dancers made in these works. The men powered through vaulting jumps and hard, fast turns, while the women picked their way through exquisite steps on point, their arms gracefully floating. The reason for these differences was partly dramatic – classical ballet had a peculiar fondness for plots where idealized, passive women are sought by ardent, active men. It was also partly cultural – ballet's conservative worlds have probably reflected even less critically than other art forms the stereotypes of their era. But there are formal reasons too why men still tend to dance differently from women in classical ballet.

Firstly, just as piano music uses a seven-octave span between very high and low notes, so the ballet vocabulary revolves around a formal contrast between female lightness and speed, and the more muscular power of the men. In visual terms too it needs to embrace a wide gamut of scale and shape, i.e. the full contrast between big men's bodies and smaller female ones. Also as an art that's historically been preoccupied with magic and artifice, ballet prizes certain kinds of physical illusion, which are created by women appearing to float on their points or being wafted through the air by men. Over centuries it has evolved extremes of male and female dancing to service these formal concerns, and these still influence the vocabulary today.

Traditionally the apportioning of dance qualities has constricted women less than men. Though they can't perform most classical lifts and are rarely required to support their partners, women do jump and turn (albeit on a smaller scale than men) as well as getting all the moves considered too dainty for their partners. Their range has also dramatically increased during this century as female technique has become more athletic. Balanchine frequently admitted that he was far more interested in choreographing for women because they had so many more movements available to them. 'Woman,' he said, 'is the queen. It is easier to make dances for men – they jump, they turn. A woman is more complicated, that is the only reason they are a priority.'

Balanchine was in fact an interestingly pivotal figure in the way he choreographed for the sexes, poised between nineteenth-century tradition and twentieth-century liberation. His great muses were all women (including Tanaquil LeClercq and Suzanne Farrell) and his choreography for them ranged from the lightning-fast classicism of *Theme and Variations* to the dreamy romanticism of *Liebeslieder Walzer*. These kinds of ballets exemplified the traditional brilliance and grace of female dance and they fitted in with Balanchine's stubbornly old-fashioned reverence for their mystique. (When he described the care he took over choreographing for women he once said, 'They are fragile like orchids. You have to know how much sun, how much water, how much air and then take them inside before they wilt.')

But even as we may wince or laugh at such sentiments, Balanchine has left us roles where women dance with far more attack, independence and power than any nineteenth-century ballerina. In fact, in *Agon* or in the 'Rubies' section of *Jewels* (1967) they are anything but delicate plants. Among the gang of contesting men in *Agon* the ballerina's limbs appear as strong and lethal as theirs and she's their equal in stamina (see illus. 12). If, in the central *pas de deux*, the man moulds and supports her body, she is also tauntingly resistant – it's an erotic game between them in which she has an equal stake. In 'Rubies' she is struttingly and triumphantly her own woman. She plays with a perverse sensuality and showbizzy pizazz (lolling hips, high-kicking legs, provocatively splayed *pliés* on point) with a power that makes Madonna look meek. She may be on display but she is in no way passive.

In the same ballet Balanchine actually choreographed one of his few great roles for men, exploiting, during its creation, the stellar talents of Edward Villella in a part that was neither cavalier nor Prince – but an urban, urbane warrior. Darting and spinning round the stage, the lead man twists and angles through choreography that flashes up images of musical hall, comedy, circus and plain sex. A circling of his foot on the floor is an insinuating taunt; a cock of his head an irresistible come on. But it has to be acknowledged that little else in Balanchine's repertoire has matched this celebration of male dancing – and a quick survey of the rest of twentieth-century classical ballet shows that women still come away with most of the best roles. (One major exception is the Bolshoi repertoire, in which works like Yuri Grigorovich's *Spartacus* (1968) and *Ivan the Terrible* (1975) have provided intense and showy vehicles for male dancing.)

There have, of course, been individual stars like Nijinsky, Baryshnikov and Nureyev who've tipped the balance away from the ballerina mystique, and helped to extend the male range. Nijinsky possessed not only an amazing jump but an exoticism and sensuousness that gave him a technical flexibility way beyond the traditionally stiff masculine vocabulary. His versatile expressiveness also made him wonderful in roles far removed from run-of-the-mill Princes – from the Golden Slave (the beautiful dumb hero in *Schéhérazade*) to poor, tortured, clumsy Petrushka. For almost the first time in history a man was presented as the emotional and erotic heart of a ballet. (Even though the eighteenth century had venerated male dancers, it was more for their technique than their dramatic mystique.)

We have no way of deciding whether Nureyev was, as many claimed, Nijinsky's equal as a dancer, but he certainly possessed a formidable determination to dance every step of the repertoire. After defecting to the West, he introduced male solos into many of the nineteenth-century classics to flesh out the supporting Prince roles, and in his own productions of ballets like *Romeo and Juliet* and *Cinderella* he created many substantial parts for men. (In the former, Juliet is ousted from the emotional and technical limelight by the combined virtuosity and mischief of Romeo, Tybalt, Mercutio and Benvolio.) Nureyev also experimented widely with modern choreography, dancing in works by Taylor, Graham and Glen Tetley which added whole new vocabularies to his range.

Baryshnikov's luminous style and aerial virtuosity made almost any role he danced a starring one, and inspired choreographers like Twyla Tharp to push his dancing towards wilder, more glittering technical excess. After his retirement from ballet in the late 80s Baryshnikov also went on to demonstrate that there was life after Princes and heroes. He formed his own company (the White Oak Project) which performed a basically modern repertoire (Graham to Morris) and showed that rhythm, line and intelligence could be as thrilling in male dancing as barrelling leaps and *entrechats* (beaten jumps).

But it was the women choreographers in the early part of the twentieth century who most dramatically rewrote the sexual roles in dance. Most of these were opening up the terrain of modern dance but one of history's most interesting exceptions was Bronislava Nijinska, who, as Lynn Garafola has argued in *Diaghilev's Ballets Russes*, choreographed classical dance from a sharply feminist viewpoint, and in *Les Biches* (1924) exposed many of the sexual clichés in ballet.

The work is set at a house party (which could almost be taken from an Aldous Huxley novel) where bright young things jockey for sexual attention and only a young lesbian couple stand apart from the general exhibitionism. The theme of decadence is understated and the atmosphere ambiguous. As its composer Poulenc wrote, it's 'a ballet in which you may see nothing at all or into which you may read the worst'.

As the characters display themselves to us and to each other, they make explicit both the narcissism and the voyeurism that underlie all dance performance. When one of them dances a variation he or she sends self-conscious glances to the audience and to the other characters, who in turn stare openly at their performance, measuring it up. (The most ludicrous offenders are the three male athletes who flex their arms and perform turning jumps with pompous exhibitionism. The absurdity of their macho competitiveness is exaggerated by the way they stop dead after each feat – as if wracking their brains for another stunt to show. It is also heightened by the fact that as men they've been reduced to an unusually passive role, objects for the women's gaze.)

The women too show off their tricks with heartless deliberation, but the Hostess, an older woman, projects a power and an independence that set her apart. She dances mostly male steps, like high beaten jumps, and her movements have the vigour and panache of a man's. An even more unsettling outsider is the Garçonne, a figure of extreme sexual ambiguity who wears a mannish jacket with her point shoes and who dances and flirts with a terrifying mechanical calm – a robot imitating the follies of its human companions.

The lack of any spontaneous human warmth in all this sexual display is scathingly demonstrated in the *pas de deux* where partners go through all the mechanics of lifting and balancing while barely exchanging a glance. By highlighting the stereotypes of classical dance, dislocating some of its familiar rhythms and reallocating steps from men to women and vice versa, Nijinska made an old, sanctified language look dangerously modern and subversive.

The early modern choreographers, though, were writing their own language from scratch – and it was very definitely a language for women. Duncan and Graham danced with a force and freedom that were unknown to their classical sisters and there were usually no men on stage to even consider carrying them around. They also developed a new set of roles for women to play, and even if Duncan's image of herself as Earth Mother, Goddess and Revolutionary was as romantically idealized as Petipa's Aurora, it also had more guts and spirit.

Graham's women were scarcely ordinary either. Yet her grieving victims, her jealous furies, her martyrs, saints and geniuses plumbed far deeper recesses in the female psyche than any male choreographer had acknowledged. They also took on the issue of power. Medea, St Joan and the Brontës weren't waiting to be woken up – they were out there fighting for control of their destiny.

Men, of course, didn't feature in Graham's early work at all, while in her middle, Jungian period they often appeared as inadvertently comic archetypes – big stiff-legged macho hunks. In her later work Graham became much more interested in how men could dance and express themselves, although this period also saw a decline in the emotional intensity of her work – which was perhaps definitively female.

Merce Cunningham side-stepped many pitfalls of gender stereotyping by making works that were only about dance – there was nothing for men to get heroic about, no reason for women to be jealous or timid. As a dancer, Cunningham also moved with some of the qualities associated with women – lightness of step, an open carriage, graceful arms – so that his choreography translated well on to both sexes. Watching a Cunningham work where many of the movements are interchangeable between men and women, we rarely feel that sex or gender is a major consideration.

The principle of gender-free dance became a live issue in the 60s and 70s. In the cool dances of Rainer, Brown and others there was, deliberately, little about the vocabulary that signified male or female. But it was in contact improvisation that equal opportunities between men and women were most physically addressed.

In ballet and much modern dance there is a brute physical logic to the fact that men mostly heft women about rather than the other way round. Since most male bodies are bigger, heavier and stronger, women simply cannot perform the kind of high-flying, high-precision lifts that many choreographers ask for. With contact improvisation, though, a whole new aesthetic of partnering allowed dancers to use any part of their body to hoist or balance their partner (including the solid muscular table of buttocks, hips or back). This combined with new techniques of lifting (using the force and momentum of bodies in motion rather than one dancer 'picking the other up' with his or her hands) meant that even the tiniest women were able to lift and control big men.

Around the same time the issue of physical stereotyping came into sharp political focus – particularly in the context of ballet. Anorexia and bulimia became recognized as professional hazards, as young women starved and vomited themselves into an increasingly slender 'ideal'. One of ballet's most public victims was Gelsey Kirkland who in her autobiography describes how in 1976 she managed to reduce herself to a skeletal 80 pounds: 'I starved by day, then binged on junk food and threw up by night; I took injections of pregnant cow's urine, reputed to be a miraculous diet aid; I stuffed myself with laxatives, thyroid pills and celery juice.'

Men dancers didn't suffer such extremes of self-disgust, but even so were obliged to find a miraculous balance between fashionable slenderness and the kind of muscle power needed for super-athletic partnering. Height also became a more sensitive issue as post-war women grew taller and men under five foot ten faced the prospect of dancing jesters, peasants or juveniles for the rest of their careers. A critical vanguard of dancers and choreographers (mostly outside the world of ballet) denounced this physical culture as body fascism and zealously began providing alternatives.

Thus when the American choreographers Bill T. Jones and Arnie Zane first started dancing together in the late 70s they were sending out very deliberate messages to the world. The first was the fact that they were gay lovers as well as partners; the second was that Jones, a luxuriantly built black man, was partnering Zane, a tiny elfin white man, and they looked fabulous together.

When Mark Morris first set up his company he made a point of using dancers who didn't look like the delicately muscled sylphs of classical stereotype. He wanted dancers with interesting minds, bodies and personalities, and he didn't mind fat on men's bellies or big muscles on women's thighs – just as long as they could think and move. Not only did his dancers, as a consequence, come in a striking assortment of sizes, shapes and colours, but Morris deliberately set moves on them that went against their physical or sexual type. As Joan Acocella notes, tiny Teri Weksler – whom Morris used to refer to as the 'paper cup' – created the big, weighted role of the lead Sailor in *Dido and Aeneas*, while 'four-square, blocklike' Donald Mouton danced the quick, feathery lark in *L'Allegro*.

As a dancer himself, Morris possesses a peculiarly equal mix of 'male' and 'female'. He can move right across the range from light, delicate and small to hard, heavy and massive. He can be an awkward cowboy in *Going Away Party* (1991) or he can be one of the most regal, tragic and erotic Didos in history (see illus. 8).

For several years Morris insisted that his company also danced on strictly androgynous principles and he never gave his men steps that his women couldn't do – and vice versa. But, as he now says, that basically meant he had to limit his duets 'to one lift' and he got bored. Yielding to the physiological truth that men can lift women in more ways than women can lift men, he now allows the latter to partner women in ways that can't always be reciprocated. But in its style, texture and imagery his work remains a constant teasing and inverting of gender. If there's kissing to be done, everyone usually gets to kiss everyone else, whatever their sex. If there's dirty, violent stuff to do, everyone does it. And if, as in *L'Allegro*, he chooses to give his men a boisterous knees-up number and his women a floaty feminine dance, it is a knowing use of type. (In private these are called 'the stupid men's dance' and 'the Kleenex dance'.)

Morris's dances are rarely political in terms of a delivered message. Yet during the 70s, when feminism first hit dance hard, many choreographers and dancers began to see sexual politics as the prime issue of their work. Some began to explore the gender of the body – using improvisation to develop 'female' movement that had been fettered by male-originated techniques. Others, like the British choreographers Jacky Lansley and Emilyn Claid, made works which addressed the roles of women in life and art. *Bleeding Fairies* (1977) celebrated the fact that ballerinas are not 'good girls' but flesh-and-(menstrual)-blood women. Lansley, originally a dancer with the Royal Ballet, also readdressed classicism in her version of *Giselle – I, Giselle* (1981) – where the heroine was no longer the passive victim of Albrecht's treachery but actually chose to die, leaving the duplicitous world of men for the powerful female world of the Wilis.

European choreographers like Pina Bausch invented a whole new vocabulary to show how women are threatened by men. In *Nelken* a man forcefed a woman with food she didn't want, while another woman was driven into a corner by three men crashing and diving across a table as they pushed it brutally towards her.

Men too have exposed male and female stereotypes and also tried to liberate themselves from them. The all-male British company The Featherstonehaughs, for instance, have explored a comically wide range of male behaviour and imagery – from lounge lizards to folk dancers, from rock and rollers to religious icons. DV8 have also presented works which explore alienation and loneliness among gay men, and expose the alcohol-fuelled aggression of macho posturing.

While many of the works performed today continue to divide down traditional male/female lines, the options of what men and women can do on stage have, during the last decades, opened wider than Martha Graham's pioneering generation could ever have imagined. Stephen Petronio can make a work where men in pink corsets partner each other, or where he and his lover (Michael Clark) embrace naked on a bed in an art gallery. Women can reveal their most masochistic fantasies in De Keersmaeker's *Bartók/Aantekeningen* or power their way through abstract virtuoso dance in Tharp's *Upper Room*.

Such is the subversiveness and flexibility of male and female roles offered by the current repertoire that they may undermine the way we look at older works. Can we still naïvely admire the heroic strength of Prince Siegfried, the quiescent loveliness of Odette and the erotic charm of Odile when we have recently been watching dance that either satirizes such gender-typing or else assumes it is part of a dinosaur past? Great performers will invest these roles with an imaginative power and credibility – but some-times when Siegfried dashes valiantly on stage to save Odette in Act IV of *Swan Lake* it's hard not to laugh.

Ballet dancers today not only have to get their bodies around a stylistic range that encompasses 150 years – from *Giselle* to William Forsythe – they also have to get their heads around the fact that they might be gentle virgins one night and inner-city androgynes on another. In recent years Adam Cooper of the Royal Ballet may have achieved the ultimate in gender-crossing and time-travelling by performing, in the space of months, Prince Siegfried in Petipa and Ivanov's *Swan Lake* and Odette/Odile in Matthew Bourne's all-male version of the ballet.

Actually in the latter the two 'female' leads were transposed to a Swan and a male Stranger, and in both Cooper, who helped to create the role, danced with a very masculine power. But as the Swan he possessed a wild beauty and lyricism that was far from classical male dancing, and he was also partnered by the Prince, which he found a bizarre novelty: 'It took me a long time to trust another man. I'm not used to being manipulated. I'm not used to falling off my leg and someone else being there to catch me.'

As the Stranger he danced with a louche sexuality that seemed directed equally at men and women, and his set-piece *pas de deux* with the Prince was rivetingly ambiguous. It was based around a tango (traditionally a dance for two men), but within this format Cooper was both a promiscuous male – wantonly gyrating his leather-clad groin – and Odile, enchanting Siegfried with the beauty of his dancing. The Prince tried to remain the dominant partner, taking Cooper's hand and supporting his weight, but, as in Petipa's original, he was helplessly manipulated by the object of his fascination. A rabbit failing desperately to be a snake.

Cooper has said that the role liberated him into subtler and more expressive ways of dancing, far removed from the distorting excesses of men who become so obsessed about the height of their jumps that they don't care 'if they look like builders' as they dance. If this ballet is part of a general trend towards depolarizing male and female roles, it's also possible to see Cooper as part of a generation of dancers who are moving towards a more androgynous style. Certainly when I look at my personal list of favourite performers several possess this quality. I find the delicacy of Mark Morris's bulk both startling and moving, while I love the joyous, muscular power of Darcey Bussell. And Michael Clark's astoundingly beautiful line has everything to do with a 'female' sinuousness, an exquisitely poised head and highly arched foot. When individual men and women cross so freely male and female it's possible to see the chemistry that can spark between two bodies actually scintillating in one.

In the studio choreographers may think that they know everything there is to know about their work. They've memorized every detail in the movement and logged every nuance in the way the dancers perform it. But once it's been relocated to the theatre, often as late as the dress-rehearsal or technical run-through, a work can look suddenly very different. The stage on which it's danced may radically affect its atmosphere and scale. And few dances go out naked into the world. A designer will have created sets and costumes to decorate the movement or enhance its drama, and these can have a formidable (and not always intentional) effect on how the work is seen. Drab outfits or dingy lighting can depress a work's spirits, while glitzy, overdecorated designs can make a work look cheap. Tight-fitting costumes, or cramped scenery, can irritatingly constrict the dancers, while badly assembled designs can make audiences jumpy with nerves as they watch seams tearing or walls beginning to sag.

READING THE CLOTHES

Dancers' costumes send out just as many signals as the clothes of ordinary people – influencing how we read their movements. A floating white tulle skirt will alert us to Romanticism, lyricism, moonlight and mystery just as a T-shirt and sweat pants makes us expect practical, no-frills dance. (Can we ever imagine Trisha Brown dressing her spare, loose-limbed movement in tutus?)

Dance also runs closely with fashion. Throughout history it's been common for designers to dress dancers in contemporary style. The cut, fabric and length of a costume can help to date a picture of a dancer just as much as the movement he or she is posing. For instance, neon-coloured Lycra tights and leg warmers will place a modern dancer firmly in the late 1970s while little black dresses will put them at around 1986. Further back, the decorous mid-thigh length of a male tunic signals late-nineteenth-century propriety, while the ornate wigs, head-dresses, masks and costumes that burdened dancers in the late seventeenth century speak flamboyantly of that period's respect for ornament.

Choreographers who don't want to give out confusing signals of character, style and period, particularly in a plotless work, will generally dress their dance in as uniform a style as possible. Plain tutus, tights, all-in-one leotards signal 'dance', But they don't intentionally commit the work to a specific time or place. Further, if all the cast wear the same outfit, we register them more as a choreographed ensemble than as individuals.

But dancers' bodies rarely look identical – even in the closely drilled *corps de ballet* of a large company – and a skin-tight leotard can reveal as much as it conceals of a dancer's identity. Audiences may often find themselves comparing various near-naked bodies in distracting detail, just at the point where they're meant to view the dancers as an abstract whole. And certain designers who work for dance dislike the leotard because they feel it has an unflattering effect on the natural lines of the body. Antony McDonald, who began inventing quirky and stylish costumes for dance in the 1980s, puts it bluntly: 'It's like dressing dancers in cling film; it squashes in all the bits and makes them look horrible.'

Danilova recalls the first time she was asked to wear a leotard and tights in the late 20s and says that although she and her fellow dancers could see the formal desirability of becoming 'naked sculptures', they 'were unaccustomed to wearing costumes that were so revealing and . . . felt uncomfortable at having our every contour exposed.'

Yet many dancers love the leotard because it's a disaster-free option with no skirts to rip, no cloaks to tangle with, no jewels or buttons to catch on. (Once when Anthony Dowell was lifting Antoinette Sibley on to his shoulder in Ashton's *Cinderella*, her tutu knickers became stuck on a hook in his tunic and he had to run off stage with her simply hanging from his chest.) And wardrobe staff adore the fact it's so simple to care for compared to the delicate fabrics and complex tailoring of nineteenth-century outfits. (Julian Braunsweg remembers the costumes for the Festival Ballet's *Les Sylphides* getting grubbier and grubbier on tour because there was no money to get them cleaned. 'It was necessary for the lighting to get dimmer as the tutus got dirtier ... talk about moonlit glade ... it [was] more like a black-out.')

Many choreographers also love the leotard-and-tights option because it's the best and simplest way of covering bodies while still giving them maximum freedom to move. In fact the development of dance technique, and of female dance in particular, can partly be written in terms of the dancers' changing attire.

It's no coincidence, for instance, that when skirts were shortened from just above ankle length to above the knee during the nineteenth century there was also a dramatic increase in the virtuosity of female dancing – with higher jumps and *arabesques* and more athletic lifts. When women threw off their constricting corsets in the late nineteenth century they also began to dance with a much more pliant torso, while the sweat pants that were introduced in the 60s allowed them to lift other dancers, to roll across the floor and race around the stage with a power that most skirts would inhibit.

Shoes too have had a crucial influence on style. The light, low-heeled slippers worn by eighteenth-century dancers showed off elegant feet and finely turned ankles, focusing attention on the brilliant footwork of the period. But they weren't supple enough to facilitate the preparations and landings of very high jumps, nor did they allow the dancers to go up on point. The emergence of the thin ballet slipper with slightly stiffened toe, however, caused a revolution in female dancing, allowing women to jump more freely and balance on the tips of their toes. This in turn relegated male dancers from star virtuosos to stolid *porteurs*, gallantly lifting and supporting their more airborne ballerinas. The boxed-toe shoe of the late nineteenth century paved the way for another quantum leap in female technique, making possible the bravura effects we now regard as standard.

When Isadora Duncan and Martha Graham threw off their shoes and danced barefoot they were thus making a very powerful statement not only about themselves but about the kind of dance they would perform. Without a thin-soled ballet shoe creating a lubricating divide between them and the floor, without a stiffened toe to perch on, they presented themselves as women of this earth, acknowledging gravity rather than floating away from it. With the fleshy naked traction of their feet against the floor, their dancing had not only a more vigorous and sensuous rhythm to it but a different kind of leverage at its base. Graham's bare feet allowed her to execute her most vertiginous spirals and falls in the knowledge that one part of her at least was securely rooted to the floor.

But there was also a potentially religious aura surrounding the bare foot – a suggestion that dancers were removing their shoes before the altar of Dance – and the sneakers favoured by the 60s avant-garde sent out a different message. Because sneakers were worn by everyone, dancers were signalling that anyone off the street might do what they did. Sneakers were also practical. Designed for speed, lightness and cushioning by sports manufacturers, they bore no connotations of art or suffering. They simply suggested that dance was a kind of task to be performed in the most practical possible way. (Given that period's affection for long passages of repetitive walking, jogging and running, sneakers must actually have prevented a lot of stress injury.)

By the 1980s choreographers had hit on another item of street fashion – the Doc Martens. These blunt, heavy rubber-soled shoes might seem like a dancer's nightmare, but they were actually the perfect accessory for the crashing momentum, violence and risk-taking of the decade. Not only did Doc Martens exaggerate the danger of dancers flying through the air – their heavy-shod heels liable at any moment to clip someone's ear – but their weight also emphasized the ferocious stop–start phrasing of the dance. They also made a lot of noise, exaggerating the force of the dancers' collective footwork.

BREAKING THE DRESS CODE OF DANCE: IMAGES FROM THE HISTORY OF COSTUME

Seventeenth-century Ballet

Basically the great court ballets of seventeenth-century Europe were elaborate catwalks for the nobility – allowing them to show off their fine manners and even finer clothes. One of the most dazzling of all the models was Louis XIV, who frequently starred in his own ballets. Pictures of him in full costume show how his outfits were designed to make him look as gorgeously decorative as possible and maximize the divinity of his status. His favourite role was Apollo the Sun-King, for which he wore a tunic stiff with embroidery, with elaborately puffed sleeves. There were bows on his shoes and jewels on his garters and his head-dress of plumed feathers radiated hugely round his head.

Other courtiers appearing in Louis XIV's ballets would have been slightly less splendidly attired. Those performing in group dances would have worn plain black masks to maintain a decorous anonymity, but expressive, stylized masks were worn by grotesque or mythic characters. Women, of course, were still fettered by long heavy skirts when they danced. So it was the men, with their short tunics and hose, who were free to make the boldest advances in dance technique.

Eighteenth-century Ballet

Pictures of two of the eighteenth-century's greatest stars, Marie Camargo and Gaetano Vestris, show them wearing the conventional dance dress of the period. For Camargo, this means that her waist is tightly corseted, her breasts plumped up, her sleeves puffed and her skirts and panniers swing out like giant bells. She is all pinched elegance and exaggerated curves. The only free parts of her body are her ankles and feet which peep from under her skirt to display her famously brilliant jumps.

Vestris's tunic is as highly patterned as Camargo's dress, and his plumed head-dress looks as encumbering as her corsets, but his body looks far less tightly squeezed and his short hooped skirt or tonlet (some sort of ancestor to the nineteenth-century tutu) allows him much more freedom to move. Both outfits are typical of a period when dance was valued less for its expressive powers than its ornamental displays of virtuosity. In the 1730s ballerina Marie Sallé had tried to inject a note of realism into her costume. Performing Pygmalion, the statue that comes to life, she abandoned her corsets and petticoats for a simple Greek tunic, letting her hair flow loosely down her back. This Duncan-like gesture made her the toast of several cities but wasn't taken up by anyone else until choreographer Jean-Georges Noverre began to campaign for more dramatic ballet stagings in the 1770s. In the name of realistic costume he managed to jettison the male tonlet and the use of masks – insisting that the dancers' own faces should register character and emotion.

Nineteenth-century Romantic Ballet

By the late eighteenth century women's fashions had become more diaphanous, and paved the way for the thin floating frocks of Romantic ballet. The fluid lines of the Romantic style were created not only by these drifting white tulle skirts, softly puffed sleeves and transparent wings, but also (if contemporary illustrations are accurate) by less ruthless corseting which allowed the dancers to bend more freely in the torso.

By eighteenth-century standards these women's frocks were almost simple – but ballet's glamour had shifted from the dancers' glittering costumes to their techniques and the stories they told. The dominant colour of their dresses was white – then a novel colour for stage design – for, as Théophile Gautier remarked, Romanticism 'brought about a great abuse of white gauze, of tulle and tarlantans, shadows melted into mist through transparent dresses. White was almost the only colour used.' Colour was employed for peasant or exotic costume, but modesty still prevailed in the simple lines of the women's skirts and in the use of aprons and ribbons for ornamentation. Flowers were very popular, circling the dancers' hair, tucked into their bodices or held in their hands, and their presence was partly symbolic – lilies signifying death, roses young love. But these heroines were themselves like flowers waiting to be plucked in their innocent freshness, all too prone to fading tragically away.

The few pictures of men from this period show them dressed in dark, vaguely medieval tunics, or gentrified versions of national costume. Compared to the dashing outfits of Vestris, their outfits look distinctly unassuming. These dancers are no threat to the real stars, the ballerinas.

Nineteenth-century Classical Ballet

By the late nineteenth century the mid-thigh tutu was standard wear for female dancers and, even though it was longer and staider than our current version, for the time it displayed a titillating amount of leg. It also provided a lot more freedom and exaggerated the formal stylization of the classical dancer's body. With its stiffly flared skirt, it exaggerated the turned-out line of the limbs and provided a frame around the dancer's hips and upper thighs – the source of all her steps. It also took up space, creating an aura around her and making her literally larger than life.

Among the top ballerinas competition was deadly, and individual success was marked not only by the number of starring roles a dancer performed, but also by the wealth and rank of her admirers. Consequently it was common for these women to go on stage displaying their latest or favourite piece of jewellery. They did this irrespective of the period, setting and nature of the role, just as they always wore a splendid tutu irrespective of the fact that other dancers on stage might be wearing costumes from another time and place entirely.

The men, however, continued to wear tunics over tights, and in Russia at least they had to observe certain codes of propriety well into the twentieth century. When Nijinsky danced *Giselle* in St Petersburg in 1911 he wore the costume which had been designed for performances in the more liberal theatres of Paris. This was a much shorter tunic than the Russians were accustomed to, and it omitted the trunks that were customarily worn over tights. To certain members of the Russian establishment Nijinsky appeared to be rudely displaying himself and his 'outrage' was considered all the more scandalous because the Dowager Empress had been in the audience.

(She, apparently, was less shockable than her ministers and said, 'I did not see anything indecent in Nijinsky's costume. If I had noticed anything shocking, then as a lady I would hardly have drawn attention to it.' But as a lady today the Dowager Empress might find herself having to maintain a careful silence over more opportunistic male displays. Since tunics now rarely reach lower than hip level and tights are very closely fitting there are occasions when audiences can't help being mesmerized by the 'line enhancement' practised by vainer men dancers.)

Twentieth-century Ballet

Nijinsky's costume was in fact inspired by Jules Perrot's outfit for the original staging of *Giselle* and was characteristic of the drive for authenticity that motivated the early Ballets Russes productions. Fokine, even while at St Petersburg, had fought passionately against his ballerinas wearing personal jewellery on stage, and had tried unsuccessfully to get his dancers to perform with bare legs in one of his early Greek ballets. Once he was with Diaghilev, and Benois and Bakst were designing his ballets, Fokine's pursuit of realism had free rein. Not only did the designs of a ballet like *Petrushka* show unprecedented attention to authentic detail but various costumes broke the mould of 'ballet dress' in bold new ways. What would the Maryinsky management have said to Nijinsky's skimpy, pink-petalled tunic in *Spectre de la Rose*, to his naked torso in *Schéhérazade* or to his dappled all-in-one leotard in *Faune*?

In some ballets the costume and design dominated the choreography, like Picasso's outfits for *Parade* which virtually reduced certain of the dancers to stage hands as they moved around in towering cubist structures. However, the costumes created by Oskar Schlemmer for his own ballets during the 1920s were even more unsympathetic to the dancers' bodies. Preferring abstractions to people, he dressed his performers in outfits that wildly distorted their natural contours. They became simply colours and shapes moving in space (see illus. 14).

Schlemmer's ideas were fuelled by a philosophy that makes Le Corbusier sound cosy. 'In the past,' he argued, 'we have neglected Form and Law in favour of the cult of mood and individualism.' But as American critic Deborah Jowitt reports, reconstructions of his works reveal an irresistible wackiness of design. She describes Schlemmer's own costume in the third part of his *Triadic Ballet* (1922), which involved one of his legs being fatly swaddled to look like a 'turkey drumstick' while the other, clad in black, was virtually invisible against the black stage. One of Schlemmer's hands was concealed under a huge bell, while the other was got up to look like a metallic club, and his pear-shaped head was painted half-pink and half-red.

The ballerina of the piece was dressed in black and thus invisible except for the gold coil that spiralled round her torso and her golden head-dress. All that could be seen of her two cavaliers also was their gold masks, the gold balls and discs that were attached to their torsos and the bizarre decoration of their legs – a series of balls enclosed within a cage of white strings. Not surprisingly, much of Schlemmer's choreography consisted of very odd and very limited steps.

In works like *Triadic Ballet* it's the costumes that dance. Individual performers are transformed into objects and illusions, and this fascination with metamorphosis has continued throughout twentieth-century dance. In Alwin Nikolais's high-tech compositions, dancers have mutated into anonymous shapes created by yards of stretchy fabric and coloured light shows, while dancers in American companies Pilobolus and Momix have been turned into giants, animal life and vegetation through costumes, lighting and the gymnastic contortions of their bodies.

But for Balanchine unadorned steps were sufficient to fill the stage. His choreography provided all the pattern, colour and imagery a work needed, and of course it had to be clearly seen. Thus the archetypal Balanchine work was danced in minimal costumes (T-shirts, leotards and tights in stark black and white). Not only did these offer a cheap, no-fuss option, but they emphasized the dancers' lean modernity, their clean lines and energy, and their bold declaration that beauty, mystery and glamour could be found in pure movement. The costumes' uniformity also declared Balanchine's allegiance to New World democracy – or rather meritocracy. In most of his ballets it was clear that dancers who got the best steps were also the best at the job. It wasn't because they were Princes or Princesses wearing the most expensive outfits on the stage.

Balanchine's preferred uniform has been much imitated and is now one of the standard outfits for a plotless ballet. Another familiar uniform, which often signifies a blander, prettier kind of neo-classicism, is the flimsy, pastel-coloured frock or tunic, while the mid-calf dress in drab shades of jersey tends to signal dance with a suffering heart and earthy peasant roots.

Between the two extremes of dancers wearing practice clothes and looking like Meccano men, the twentieth-century ballet wardrobe now embraces a huge set of options. Choreographers can choose between the modern variant of the nineteenth-century tutu or jeans; they can opt for the subversiveness of on-stage nudity or the reassuring panoply of full historical dress.

Modern and Post-modern Dance

When Isadora Duncan bared her feet and sometimes her breasts she was trumpeting the naturalness of her dance and the power of her own body. 'I believe,' she was wont to declare, 'in the religion of the beauty of the human foot.' Given the tightly corseted nature of late-nineteenth-century society, some of the public must have flocked to Duncan's shows for titillation rather than spiritual uplift. But her gestures paved the way for other dancers like Martha Graham to dance barefoot and to strip their image of feminine frippery. The plain jersey frock favoured by Graham was very severe – emphasizing the stark lines of her choreography. But Graham was personally vain and theatrically astute. Her tight-fitting bodices were cut very low and very beautifully, while the wide swing of her skirts moved sensuously with the movement, falling into almost sculptural folds that amplified the dynamic of the dance.

Merce Cunningham, whose own movement was both more detailed and less vehement than Graham's, preferred to dress his dancers in leotards and tights or unitards – the ultimate second

skin that allowed them maximum freedom with minimum distraction.

With the universal advent of Lycra in the 70s, unitards started
to appear in a glossy, acid-bright assortment of colours. These
were particularly favoured by choreographers of the more athletic
school of modern dance. As light gleamed off the dancers' sleekly
clad limbs, the extreme lines and acrobatic distortions of their
bodies seemed like the language of a super-race. This was the
age when dance became – willingly or otherwise – part of a global
cult of physical fitness. Acolytes sweated in the gym or aerobics
class to achieve the dancer's lean thigh, washboard stomach, taut
muscle tone and supple spine. Boutiques sold leotards and leg
warmers by the million. They were worn at parties and discos.
They spelt fitness and sex.

By contrast the intellectual aesthetic of choreographers like
Rainer and Brown was functionally dressed in sneakers and sweat
pants – or sometimes in chaste near-nudity. If their spare, understated choreography could be summed up in a single phrase, it
would be anti-gloss. Twyla Tharp once retorted to a caretaker
who chided her and her dancers for rehearsing on a Sunday that
they 'were just a bunch of broads doing God's work'. Late-60s
avant-garde dance clothed its puritan work ethic in puritan dress.

By the mid-70s one strand of minimalist dance had started to
look East. Choreographers made works whose dreamily repetitive
turns and T'ai Chi-inspired stillness were designed to induce a
meditative calm in its audience. Appropriately the performers
tended to wear loose-fitting pyjama trousers, simple tops, bare
feet or Chinese slippers – Zen dress for Zen dance.

By the 80s the concept of the 'ordinary' or the anti-dance uniform had become more glamorous. Dancers (particularly in
Europe) were no longer dressed in androgynous sweat pants. The
cut of the women's frocks and of the men's trousers was notice-
ably more stylish and most women wore lipstick. Dance might
be displaying the violence and alienation of inner-city life, but it
was also displaying the chic. At one extreme end of the spectrum
street fashion turned to club style as dancers wore outfits that
would have graced the staircase of clubs like London's Kinky
Gerlinky (and often, after shows, did). Michael Clark, for instance,

might wear a dragon's tail or a frilly apron, bubble wig and dildo. Genders were bent, fantasies ran rampant in clothes you often couldn't even give a name to. This was dance as counter-culture with a fashionable vengeance.

DANCE STAGES AND SET DESIGNS

If the dancers' clothes can give us important clues about what kind of people (or bodies) they are, then the stage on which they perform and the design of the scenery both tell us about the world they inhabit. Stage and setting can put the dance into a specific period or place and they can help define its atmosphere. They also create the frame within which the choreography and its dancers are viewed. And, as with any well or badly hung painting, this frame can have a flattering – or distracting – effect on the work.

The Stages

When choreography is performed on a proscenium arch stage and seen from the hushed darkness of an auditorium, the audience may feel as if it's in a magic box, primed and ready for illusion. But despite the mystique of the venue, the actual size and type of stage may make or break a work's power. A too-small stage will cramp and stifle a large-scale dance, while a cavernous stage may swallow an intimate solo. An unfamiliarly sharply raked stage can throw the dancers off balance, while a flat, hard stage can bully the bounce out of them. (When Mikhail Baryshnikov and Gelsey Kirkland performed together at the Paris Grand Opéra, Kirkland, used to flatter American stages, was badly affected by its steep rake. At one point she started to skid backwards and would have fallen off the stage, had Baryshnikov not grabbed her by the tutu and pulled her back.)

Nor is it just the dancers' nerves that are frayed by the unpredictability of venues. Choreographers also suffer as the piece they've made to fit a particular space has to have its spacing and dynamics readjusted to fit different stages. Shobana Jeyasingh's

experience is typical. When her works go on tour they're performed in a wide range of theatres, which may not all be specially
suited to dance. It is, as she says, 'like asking a painter to keep
moving his or her work from one frame to another and still expect
them to be contented with the effect'.

But it's not only the shape and size of venue that affect the
work, it's also the atmosphere. When we watch a performance in
a hall or gym, the sweating, panting performers are much closer
to us than in a conventional theatre, so that we feel the work's
physicality, its effort and its graft. Dance performed outdoors,
however, is like music, and tends not to travel well – its effects
dissipate in the distance and fresh air.

A non-theatrical venue can, though, interact potently with
dance. When Trisha Brown staged her early rooftop pieces in 60s
New York the sight of the dancers' tiny figures against the vaulting Manhattan skyline must have thrillingly jolted the audience's
sense of human scale. Equally when Daniel Larrieu's dancers took
over various European swimming pools for his work *Waterproof*
(1986) the juxtaposition of dance and water, of choreography
and swimming, of music and sports hall echo was uniquely
surreal.

And, of course, the scenery or set design of any work is as
much a part of the frame as the stage – dramatically influencing
our view of the choreography, whether it be the gothic lakeside
scenery of *Swan Lake* or the austere sculptural forms of Isamu
Noguchi's sets for Martha Graham.

The Sets

Audiences for the court ballets of the sixteenth and seventeenth
centuries would have been as interested in the theatrical frame
as in the dance. Kings and nobility not only lavished money on
opulent costumes and disguises, they also commissioned scenery
that involved state-of-the-art machinery and fantastical decoration. In the allegorical *Mountain Ballet* performed at Louis XIII's
court, for instance, the scenery consisted of five huge mountains,
whose sides opened to allow quadrilles of dancers to enter the

stage. The settings of these ballets were essentially designed to be gawped at.

But when ballet moved on to theatre stages, designers began to create more intimate, self-contained worlds. The introduction of gas lights in the early nineteenth century meant that soft, flickering light could transform hard-working, sweaty ballerinas into hovering sylphs; it could conceal the mechanisms of wires and harnesses that flew sprites and Wilis through the air; and it could make flat, painted scenery look as if it concealed groves and caves. Whether designers were re-creating the Indian temples of *Bayadère* or the *faux* Versailles of *Sleeping Beauty*, they were aiming for a realism that would set the story in a believable place as well as give colour and detail to the plot. With today's computer-operated stage machinery and lighting, and with the versatility of materials available to designers, audiences can now be transported to the busy streets of Shakespeare's Verona in Nicholas Georgiadis's designs for MacMillan's *Romeo and Juliet* as convincingly as to the cold, glittering ice palace of Terry Bartlett's designs for David Bintley's *Snow Queen* (1986).

Good dance design, however, like good opera or theatre design, has to yield precedence to the material. Too much busy detail in costumes, props and scenery can make the dance very hard to see, swamping the patterns of the choreography in a generalized blur. (Running too hard after realism can also be impractical. When Nicholas Beriosoff choreographed a version of *La Esmeralda* for Festival Ballet in 1954 he was very keen to have a goat accompany his gypsy heroine's first entrance. But the goat, which was loaned by London Zoo, reacted very intimately to one of the ballerinas, Natalie Krassovska. As the company's director Braunsweg recalled, 'Every time Tata went on with the goat, it peed all over her. She stood centre stage, looking beautiful, while the goat wet her legs and point shoes and the pool of water grew larger and larger.' After four performances the goat was sent back to the zoo.)

Ideally in any dance design there should be some concept, visual or poetic, that reacts with the choreography and shows it to us freshly. Yet designers have to resist the temptation to re-write the work, and a couple of recent British productions of

nineteenth-century classics illustrate how even the best inten-
tioned can end up quarrelling with the choreography.

When the English National Ballet updated its *Giselle* to a 20s
Alpine setting, in 1995, they were aiming to give us new views
on a familiar ballet, and at certain points they succeeded. The
aristocratic hunting party in Act I looked startlingly intimidating
when they entered in their furs and skis, their expensive twentieth-century accessories making Giselle and her mother seem
part of an exaggeratedly old-fashioned, innocent world. But
wrenching the ballet out of its original context also threw up
problems of logic. When Albrecht drove up to Giselle's hut in a
gleaming limo which he left parked in full view, it wasn't a good
basis for a man pretending to be a simple peasant. And when
Hilarion mimed to himself the traditional set passage – 'I've seen
Albrecht's sword and I've seen his cloak, he has to be a nobleman'
– there was something comical about the choreography's inability
to take into account the most blatant status symbol of them all –
the huge car at the back of the stage.

In the Royal Ballet's production of *Sleeping Beauty* (1994)
designer Maria Bjørnson took some dizzying risks in her efforts
to underline certain themes in the ballet. In the Prologue and
Act I she demonstrated, visibly, that something was rotten in the
self-congratulatory court of King Florestan by distorting all the
angles of the palace interior. Pillars crowded at odd angles, balus-
trades spiralled into a queasy vortex and a banqueting table
threatened to tilt its load of candelabras on to the floor. Only
when Evil (Carabosse) was acknowledged and then vanquished
in the ballet did the perspectives gradually right themselves. But
in the process the designs continued, rather spectacularly, to tell
the ballet's story. The hunting scene of Act II was, unusually, set
in winter, as if 100 years after Carabosse's curse the whole world
was still frozen by her spell. The circle of bleak sky at the apex
of the scene closed like a giant eye when Florimund set off to
find Aurora, and when it opened it revealed the misty palace, the
distant object of his quest. At the close of Act II the action cut to
the interior, where Aurora was tangled in spiders' webs that
ripped dramatically apart with Florimund's kiss.

Bjørnson's critics objected to her presumption in taking over so much of the ballet's story-telling, while her admirers found her effects unusually magical. But even the latter had to admit that her sets made the first half of the ballet difficult to see. The plot of *Sleeping Beauty* may deal with chaos and evil, but Petipa's choreography never deviates from its perfect symmetries, and against the crazy angles of Bjørnson's set, the exquisitely orderly dance patterns were often lost. The dancers too were dwarfed by the emphatic lines of the palace interior. They seemed in severe need of fresh air.

It's arguable that we've become so reliant on ingenious stage devices and beautiful costumes that we no longer see how well dance can tell its own story and how cunningly it can spin its own patterns. *Swan Lake* or *Sleeping Beauty* can actually look impressive danced against a black velvet curtain. And when William Forsythe assaults ballet convention, part of his attack involves stripping opera house stages of their traditional glamour and illusion. When in *Firstext* the stage was taken right back to bare bricks, the dance looked both fragile and apocalyptic in the echoing spaces that were opened up.

Such devices can only shock once in a generation, though – because fashion shapes the way we look at all designs. Some of the grey-and-chrome sets that were voguish during the 80s now look as *passé* as that decade's designer living rooms, while some folkloric designs for *Giselle* or *Coppélia* (1870) can seem fusty and twee. At the same time, potentially excruciating past design can look charming or period when revived at the right time. A 1992 revival of Ashton's 1968 *Jazz Calendar* with designs by the late Derek Jarman happened to coincide with a 60s retro trend in fashion – so while its plastic materials, Day-Glo colours and playschool shapes might have looked laughable a decade before, they actually appeared surprisingly current and sharp.

Diaghilev was the last person to underrate fashionable taste – but his practice of commissioning designs from painters and sculptors guaranteed that some of his ballets retained the lasting impact of works of art. Picasso, Matisse, Gris, Bakst and others were not just creating cardboard imitations of the real world, they were bringing a live painterly vision to the ballet. The dappled impressionism of Bakst's designs for *Faune*, Picasso's hot, witty

Spanish designs for *Le Tricorne* (1919), the dark expressionist power of Rouault's setting of *Prodigal Son* – all of these were, and are, canvases in their own right. Not only do they profoundly define the ballets' identity, they can be studied as pleasurably as works in a gallery.

At times Diaghilev's designers threatened to hijack the dancing, so it's hardly surprising that when Balanchine began to strip his own choreography down to lean, neo-classic lines he usually chose to do so on a bare stage. Not only was visual competition from enthusiastic designs the last thing he wanted, but the presence of elaborate scenery and props would have denied the axiomatic basis of his work – which was that dance creates its own world in its own space.

Isadora Duncan also knew the value of the empty, if artfully draped, stage to show off her own recitals. As a dancer, she knew she could create quite enough theatrical interest by herself. Martha Graham also started out making dances on bare stages – lack of money meant she had little choice. But as her budget expanded, so she appreciated the value of sharing her stage with beautifully designed sets and props. The shapes of her dancers' bodies would have other complex physical forms with which to connect; their energy could bounce off the energy of other objects.

The sets which Graham commissioned from Isamu Noguchi were in part beautiful sculptures resonating within the dance. But they were also hard-working and functional sets. They provided surfaces around which the dance could move; they divided up the stage into small secret spaces or open areas. They often gave the bare suggestion of location (like the little fence that marked out the farm perimeters in *Appalachian Spring* (1944)) and they yielded important symbolic clues to the work – like Medea's flaming wire cage in *Cave of the Heart* that suggested fire and sun, imprisonment and magic.

Merce Cunningham's late work tends to be danced on a bare stage, but his earlier dances were often crammed with odd props (a television or a potted plant) or some huge installation. Like his music, these designs were a strictly independent ingredient in the performance mix. Their role wasn't planned when the choreography was made. If Andy Warhol's silver helium-filled balloons scudded under and over the feet of the dancers in *Rainforest*, or if his choreography had to fit itself around Jasper Johns's large Perspex rectangles in *Walkaround Time* (1968), Cunningham didn't complain that the designs got in the way. They were interesting, beautiful objects which he'd invited in (see illus. 13). (He once said about the Johns designs for *Walkaround Time*, 'I had no idea how big they were going to be because I never saw them until the day of the performance.' As he went on to admit, cheerfully, 'They limited very much what one could do in the space.')

In much of today's dance the design element has become so dominant that the work has to be choreographed around it – it can't physically exist without it. In D V 8's *Strange Fish* some of the most astonishing images were only made possible by the set (designed by Peter Davison). Huge wooden walls with built-in cubby holes, doors and footholds allowed the dancers to leave and enter the action with shocking abruptness, as well as facilitating the various climbing and balancing acts that were part of the characters' ritual methods of attention-seeking and destruction. A water tank beneath a false floor allowed two characters to immerse themselves in a watery spiritual baptism; a giant cross supported a female Christ figure and a trap door opened up to send torrents of white rocks spilling over the stage – rocks over which a woman painfully racked her body after a humiliating sexual encounter.

The works of Japanese choreographer Saburo Teshigawara generally take place in even more immaculately assembled pieces of installation art. In *Bones in Pages* (1993), 1,000 books lined the walls of the stage facing outwards with their pages ruffled to create a textured light-reflecting pattern. Down one side of the floor 1,000 shoes were mathematically lined up to cut a huge shadowy swathe. Sections of furniture were stuck at odd angles on to large Perspex screens. Everyday objects were reduced to shapes and ideas, light and shadow.

As in much of Teshigawara's work, the choreography was geared towards dismantling this abstract world. The dance began with Teshigawara slumped over a table covered with shards of plastic glass until suddenly, and from nowhere, a black crow flopped down crashing and stumbling over the glass fragments.

This shocking moment activated Teshigawara into a frenzy of self-berating dance and then into a ritual destruction of the stage – ending in a blizzard of torn pages and storm of thrown shoes. The dance would have meant nothing without its set.

But some of the most magical effects in dance can be created by pure light. Designers like Jean Rosenthal and more recently Jennifer Tipton have developed lighting far beyond its simple ability to cue day and night, indoors and outdoors, cheerfulness and gloom. It has become intrinsic to the design of the movement, to the degree that in a work like *Necessary Weather* (1994), performed by Dana Reitz and Sara Rudnor, Tipton is actually listed as co-choreographer. Throughout this piece her light creates a constantly changing structure within which the dancers move. At one point it quarters the stage into four pools that draw the two women in from the surrounding darkness; at another it streams from floor to ceiling in a column of gold that holds Reitz captive as she stands in its beam. It also works an alchemical reaction with the movement. When it throws the dancers into high definition it seems to blast up the volume of their energy; when it casts them into silhouette or gilds them with a rosy glow they become figures of mystery and reticence.

Bad lighting is everybody's nightmare. It can flatten the dance or throw it into obscuring gloom; it can cast an unflattering glare on the dancers' faces and bodies. But part of the magic of good lighting is that its effects work in ways that are similar to dance. They are created out of space and moving energy, out of images that may appear stable but are actually ephemeral. They create poetry out of air.

Chapter Fourteen: **FILMING DANCE**

Dance has traditionally been the most theatrical of art forms, existing only at the moment of the live performance. But during the twentieth century television and cinema have developed increasingly sophisticated ways of getting movement down on film. Audiences no longer have to travel to theatres to see dance – it can be delivered to their sitting rooms. A single TV screening of *Nutcracker* or *Sleeping Beauty* may be seen by more people than those attending a whole season of live performances, while audiences living in the Australian outback or Scottish Hebrides may come to have similar access to dance as those living in London, Paris or New York.

We may be entering a brave new era of televised dance, and the benefits for choreographers may sound as heady as those for audiences. Not only can more people see their work, but the camera can offer an imaginative freedom far wilder than that dreamed of by the early Romantics.

It can, for example, show us six bodies floating slowly through an open window – dreams or memories who come in from the night to haunt a man in an empty room.

It can show us a lone, desperate woman dancing on the top of a skyscraper, her body arching sickeningly backwards into empty air as her feet skitter to retain her balance.

It can show us a young man walking down a train carriage who blinks and suddenly realizes that all the passengers round him are nodding their heads, flapping their hands and bouncing their knees in a tightly choreographed, Busby Berkeley-style routine.

In these and a thousand other examples of television dance, choreographers have been allowed to dispense with gravity, to travel the world and to liberate themselves from the laws of probability. They have also been given the opportunity to record their works for the future. When dance is put on film its survival is no longer dependent on written notation, or on people's memories. When star performers dance for the camera, their legends too can be nailed down for posterity.

Or can they?

Keith Money's 1968 film of Margot Fonteyn performing Act I of *Sleeping Beauty* with the Royal Ballet is acknowledged as a treasure of the archive. Here, on celluloid, is Britain's most famous ballerina dancing her definitive role with a company at the peak of its form. Here, preserved for all time, is the classic simplicity of Fonteyn's line, the clear shape of her phrasing, the loveliness of her smile.

But even as we marvel at this flashback into history, we find that Money's filming techniques can intrude on the way we see the dance. We have to ignore his rather laboured direction – the dogged way he cuts back and forth from a full frontal shot to an extreme diagonal as well as the predictability with which he underscores every big moment with a close-up. And we also have to discount the merciless way that the film (like all films) exposes ragged dancing and eccentricities of style. We note with unsettling clarity how the *corps* are not dancing every step together, how small they look compared with the leggy athletes we've become accustomed to, and even how strangely 60s their make-up appears.

Even Fonteyn's 'magic' has to be deliberately constructed: we note her qualities, they don't blaze off the screen. Of course, she wasn't performing in front of a live audience here. Nor was she dancing at the height of her technical powers. But the fact is that while the techniques of film and video can create their own illusions (like dancers flying eerily through windows), they can't fully capture the illusion of the stage. Charisma, personality, physical beauty, style – all these are diminished when they're converted from flesh and blood into electronic signals, even when we're viewing dancers of our own time.

Research has actually shown that watching dance on film is a very unphysical experience. Audiences sitting on sofas don't perform those tiny twitchy moves which they make when they're watching live bodies. And the reason why they don't dance along with the performance is not just the absence of live flesh – it's the fact that dance is taking place in an entirely different environment.

Firstly the screen is much smaller than the stage (20 inches square compared with 30–60 feet square) and it only has two dimensions, which means that TV dance inevitably looks diminished. When we watch dance on the 'big stage' our eyes can track backwards and forwards and from side to side as well as change focus with incredible speed, so that they take in a huge amount of information. They also respond intensely to the movement, widening with any dramatic stimulus. Not only do we 'read' the dance in lively ways, we connive in its dramatic effect.

TV dance, by contrast, gives us only an edited version of the live event. A camera crew can only reproduce a tiny proportion of the information we read from the stage, and it can only do so with laborious effort – positioning cameras, planning shots and then painstakingly editing the material into a finished film.

Every image that is shot in a dance film also kills off a hundred others. If the camera zooms in for a close-up, it will capture the detail and intimacy of a move but also lose its relation to the rest of the dance. If the camera retreats to take in the whole stage, it will capture pattern and mass but lose the clarity of the steps and the individuality of the dancers. Twenty or thirty figures on a big screen are little more than sticks.

Television perspective also works very differently from stage perspective. When live dancers move backwards they can still be impressive at the back of the stage. But on screen a dancer only has to travel back a few steps to shrink dramatically. Similarly when dancers close to the camera move from side to side they're only in shot for a couple of steps before they're lost from view.

Another issue is time, which affects us differently in filmed dance than it does in live performance. It may be that we're used to concentrating more intently in the theatre, so that time passes quicker, or it may be that we're used to television assaulting us with rapid, high doses of imagery. But frequently the work that grips us in the theatre becomes a dull plodder in the sitting room.

Of course, directors have many ways of compensating for the limits of their medium. They can physically move the camera alongside the dancers to generate extra energy. They can shoot from different angles to keep the choreography surprising (dancers tilting hugely as they're shot from below or bodies glimpsed quirkily past elbows and between legs). They can incorporate dramatic lighting changes to underline changes in pace or structure. They can play with montages or dissolves to try and mimic the simultaneity of live viewing. They can make dull movements look fascinating with a zooming close-up. They can zap up the pace with speedy editing. In all sorts of ways they can make extremely inventive and interesting film – but the choreographer may not recognize it as his or her dance.

Most choreographers have now resigned themselves to the catch-22 of TV dance, which is that a scrupulous record of their steps will produce a very dull film, while a fresh and lively screen version is bound to take liberties with their work. The camera can't record dance in ways that are both interesting *and* faithful.

There are two ways out of this dilemma. The choreographer can either work closely with the director, re-creating the stage dance as a two-dimensional screen event, or make work directly for the camera – exploring the brand new genre of television dance.

It's not surprising that Merce Cunningham, the most technophile of all choreographers, was one of the first to start exploring this option. Even back in the late 70s he was saying, 'Several years ago, I had a feeling that, good or bad, there was going to be more dancing on television and that I had better find out about it.' And he's gone on to make a number of TV dances where the camera works for, rather than against, his choreography.

In *Points in Space* (1986), for instance, he and director Elliot Caplan made a special virtue out of the fact that televised dance often looks as if it's happening in limbo – a space without boundaries or walls. During filming Cunningham put his dancers in a huge circular arena and choreographed the movement so that it faced all directions, and Caplan's cameras too roved all round the dance. This meant there was no front, back or side to the choreography and no 'front view' for the camera – and the dancers as a result appeared, magically, to occupy limitless space.

When they were actually in shot, they seemed to be held fast in the camera's eye, and often the camera moved with them, creating an exhilarating sense of speed. The relationship between dance and lens felt very physical. But when the dancers moved out of shot it seemed as if they'd zoomed back off into space and were continuing to perform their intricate dance somewhere else among the stars.

(It was typical of Cunningham that he should then reverse the usual stage-to-screen logic and adapt *Points in Space* to the theatre. The difference was astonishing. On stage, the work seemed to have moved into a pressure chamber, a small box with dark walls, and the originally free-spirited dancers now appeared much more vulnerable and confined.)

It is difficult, though, to astonish your audience with pure dance on camera and much easier to exploit the variety of location, props and special effects that can be used when filming more theatrical dance. In the screen adaptation of DV8's *Strange Fish* director David Hinton enriched the dance by relocating it to a disused factory which was rebuilt to look, in some sections, like a social club and, in other sections, like symbolic space, with various doors and corridors marking out the internal geography of the characters' minds (different fantasies and personae occupying different rooms).

When Hinton directed the screen version of DV8's *Dead Dreams of Monochrome Men* his camera dealt with the loss of live impact by its own extreme effects. In the trust-and-dare sequence in *Dead Dreams* (where Nigel Charnock repeatedly climbs to the top of a wall several times his height and then throws himself down at Russell Maliphant), he captures the sickening physical tension of the live version by having the camera move to the top of the wall and then plunge down to Maliphant – the cutting of the shots and the speed of the zoom intensifying the fall.

Obviously where choreographers create works direct for television the possibilities become even more explosive. The writer Walter Benjamin once famously argued that 'Even the most perfect reproduction of a work of art is lacking in one element: its presence in time and space, its unique existence at the place where it happens to be.' But in dance made specially for camera choreographers can create a new 'unique existence' that is the film. British companies The Cholmondeleys and The Feather-stonehaughs have danced on cross-Channel ferries and on the beaches of France; the Royal Ballet have apparently danced on a storm-tossed galleon in *The Rime of Ancient Mariner*. And when those six bodies float horizontally through the window in Gilles Maheu's *Le Dortoir*, past and present, dream and reality, space and time dissolve into a logic that exists only within those few extraordinary shots.

Despite its range, inventiveness and edge TV dance is rarely ranked alongside theatre dance as Serious Art. It's still considered a hybrid and a novelty. In the same way comic ballets also tend to be regarded as diversions – unable to match the high tragedies or abstract works in the repertoire for substance and vision. Yet comedy in dance is underrated and under-reported and goes far beyond the routine clichés of the eyelash-batting, pouty male dancer and the wobbly, fat ballerina. The fact that dance is a physical art with intensely inbred conventions makes it a rich source of humour. And, as works like Tudor's *Gala Performance* (1938), Jerome Robbins's *The Concert* (1956) and the repertoire of Les Ballets Trockadero de Monte Carlo show, some of the best jokes cracked about dance are by dancers and choreographers.

Of all Western dance, classical ballet is probably the most vulnerable to comedy. It aims so relentlessly for perfection that any human lapse or frailty can seem exaggeratedly funny. In real life, when things go wrong for dancers, most viewers are caught halfway between sympathy and hilarity. The ardent Prince who vaults off stage in search of his Princess and is then heard crashing straight into an unseen obstacle in the wings, becomes instantly ludicrous – his heroic pretensions deflating along with the climax of his leap. The two dancers criss-crossing the stage in the *corps de ballet* who get out of line and bump into each other are no longer Swans or Wilis but clowns.

At such moments the superhuman perfection of the choreo-graphic mechanism is suddenly revealed as fallible – and the jokes in Robbins's comedy ballet *Concert* come very close to the bone in showing how individual dancers may be elegantly and com-placently navigating the patterns of the choreography while at the same time being fatally out of sync with each other. Natalia Makarova still remembers how bad this can feel in real life, recalling the performance when as a fledgeling dancer in the Kirov's *corps* she found herself out of rhythm with everyone else. 'I was so much concentrating on the steps ... that I messed up the whole thing, everyone was down while I was up and everyone up when I was down. The public was hysterical and I didn't even realize that they were laughing at me. I thought I would be fired, but instead they never put me in the *corps de ballet* again.' (The nightmare dance was the Parrot Waltz in *Bayadère*. When Makarova staged her own version she edited it right out of the ballet.)

At the same time, when ballet looks too mechanical – when individuals appear too subordinate to the choreographic process – dancers can equally look comic. Few performances of the Cygnets' *pas de quatre* in Act II of *Swan Lake* escape without a giggle from somewhere in the audience. The precision-perfect timing of their little jumps, crossed arms and nodding heads is so briskly drilled that the dancers look as if they've been wound up by clockwork.

Ballet also teeters on the edge of the ridiculous because of the extravagance of its manners and the extremity of its characters, emotions and plots. If we aren't entirely convinced by the tragedy of Siegfried's deception by Odile, then we find it hard to keep a straight face when he goes running to his mother in anguished panic – 'Look, Mummy, what the nasty woman's done to me.' If we don't buy the image of the grand ballerina, we can find a dancer's mid-scene curtseying and milking of applause either outrageous or absurd. If we can't accept the period kitsch of a ballet like *Bayadère*, then we will find its parade of stuffed tigers and elephants, its aviary of parrots perched on the shoulders of the *corps de ballet*, its solemn cartoon mime preposterous.

The question of where ballet's extravagance slides into camp has been marvellously addressed by Les Ballets Trockadero de Monte Carlo. This all-male American company (with its star cast of Mesdemoiselles Gladiolova, Leftova and Bolshoya, etc.) presents a repertoire of delinquently revised classics from the Romantic period to Martha Graham. And what makes the dancers so funny is their blend of incongruity (chest hair and point shoes);

extremism (conventions parodied to a merciless degree of absurdity) and accuracy. These men know ballet inside-out, and they all want to be ballerinas. What they show us is a fine line between ballet as it almost is and ballet sent up to extinction.

Their version of Perrot's *Pas de quatre* (1845) parodies the conventions of Romantic style, so that we can hardly see the steps for period mannerism – the winsome pretence of fragility, the droopy arms and delicate, girlish footwork. It also gets hilarious mileage out of playing up the vulpine rivalry that existed between the four original ballerinas for whom the ballet was made, with an imperiously cross-patch Marie Taglioni stalking the stage while Lucie Grahn, Carlotta Grisi and Fanny Cerrito fight to steal her limelight with a battery of fluttering eyelashes and fixed smiles.

In *Swan Lake* the Trocs take evil mickey out of the more arcane mime conventions of nineteenth-century ballet. When Odette has to explain to the Prince the complex history of how she and her fellow princesses were turned into swans, it's all done as a tortuous game of charades. As for the four Cygnets, the dancers can barely fit into the Wendy house steps of the choreography, so big are their feet and so bulging their biceps (see illus. 15).

Yes, Virginia, Another Piano Ballet (1977) pounces on every cliché that's ever graced a Chopin ballet – the drifting Isadoras, the joyous folk steps, the studiedly dreamy expressions – and it reaches a deliriously comic climax when Gladiolova's rapturous excesses send her crashing into the side of the piano. But perhaps their most interesting parody of all is the generic 'Ballerina'. Two dancers in particular, Enimenimynimova and Grudj have mimicked to perfection all the devices by which She becomes an art form in her own right, the piously unworldly gaze that never leaves her face, the ritual of the curtain call where Her voracious egotism has for decency's sake to be concealed under a veneer of tremulous humility.

Accuracy is crucial even to a joke as extravagant as the 'Dance of the Hours' ballet in Disney's *Fantasia*, which is performed by ostriches, hippos and alligators. When the Disney animators worked on these images they used real-life ballet stars as models – Irina Baronova for the ostrich ballerina, Tatiana Riabouchinska for the hippo ballerina and David Lichine for the lead alligator.

Thus the skinny-legged ostrich and her *corps* are capable of virtuoso feats even as they make absurd all that we're used to admir-
ing. Their feet are unnaturally large in the way dancers' feet in
point shoes are – like ducks' feet out of water – and the ballerina's
in particular are gorgeously and rubberily articulate as she goes
up and down from point or crosses her ankles in beaten jumps.
The hippo ballerina, unlike her grand ostrich sister, has the dippy
feyness of a Romantic wannabe, dreaming of beauty and nature
as she dances, while at the same time remaining placidly and
benignly hippoish. The male alligator is all Sir Jasper cynicism and
smoothness, coming on to the defenceless hippos with hypnotic,
dangerous eroticism and capturing the more lurid sexual under-
tones of nineteenth-century ballet – hapless virgins ensnared by
evil, sex covertly corrupting innocence.

In the human ballet zoo, Tudor's *Gala Performance* remains not
only one of the repertoire's comic gems, but also a good source
of information about ballet history. The scenario revolves around
three ballerinas – French, Russian and Italian – who are all jockeying for star status. The accurate observations of gesture and
motive that made Tudor's serious works so real are here exploited
to brilliant comic effect and also give us succinct lessons in
national style.

The Moscow ballerina even now functions as a wicked parody
of Bolshoi excess as she milks every moment for emotional and
physical drama. Her *pirouettes* revolve with pedantic slowness so
that she can flash a smile at each turn; whenever she prepares
for a virtuoso jump or balance, her torso bends agonizingly forward under the burden of her artistic temperament, and when
she finishes a phrase she adopts a pose of shameless sensational-
ism, her back arched, her wrists exquisitely cocked, her mouth
almost snarling with triumph.

The Italian is all stately elegance and icy self-command. Conscious only of her sublimity, she expects her audience to dissolve
in raptures whenever she so much as points an exquisite toe, and
she totally ignores her hard-working partner as he scurries round
her to support her endless balances.

The French is a study of blown kisses, giggles and pretty footwork, her finger constantly caressing her face with delicate

narcissism, her eyes beaming seductive glances at anyone she happens to notice.

Dancers can be very funny about their own art – but, because they're so disciplined in the art of gesture, they can be brilliant physical comics even when their subject isn't dance. Gentle as the comedy usually is in Ashton's ballets, it's made funny and poignant by the musical stress of the timing, by the carefully judged deformation of steps and by the humanity of the observation.

The hoodwinked lovers in *The Dream* are at their most foolish when – wrought to a pitch of confusion – the men start dealing out the women like a pack of cards, trying to make the pairing of their choice. Demetrius picks up Hermia, puts her next to Lysander, then reaches out to put Helena in her place. Simultaneously Lysander picks up Hermia and plops her at the end of the line, reaching out for Helena. The timing is so precisely on the beat of the music, the men's actions are so lumpenly stubborn and the women so stiffly and idiotically helpless that we despise them just as much as Oberon and Puck do.

In *Fille mal gardée* when the simple-witted Alain tries to partner the heroine Lise or to perform his own virtuoso solo the jokes are partly cracks about ballet technique – like the bungled lifts that send her keeling over with her bottom to the audience or the *entrechats* that end in a knock-kneed, flat-footed tangle. But the oddities of his timing (these are not fluent parodies but straining heartfelt efforts) and the fact that his steps come within some whiskers of technical accuracy mean that they are also painfully about Alain's hopeless aspirations towards the poetry of love, his deluded desire to leap manfully and beautifully into the shoes of the hero, Colas.

During DV8's piece about macho stereotypes *Enter Achilles* there's a moment where one member of a group of drinking, brawling men dares to reveal a more sensitive nature than the others. He is cruelly guyed, but when his tormentors move in to attack him physically, he transforms himself into every boy's superhero. He whirls round and round, trouncing his attackers as his clothes fall from him to reveal a Superman suit. The moment generates blissful laughter from the audience – not only because the tilting into fantasy is so unexpected and so deft, but also because the dancer is able to turn with such speed, to mimic with such accuracy the angle of Superman's flying torso and at the same time make his face so bright with childlike ecstasy. In his performance we see Superman, regression and the illusion of flying all in one.

The wit in Mark Morris's work is often straight visual incongruity as in *L'Allegro*, where we shout with laughter at a sudden vision of men pretending to be hounds peeing on bushes. It's partly the neatness of the image's timing – the men's legs cocked so perkily mid-phrase; it's also the prosaic literalness of the action set within the pastoral landscape of Milton's poetry and Handel's music. But Morris's humour also comes dirty – like the moment in *Going Away Party* where the dance is happily miming the song's lyrics and the singer starts crooning about his girlfriend's lips pressed against his. In almost innocent obedience the women instantly jump up so that their legs straddle their partners' shoulders and their knickers are right up against the men's faces. The frankness of it makes the joke both outrageously smutty and rather sweet. In the same piece the humour can also turn formal where certain moves are set right on the beat of the music and then repeated and repeated with dumb determination along with the score. If you want Mickey Mousing, says Morris, beat this.

There is, of course, a whole history of dance humour that is basic slapstick – brawls and falls, mistaken identities, mugged overreactions to disaster, drink or desire. As in verbal humour the line between the comic and the crude has everything to do with timing, context and surprise. And, of course, with performance. A role like Kitri in Petipa's *Don Quixote* (which is 99 per cent pure dance) can be entirely unfunny when it's danced by a ballerina with no comic sense. But it can have audiences laughing out loud at the mock fury of her reactions to Basilio's flirtation, at her horrified withdrawal from the advances of the popinjay Gamache and at her dry and flighty high spirits.

Finally the audience gets to see the finished work – either on stage or on the screen. The dance has been choreographed with loving invention, it has been beautifully dressed and designed, and it has been performed with passionate accuracy. Yet for all the people in the audience who are moved and enthralled by it, there will be others who are indifferent and still others who think it is rubbish.

'Imaginative, witty, moving . . . it was hard to hold back the tears' – *Le Figaro* (Paris).

'Flatulent, heartsinkingly awful' – *Evening Standard* (London).

The above reactions were to *Mr C*, a ballet made by French choreographer Maurice Béjart in 1992, and, as they demonstrate, audiences and critics can disagree so wildly it's as if they've seen different shows. As it happens Béjart himself is probably one of the most violently loved and loathed artists of our time. The arguments that divide his audiences are not simply about whether he makes pleasing steps or not, they also aspire to a moral debate. Those who adore Béjart claim that he takes dance into a sphere of cosmic profundity – dealing with Life, Death, Spirituality and Art. Those who don't, claim he's a charlatan who treats these notions with the depth of advertising copy and who trashes the values of music and dance.

But who sets the agenda for what these values are? What makes us like or dislike a dance?

When we judge a piece of choreography it obviously feels like a personal matter – based on whether we enjoy this way of moving, admire that choice of music, prefer story ballets to plotless ones. The private nature of our response may also feel exaggerated by the speed at which it's been formed. Most judgements about dance have to be based on a once-only viewing and they often have to process a lot of information in a shortish time. If we compare the amount we have to take in during a thirty-minute piece by Cunningham with what we need to absorb in a painting by Cézanne (which sits still), it's clear that we can only ever hope to see a proportion of Cunningham's material at one viewing. Even if my neighbour and I both like or dislike the work equally, we'll have based our views on different viewings of the choreography.

In any case, we can rarely study a dance with the same detachment as an art object. Dance exists through its performers and the movement is filtered through human elements over which the choreographer has incomplete control. Even if we admire the steps, our pleasure may be dissipated by our irritation with certain dancers (one man's strained shoulders or another's fixed smile). Even if we despise the movement, we may enjoy it for the sake of a favourite performer.

But however personal the base line of our judgements feels, other factors come into play. The Béjart issue, for instance, highlights a divide in national taste that certainly influences some critics, if not all viewers. The British tend to be impressed by sophisticated, self-contained choreography and are suspicious of dance that's juiced up by the kind of theatricality beloved by Béjart (dancers declaiming bits of Nietzsche or worshipfully applauding a photo of Charlie Chaplin, or the choreographer himself reading from his diary during a performance). They also have a real terror of pretension. When Béjart claims that in a *pas de deux*, 'flesh and soul striv[e] to recover the primitive Adam', or when he stages a four-and-a-half-hour dance version of *The Ring* which he hopes will 'grasp the metaphysical content, the philosophical condition, the psyche of the main characters' – the British wince.

The Americans – at least those steeped in the pure-dance tradition of Balanchine, Cunningham and Morris – view Béjart even more harshly as an arch exponent of 'Eurotrash'. This is everything that's not Balanchine – in other words stunt-filled choreography, loosely connected structure, scores that carve up existing music (i.e. that might segue a Bach Mass into a tango) and glossy sex (i.e. men as brawny athletes, women as bendy Barbie dolls).

On the Continent and in Japan, however, Béjart is widely regarded as the Emperor of modern dance. He puts on a stunning show, with state-of-the-art lighting and flamboyant costumes. He embraces high and low art with unembarrassed appetite. He's ambitious about the kind of big statements dance ought to be making. Plus he has fabulously strong and beautiful dancers whose wildly angled limbs and bold attack can raise the hair on the back of your neck. Béjart is a total experience. His supporters insist that it's only uptight Anglo-Saxon puritans who don't get it.

The ferocity with which dance passions can rage was illustrated in the late 80s when Béjart was outmanoeuvred from his long reign as resident choreographer of Brussels' Monnaie Opera House and Mark Morris was installed in his place. Though Béjart is French, he'd been in Brussels for twenty-seven years and had accustomed Belgian dance-goers to his high-octane mix of athletics, cosmology and spectacle. Morris, with his ordinary-looking dancers, his plain-spoken emotions and his passion for music and structure, bewildered, and angered, certain influential sections of the dance public. The women in Morris's company were constantly nagged to shed a few kilos and wear more lipstick. The works were criticized for their lack of 'virtuoso' dance. And when Morris performed the sacred female role of Dido, or had his dancers strip gauchely in *Striptease* (1986), this wasn't considered profound, sexy or fun. Just plain outrageous. Headlines in the Belgian press screamed 'Mark Morris go home' even while adoring British and American fans continued to make pilgrimages to his every Brussels première.

Of course, xenophobia comes into all our critical judgements, since most of us start off with a sense of our home style being 'natural' and 'right'. The works and the dancers that we regularly see colour the way we look at everyone else. English ballet-goers, for instance, accustomed to lyricism and ease in dramatic expression, have traditionally complained that New York City Ballet dancers 'lack personality', have 'wooden' arms and a 'forced' line. These prejudices often harden when NYCB dancers try to perform Ashton or the nineteenth-century classics – while it's generally agreed among Americans that the British are far too prissy to dance Balanchine.

Some dancers, though, may be issued honorary passports to another country's style: Darcey Bussell's performances of Balanchine have impressed even New Yorkers; Londoners adored Gelsey Kirkland's Aurora while Irek Mukhamedov, who seemed destined to enter the history books as an archetypal Bolshoi star, defected to England and became an acclaimed MacMillan dancer. And when things go wrong there's nothing so vindictive as a public who feel they've been let down by their own. No one can be as rude as the New York City Ballet fans who saw the company on a downward slide after Mr B's death, or the British who believed the Royal could no longer dance Ashton. When a disappointed balletomane is looking for sticks to beat the local dancers, nothing becomes more overwrought than their praise for another company – the purity of the Kirov, for instance, or the elegance of the Paris Opéra.

In modern dance, loyalties and prejudices are exacerbated by the constant imperative to reinvent the language, an Oedipal climate which tends to make each generation scorn the prevailing style. Just as Graham rejected the floaty orientalisms of Ruth St Denis, so Cunningham spurned Graham's earth-bound anguished approach. Just as the 60s minimalist choreographers found Cunningham too technically dancerly, so the late 80s and 90s moved round towards a more urgently emotional expression.

Not only does one generation move forward by rejecting the previous generation's aesthetic, but individual artists who don't travel with their generation can make themselves difficult to see. When Taylor abandoned his stark, playful experiments in the 60s for full-bodied dance, a whole generation believed bitterly that he'd sold out and refused to look closely at what he was doing instead. When Mark Morris performed in London in 1985 many in the audience (including myself), who were still tuned to the austerely abstract aesthetic left over from the late 70s and early 80s, found his vivid personality, his jokes, his savagery, and, above all, the way he danced to music impossible to place.

The things we love can blind us to the virtues of other styles. Ballet fans may comprehend that post-modern dance isn't about brilliant footwork or purity of line but still be unable to thrill to its rawness or danger. And it can get harder to see dance the further it is from our own culture and the less skilled we are in reading its conventions and body language. In classical Indian dance the demeanour of many women performers can strike the unaccustomed Western viewer as disconcertingly girlish. The dancers' bright clothes, jewels and flowers, their darting glances and sweet smiles can appear downright coquettish. In fact their dress is not meant to be flirtatious distraction; it is part of the intense visual detail of the classical Indian aesthetic, while their heightened facial expressions are part of a stylized repertoire of mime. The dancers are not simpering but telling an honoured story.

In the same way, viewers whose taste is formed by the extreme slenderness of Western ballet dancers may admit to problems in adjusting to the solid fleshiness of many flamenco women, while those addicted to the space-devouring energy of mainstream Western dance may have to school themselves to patience when they watch the tremulous slowness of South-east Asian dance. Western audiences used to star dancers and virtuosity may also be uncertain how to value much traditional African dance. Since much of this is social rather than theatrical in origin, it tends to focus on group dynamics rather than individual starriness, and its brilliance is more about rhythmic intricacy and subtle isolation of muscle groups than about the stunts most Western audiences understand – like *pirouettes* or lifts.

If dance tends to be about the here, it also tends to be about the now. Choreography may be even more vulnerable than the other arts to swings in fashion – the dance we loved in the 70s we may hate in the 90s with its 'awful cosmic rock' score, its 'garish' Lycra and its 'pretentious' angst. But it is difficult to see a work that is more than a decade old in the way it was first performed. Graham originally made dances for a company that practically lived her philosophy and style. Now that she's dead, it is impossible for dancers with very different minds and bodies to perform those dances faithfully. Today's dancers are serious about different issues; they move with less weight and force and their bodies look more lithe. How deeply can a twenty-five-year-old impersonate someone from a generation that was young half a century ago?

Judging the revival of any work is always fraught with memory and nostalgia. 'They can't dance it now', 'They don't understand it' are the understandably pained responses of those who see a once-loved work looking somehow thinner, more vulnerable than they remember. So much can have happened to it. The work may not have been well mounted – so that essential details of the style or even essential steps haven't been transmitted to the new cast. The work may not suit the dancers or may be difficult or strange for them. And the audience may simply have changed, so that what once looked daring now looks tame, what was funny now looks gauche, what was revolutionary now looks obvious. (The flamenco-inspired choreography of Massine's *Tricorne*, for instance, which sent fashionable London into a rage for everything Spanish, no longer looks exotic or tempestuous. So many real flamenco artists now regularly tour the world's stages that a 'ballet' imitation looks insipid.)

Even when works become canonized as 'classics' – like the handful of Petipa ballets that carry the name – we are far from seeing the choreography in its original form. *Sleeping Beauty, Swan Lake, et al.* have now passed from living memory; in other words, new productions can no longer be referred to the recollections of people who knew the 'ur-text'. Essentially we now re-create those ballets, or even reinvent them, to suit ourselves. Anatole Vilzak, who danced with the pre-revolutionary Maryinsky ballet from 1915, was one of our closest surviving links to the original Petipa repertoire, when he spoke scathingly in 1979 of all the changes that have been introduced.

Step by step now everything changes. *Swan Lake* is now very different all over. I don't like it so much. Erik Bruhn did a *Swan Lake* . . . And in that production, did you see a swan? Did you see a lake? No, it's gone. Why? In the Maryinsky production, you could see the swan and the lake before anybody comes out, and then Odette appears . . . That's so romantic, so beautiful. Why change that?

Though some productions may make closer reference than others to surviving source material (like choreographers' notes, sketchy notation of steps, and so on), we still look at them through the lens of contemporary taste. Notions of authenticity and acceptability change (just as in music different generations have very different ideas about how to interpret past scores). Petipa's little known ballet *Bayadère*, for instance, recently became very popular in the West after Natalia Makarova staged it for the American Ballet Theatre and the Royal Ballet and after the Kirov started touring their own 'authentic' 1992 production. There are elements in this work that seem wildly kitsch to us – like the stuffed tigers and elephants parading the stage. But most of us laugh with pleasure at them, because we've learnt to accept them as part of a dance tradition that was once closely linked to music hall. However, forty years ago, when dancers in the British-based International Ballet began rehearsing a putative production, it was impossible to get them to perform it seriously. They kept bursting out laughing. What's an embarrassment to one generation becomes history to another.

And what is dance to some is, also, not dance to others. The commonest put-down by any critic – professional or otherwise – is that a 'bad' work is not 'real dance'. When the Belgian press complained that Mark Morris's *Marble Halls* (1985) looked as if someone had 'put a bunch of chimpanzees in shorts on stage to prove that they could hop to the beat', or American balletomane Lincoln Kirstein dismissed Martha Graham's early works as 'an idiot's games', they were essentially saying that the choreography was beyond serious appraisal as dance.

This point-blank denial of a work's 'dance' status isn't just a critic's trick; it can, more seriously, be an effective strategy for any establishment trying to repress something that offends against official ideology. At many points in history dance (like all the arts) has been denied because it dares to show things that threaten the state. (It wasn't simply popular taste that made Petipa limit his ballets to myth and fairy-tale – the Tsar would never have permitted anything more challenging.)

In Nazi Germany, for example, the great German expressionist choreographer Mary Wigman had her school taken away from her because her 'distortions' of the human body were viewed as an offence against pure Aryan art. In 90s Britain works by DV8 which explored homosexual experience also came under official pressure. In 1993 the tabloid press and at least one MP tried to get a ban on *MSM* (an exploration of gay cottaging), which it is claimed 'flushed public money down the toilet', and there was an attempt to black out the television film of *Dead Dreams*. In America the moral backlash that began in the 80s made it increasingly difficult for art to get state funding if it was considered offensive to the majority view (i.e. if it was gay, lesbian, libertarian, or just plain difficult).

But even when the issues aren't overtly about banning or denying work, judgements about what is or isn't dance, what is acceptable or not, filter through the media and other networks to create a general climate in which individual works are viewed. Our personal judgements are infiltrated by contemporary notions of good and bad art as well as by publicity, gossip, news, etc.

This was demonstrated recently by a major dance controversy in the American, and ultimately the world, press which was sparked by *New Yorker* critic Arlene Croce's response to Bill T. Jones's 1994 piece, *Still/Here*. Croce had refused to see this work for reasons outlined below, but had written at scathing length about it. By the time *Still/Here* reached Britain, several months after it was made, few in the audience could watch it without also responding to the storm of arguments it had raised.

Jones's work has always made statements about his own life and beliefs – and has been open about the fact that he is gay, black and personally involved in the global tragedy of AIDS. *Still/Here* was an attempt to deal with – even to celebrate – the process of dying, and it was inspired by a series of workshops with patients suffering from terminal illness. It included videos of these patients talking about themselves, while its choreography was based on their gestures and its song lyrics grew out of their words.

Croce argued that she couldn't review this work because it was 'victim art'. She believed that its presentation of real-life suffering was so raw, so untransmuted into 'art', that it couldn't be judged dispassionately. No one could call it bad art without appearing to be a bad person. In actual fact, the work that Croce imagined was not the work that appeared on stage – which some actually criticized for having insufficiently 'raw' material. But her article generated a larger debate about art and politics which touched nerves all round the world.

One of her central points was that *Still/Here* typified a whole (bad) trend of art-making that exploited pain. Keats didn't stoop to writing an 'Ode to Consumption', but sublimated his sickness into his art. Victim art, by contrast, isn't interested in craft or vision but operates by striking politically correct attitudes and pushing emotionally hot buttons.

Supporters of Croce's argument rushed in to swipe against a whole range of bogeys in contemporary art – the decline in classical values and the 90s plague of political correctness. Her detractors meanwhile viewed her as part of a right-wing conspiracy to deny art's political power and to suppress minority voices. The argument became a caricature of aesthetes *v.* activists – with both sides prescribing what dance should or shouldn't be.

In fact, the issue also highlighted something that arts professionals easily forget – which is the messy complex of motives that send most people to galleries, theatres or concert halls. They – we – rarely go simply to judge the work as art, but to take time out, to indulge in fantasy, to meet friends, to buy into a fashionable event and to see something new.

Dance is particularly good at letting us indulge our desires and imaginations, for as the painter Matisse wrote, it is 'an extraordinary thing, life and rhythm'. Its richly ambiguous language puts up less of a fight against the dreams and feelings we may project on to it than the text of most plays or the images of most films. It's more accommodating in letting us get from it what we're looking for.

Thus when Balanchine saw Isadora Duncan and believed himself to be watching a 'drunken fat woman . . . rolling around' his judgement of her performance was no more or less correct than Ashton's, who felt he'd seen one of the world's most inspiring dancers. Ashton simply had something to take from Duncan, and Balanchine did not. And the same is true of choreography. Audiences hungry for messages or emotion may find the limpid, formal compositions of Merce Cunningham arrogantly unfeeling, while audiences who thrive on the cold, sharp air of intellectual challenge will find the familiarity and comfort of classical ballet suffocating.

Ultimately this book is not only about how we understand what we see in dance, but also about how we understand what we *want* to see. It's obvious that the more skilled we are at reading different dance styles and at comprehending how dances are put together, the more confidently we can navigate the historical, geographical and formal extremes of today's repertoire. But being dance-literate may also reveal our own taste to us more vividly too. It may explain why some rhythms excite and ease us more than others; why some steps speak clearly to us; why some dances get under our skin and hang around our minds. Being dance-literate may show us the reasons why some dances, however bleak or difficult they may be, feel to us like home.

Sources

Many of the quotations used in *Reading Dance* are taken from personal interviews with the artists. However, many books have also provided important material:

All quotations from Merrill Ashley, Christopher Gable, Toni Lander, Lynn Seymour, Moira Shearer, Igor Youskevitch and Anatole Vilzak and most from Antoinette Sibley (but also see below) are taken from the second edition of Barbara Newman's *Striking a Balance*, 1992 (Limelight Editions, New York) and reprinted here by kind permission.

Anecdotes by Julian Braunsweg (including that about the would-be impressario on p. 38) come from *Ballet Scandals*, 1973 (George Allen & Unwin).

Quotations from Trisha Brown are taken from the Channel 4 documentary *Just Dancing Around*, 1996.

Quotations from Arlene Croce (including the Balanchine quotes on pp. 204 and 205) come from her three volumes of dance criticism *After-images*, *Going to the Dance* and *Sightlines*, 1977, 1982, 1987 respectively (Knopf).

The Merce Cunningham quotation on p. 8 is taken from *The Dancer and the Dance: Merce Cunningham in Conversation with Jacqueline Lesschaeve*, 1985 (Marion Boyars).

Recollections of Alexandra Danilova come from *Choura*, 1987 (Dance Books).

Quotations from Edwin Denby come from *Dance Writings of Edwin Denby*, 1986 (Knopf, New York). Copyright 1986 by Yvonne and Rudolph Burck-hardt. Used by permission of Yvonne and Rudolph Burckhardt.

The Isadora Duncan quotations are taken from *What is Dance?* by Roger Copeland and Marshall Cohen, 1983 (Oxford University Press).

Margot Fonteyn's comments are taken from her autobiography *Margot Fonteyn*, 1975 (W. H. Allen).

Quotations from Théophile Gautier are from (p. 21) *Time and the Dancing Image*, 1988 (William Morrow); (p. 22) *The Art of Dance in French Literature* by Deirdre Priddin, 1952 (A. & C. Black); and (pp. 192 and 219) *What is Dance?* by Roger Copeland and Marshall Cohen, 1983 (Oxford University Press).

Agnes de Mille's descriptions of Martha Graham come from *Martha*, 1991 (Random House), as do Paul Taylor's comments on pp. 126–7. I have also quoted (p. 62) from her book *Speak to Me, Dance with Me*, 1973 (Little, Brown).

Quotations from Deborah Jowitt (including the Hans Christian Andersen and Oskar Schlemmer quotes, and the Merce Cunningham quotes on pp. 85 and 122–3) come from *Time and the Dancing Image*, 1988 (William Morrow).

Quotations from Gelsey Kirkland are from her autobiography *Dancing on My Grave*, 1987 (Hamilton Hamilton).

Quotations from Andre Levinson are taken from *Ballet Old and New*, trans. Susan Cook, 1982 (Dance Horizons).

The quotations from Maude Lloyd and Hugh Laing come from *The Ballets of Antony Tudor* by Judith Chazin-Bennahum, 1994 (Oxford University Press).

Irek Mukhamedov's recollections are taken from *Irek Mukhamedov: The Authorized Biography* by Jeffrey Taylor, 1994 (Fourth Estate).

The quotation from Lloyd Newson on p. 115 is taken from *Dance Theatre Journal*, vol. 10, no. 4, 1993.

The quotation from Bronislava Nijinska (p. 44) and Nijinsky's comment on Isadora Duncan (p. 71) come from Nijinska's *Early Memoirs*, translated and edited by Irina Nijinska and Jean Rawlinson, 1982 (Faber & Faber).

I have taken Yvonne Rainer's manifesto from *Terpsichore in Sneakers* by Sally Banes, 1987 (Wesleyan University Press).

Quotations from Marie Rambert are from her autobiography *Quicksilver*, 1972 (Macmillan).

The quotations from Jacques Rivière and Auguste Rodin come from *Nijinsky* by Richard Buckle, 1971 (Weidenfeld & Nicolson).

Hubert Saal's description is taken from *The Mikhail Baryshnikov Story* by Barbara Aria, 1989 (Robson Books).

Antoinette Sibley's comments on p. 124, and Leslie Edwards's and Anthony Dowell's on p. 197 are taken from *Antoinette Sibley: The Authorized Biography* by Barbara Newman, 1986 (Hutchinson).

The Lydia Sokolova quotations are taken from *In the Wake of Diaghilev* by Richard Buckle, 1982 (Collins).

Nancy Stark Smith's comment is taken from 'Taking No for an Answer' in *Contact Quarterly*, vol. XII, no. 2, 1987.

The comments by Twyla Tharp come from her autobiography *Push Comes to Shove*, 1992 (Bantam Books).

The quotation from David Vaughn is taken from *Frederick Ashton and His Ballet*, 1977 (A. & C. Black).

Bibliography

Acocella, Joan, *Mark Morris*, Farrar, Straus & Giroux, 1993
Aria, Barbara, *The Baryshnikov Story*, Robson Books, 1989
Au, Susan, *Ballet and Modern Dance*, Thames & Hudson, 1988
Banes, Sally, *Terpsichore in Sneakers: Postmodern Dance*, Houghton/Mifflin, 1983
Braunsweg, Julian, *Ballet Scandals*, George Allen & Unwin, 1973
Buckle, Richard, *Nijinsky*, Weidenfeld & Nicolson, 1971
—*Diaghilev*, Weidenfeld & Nicolson, 1979
—*In the Wake of Diaghilev*, Collins, 1982
—*George Balanchine: Ballet Master*, Hamish Hamilton, 1988
Chazin-Bennahum, Judith, *The Ballets of Antony Tudor*, Oxford University Press, 1994
Cohen, Selma Jeanne, *Next Week, Swan Lake: Reflections on Dance and Dancers*, Wesleyan University Press, 1982
Concise Oxford Dictionary of Ballet, ed. Horst Koegler, 1987 (currently being updated)
Copeland, Roger, and Cohen, Marshall, *What is Dance?*, Oxford University Press, 1983
Groce, Arlene, *Afterimages*, Knopf, 1977
—*Going to the Dance*, Knopf, 1982
—*Sightlines*, Knopf, 1987
Danilova, Alexandra, *Choura*, Dance Books, 1987
de Mille, Agnes, *Martha*, Random House, 1991
Denby, Edwin, *Dance Writings of Edwin Denby*, Dance Books, 1986
Fonteyn, Margot, *Margot Fonteyn*, W. H. Allen, 1975
Garafola, Lynn, *Diaghilev's Ballets Russes*, Oxford University Press, 1989
Jowitt, Deborah, *Time and the Dancing Image*, William Morrow, 1988
Kirkland, Gelsey, *Dancing on My Grave*, Hamish Hamilton, 1987
Lesschaeve, Jacqueline, *Merce Cunningham in Conversation with Jacqueline Lesschaeve*, Marion Boyars, 1985
Newman, Barbara, *Antoinette Sibley: Reflections of a Ballerina*, Hutchinson, 1986
—*Striking a Balance*, Limelight Editions, 1992

Nijinska, Bronislava, *Early Memoirs*, trans. and ed. Irina Nijinska and Jean
   Rawlinson, Faber & Faber, 1982
Perlmutter, Donna, *Shadowplay: The Life of Antony Tudor*, Viking, 1991
Priddin, Deirdre, *The Art of Dance in French Literature*, A. & C. Black, 1952
Rambert, Marie, *Quicksilver*, Macmillan, 1972
Robertson, Allan, and Hutera, Donal, *Dance Handbook*, Longman, 1988
Taylor, Jeffrey, *Irek Mukhamedov: The Authorized Biography*, Fourth Estate,
   1994
Tharp, Twyla, *Push Comes to Shove*, Bantam, 1992
Tufnell, Miranda, and Crickmay, Chris, *Body Space Image*, Virago, 1990
Vaughn, David, *Frederick Ashton and His Ballet*, A. & C. Black, 1977

Index

The numbers appearing in bold refer to the inset pictures.